CAMBRIDGE

AMERICAN EMPOWER

STUDENT'S BOOK WITH DIGITAL PACK

C1

ADVANCED

Adrian Doff, Craig Thaine
Herbert Puchta, Jeff Stranks, Peter Lewis-Jones
with Mark Hancock and Wayne Rimmer

CAMBRIDGE

AMERICAN EMPOWER is a six-level general English course for adult and young adult learners, taking students from beginner to advanced level (CEFR A1 to C1). *American Empower* combines course content from Cambridge University Press with validated assessment from the experts at Cambridge Assessment English.

American Empower's unique mix of engaging classroom materials and reliable assessment enables learners to make consistent and measurable progress.

Content you'll love. Assessment you can trust.

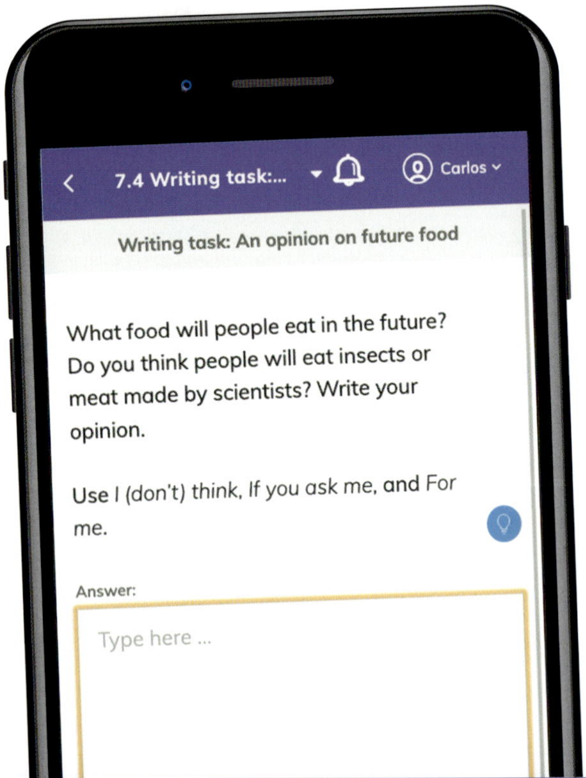

Better Learning with *American Empower*

Better Learning is our simple approach where **insights** we've gained from research have helped shape **content** that drives **results**.

Learner engagement

1 Content that informs and motivates

Insights
Sustained motivation is key to successful language learning and skills development.

Content
Clear learning goals, thought-provoking images, texts, and speaking activities, plus video content to arouse curiosity.

Results
Content that surprises, entertains, and provokes an emotional response, helping teachers to deliver motivating and memorable lessons.

6A WE ALL SEEM TO LOVE TAKING PICTURES

Learn to describe photos and hobbies
- G Simple and continuous verbs
- V Adjectives: describing images

1 SPEAKING AND READING

a Answer the questions.
1. What do you usually use to take photos – your phone or a camera?
2. Do you take a lot of photos? Why / Why not?
3. What do you usually do with the photos?
4. Do you think you're good at taking photos? Why / Why not?

b Have you ever heard of the photographer Elliott Erwitt? Read the fact file on p. 69. What kind of photographs does he take?

c What do you think are important skills for photographers? Think about these things:
- what you choose to photograph
- the way the photos look
- the equipment you use
- your attitude and personality.

d Read the article. Are any of your ideas from 1c mentioned?

e Read the article again. Answer the questions.
1. Why shouldn't street photographers plan much?
2. What should be the aim of a street photograph, according to Elliott Erwitt and the writer?
3. What do you think Elliott Erwitt means by visual garbage?
4. What attributes does the writer think are most important in a street photographer?
5. What does the writer mean when he talks about keeping an alien mindset?

f Answer the questions.
1. How are Erwitt's methods and style evident in the photo of the Villa Borghese Gardens? What do you think of the photograph?
2. Answer the question at the end of the article: As an alien – what would you find intriguing, amusing, or nonsensical?
3. Look at the titles of the "lessons" (1–4) in the article. Are they relevant to other skills and/or jobs that you know about?

2 VOCABULARY Adjectives: describing images

a Work with a partner. What do the highlighted adjectives in the article mean? Check your ideas in a dictionary.

b Now go to Vocabulary Focus 6A on p. 163.

Villa Borghese Gardens, Rome 1969 by Elliott Erwitt

68

UNIT 6

ELLIOTT ERWITT PHOTOGRAPHER FACT FILE

- born in Paris, brought up in Italy, moved to the U.S. at age 10
- began photography career in the 1950s
- known for advertising and street photography, particularly ironic black-and-white shots of everyday life
- invited to join the internationally famous photography agency Magnum in 1953

Lessons Elliott Erwitt Has Taught Me about STREET PHOTOGRAPHY

by Eric Kim

If you are not familiar with the work of Elliott Erwitt, you may perhaps have seen some of his iconic work from around the globe (the picture opposite was taken by him). He had one of the longest careers of any photographer, spanning over 50 years.

What I most appreciate about Elliott Erwitt is his wry sense of humor when looking at the world – as well as his straightforward philosophies about photography. In this article, I share some of his thoughts and advice.

1 DON'T PLAN TOO MUCH – WANDER AROUND

I think that as a street photographer, sometimes I fall into a trap of planning too much. I generally try to focus my attention on projects (having a preconceived project in mind when shooting in the streets), but I often find it also takes away from the shooting experience. One of the best things about street photography is to be a flaneur – someone who wanders around without a specific destination in mind.

ERWITT *I don't start out with any specific interests; I just react to what I see.*

Takeaway point: Let your curiosity lead you. Just go out and shoot whatever you find interesting. Go down roads that may seem a little foreign, and you might be lucky enough to stumble upon great street photography shots.

2 FOCUS ON CONTENT OVER FORM

Great photos are a combination of content (what is happening in the frame) as well as form (composition). But which is more important? Content or form?

ERWITT *My wish for the future of photography is that it might continue to have some relevance to the human condition and might represent work that evokes knowledge and emotions. That photography has content rather than just form. And I hope that there will be enough produce to balance out the visual garbage that one sees in our current life.*

Takeaway point: We often find fascinating characters in the street and take photos of them, but the compositions may not be so good. On the other hand, we might take well-composed photos of a street scene, but there is nothing going on in the photo – it is boring and without soul.

I agree with Erwitt that we should, as street photographers, put more emphasis on content over form. I feel that photos that evoke emotions and the human condition are far more powerful and meaningful than just photos with good composition.

3 DON'T TAKE THINGS TOO SERIOUSLY

When one thinks about the photography agency Magnum, some adjectives that come to mind are *gritty* and *raw*.

However, Erwitt's style was vastly different. He didn't go out and take photos in conflicts or war. His photos tended to be more playful, humorous, and amusing.

ERWITT *Well, I'm not a serious photographer like most of my colleagues. That is to say, I'm serious about not being serious.*

Takeaway point: Don't take yourself and your street photography too seriously, and remember – at the end of the day you want to enjoy yourself.

4 HONE YOUR SKILLS OF OBSERVATION

Erwitt was inspired to go out and take pictures when he saw a photograph by master photographer Henri Cartier-Bresson. He realized it was an act of observation that made the photo great and that he could do something similar.

ERWITT *The picture seemed evocative and emotional. Also, a simple observation was all that it took to produce it. I thought, if one could make a living out of doing such pictures that would be desirable.*

Takeaway point: One of the things that is the most beautiful about street photography is that it doesn't rely on having an expensive camera or exotic lenses. Rather, it comes down to having an observant and curious eye for people and the world around you.

Therefore, cultivate your vision and way of seeing the world. I recommend that you always carry a camera with you because you never know when the best street photo opportunities will present themselves to you.

A fun exercise: Pretend that you are an alien from another planet, and you have come to the planet Earth for the first time. Imagine how strange human beings would seem – and the urban environment they have built for themselves. As an alien, what would you find intriguing, amusing, or nonsensical?

Always keep that mindset to be amazed by what you see around you.

69

2 Personalized and relevant

Insights
Language learners benefit from frequent opportunities to personalize their responses.

Content
Personalization tasks in every unit make the target language more meaningful to the individual learner.

Results
Personal responses make learning more memorable and inclusive, with all students participating in spontaneous spoken interaction.

> *"There are so many adjectives to describe such a wonderful series, but in my opinion it's very reliable, practical, and modern."*

Zenaide Brianez, Director of Studies, Instituto da Língua Inglesa, Brazil

Measurable progress

1 Assessment you can trust

Insights

Tests developed and validated by Cambridge Assessment English, the world leaders in language assessment, to ensure they are accurate and meaningful.

Content

End-of-unit tests, mid- and end-of-course competency tests, and personalized CEFR test report forms provide reliable information on progress with language skills.

Results

Teachers can see learners' progress at a glance, and learners can see measurable progress, which leads to greater motivation.

Results of an impact study showing % improvement of Reading levels, based on global *Empower* students' scores over one year.

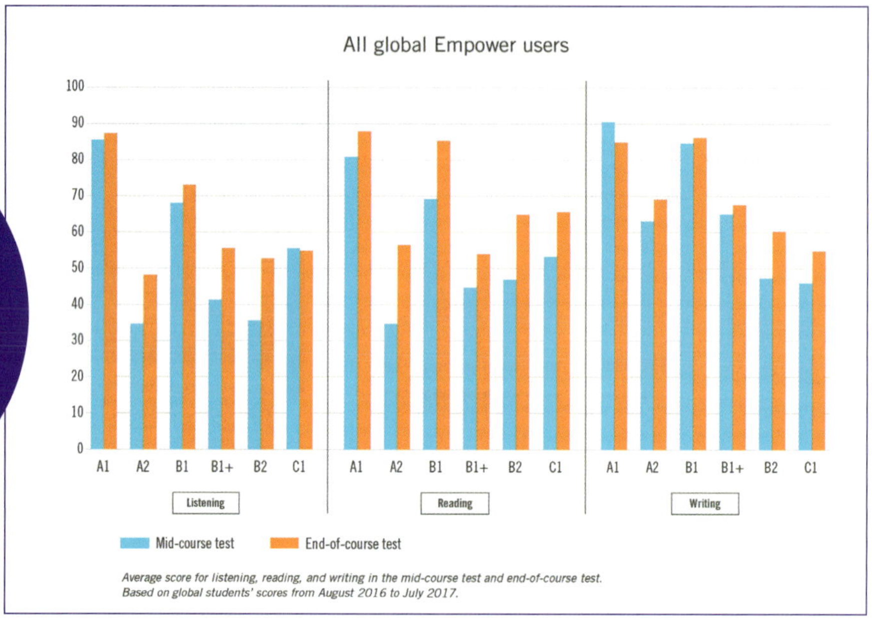

Average score for listening, reading, and writing in the mid-course test and end-of-course test.
Based on global students' scores from August 2016 to July 2017.

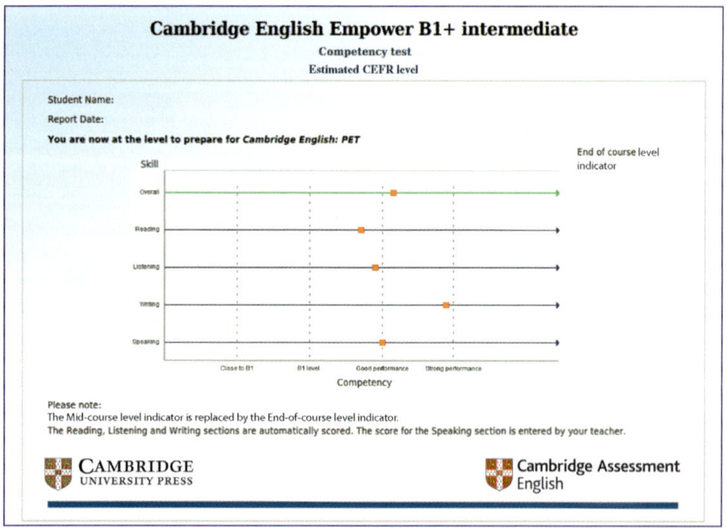

Cambridge English Empower B1+ intermediate

Competency test

Estimated CEFR level

Student Name:

Report Date:

You are now at the level to prepare for *Cambridge English: PET*

Skill: Overall, Reading, Listening, Writing, Speaking

End of course level indicator

Close to B1 | B1 level | Good performance | Strong performance

Competency

Please note:
The Mid-course level indicator is replaced by the End-of-course level indicator.
The Reading, Listening and Writing sections are automatically scored. The score for the Speaking section is entered by your teacher.

CAMBRIDGE UNIVERSITY PRESS

Cambridge Assessment English

> *We started using the tests provided with* Empower *and our students started showing better results from this point until now.*

Kristina Ivanova, Director of Foreign Language Training Centre, ITMO University, Saint Petersburg, Russia

2 Evidence of impact

Insights

Schools and colleges need to show that they are evaluating the effectiveness of their language programs.

Content

Empower (British English) impact studies have been carried out in various countries, including Russia, Brazil, Turkey, and the UK, to provide evidence of positive impact and progress.

Results

Colleges and universities have demonstrated a significant improvement in language level between the mid- and end-of-course tests, as well as a high level of teacher satisfaction with *Empower*.

Manageable learning

1 Mobile friendly

Insights
Learners expect online content to be mobile friendly but also flexible and easy to use on any digital device.

Content
American Empower provides easy access to Digital Workbook content that works on any device and includes practice activities with audio.

Results
Digital Workbook content is easy to access anywhere, and produces meaningful and actionable data so teachers can track their students' progress and adapt their lesson accordingly.

"I had been studying English for 10 years before university, and I didn't succeed. But now with Empower *I know my level of English has changed."*

Nikita, *Empower* Student, ITMO University, Saint Petersburg, Russia

2 Corpus-informed

Insights
Corpora can provide valuable information about the language items learners are able to learn successfully at each CEFR level.

Content
Two powerful resources – Cambridge Corpus and English Profile – informed the development of the *Empower* course syllabus and the writing of the materials.

Results
Learners are presented with the target language they are able to incorporate and use at the right point in their learning journey. They are not overwhelmed with unrealistic learning expectations.

Rich in practice

1 Language in use

Insights

It is essential that learners are offered frequent and manageable opportunities to practice the language they have been focusing on.

Content

Throughout the *American Empower* Student's Book, learners are offered a wide variety of practice activities, plenty of controlled practice, and frequent opportunities for communicative spoken practice.

Results

Meaningful practice makes new language more memorable and leads to more efficient progress in language acquisition.

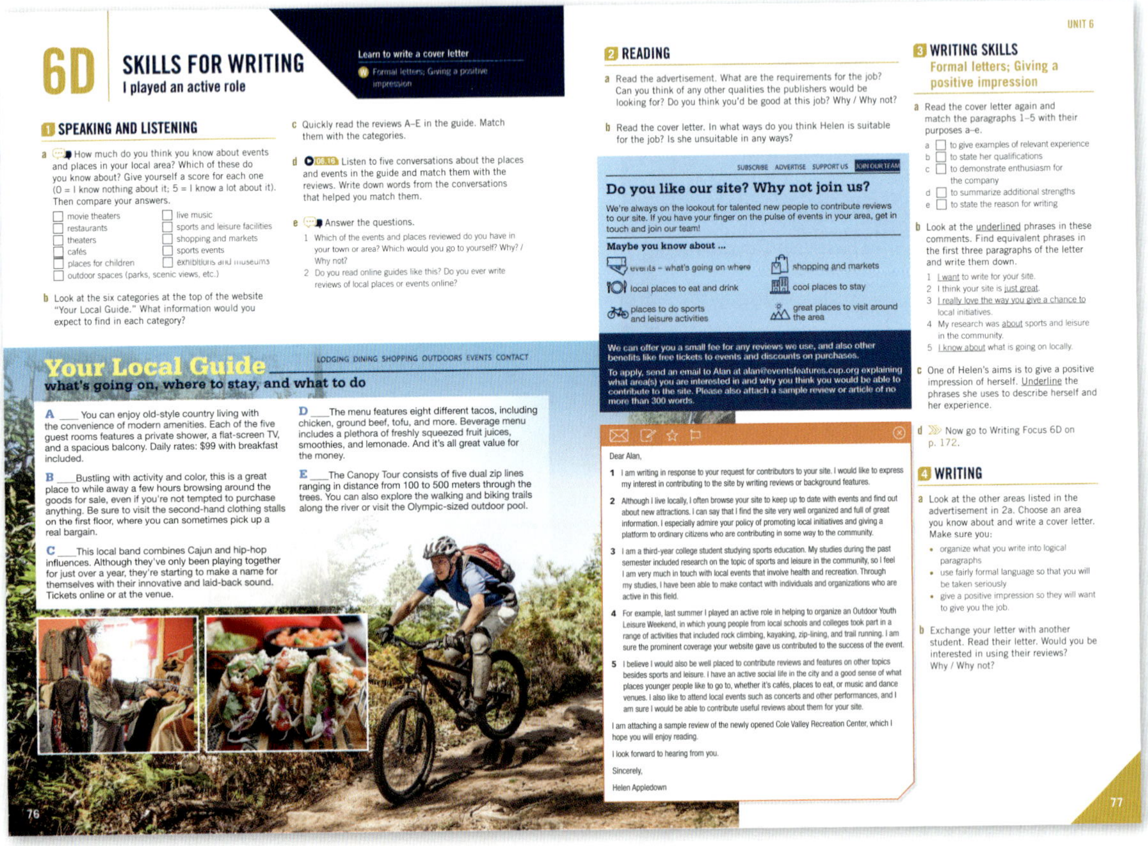

6D SKILLS FOR WRITING
I played an active role

Learn to write a cover letter
W Formal letters; Giving a positive impression

1 SPEAKING AND LISTENING

a How much do you think you know about events and places in your local area? Which of these do you know about? Give yourself a score for each one (0 = I know nothing about it; 5 = I know a lot about it). Then compare your answers.

- [ ] movie theaters
- [ ] restaurants
- [ ] theaters
- [ ] cafés
- [ ] places for children
- [ ] outdoor spaces (parks, scenic views, etc.)
- [ ] live music
- [ ] sports and leisure facilities
- [ ] shopping and markets
- [ ] sports events
- [ ] exhibitions and museums

b Look at the six categories at the top of the website "Your Local Guide." What information would you expect to find in each category?

c Quickly read the reviews A–E in the guide. Match them with the categories.

d 06.16 Listen to five conversations about the places and events in the guide and match them with the reviews. Write down words from the conversations that helped you match them.

e Answer the questions.

1 Which of the events and places reviewed do you have in your town or area? Which would you go to yourself? Why? / Why not?
2 Do you read online guides like this? Do you ever write reviews of local places or events online?

Your Local Guide LODGING DINING SHOPPING OUTDOORS EVENTS CONTACT
what's going on, where to stay, and what to do

A ___ You can enjoy old-style country living with the convenience of modern amenities. Each of the five guest rooms features a private shower, a flat-screen TV, and a spacious balcony. Daily rates: $99 with breakfast included.

B ___ Bustling with activity and color, this is a great place to while away a few hours browsing around the goods for sale, even if you're not tempted to purchase anything. Be sure to visit the second-hand clothing stalls on the first floor, where you can sometimes pick up a real bargain.

C ___ This local band combines Cajun and hip-hop influences. Although they've only been playing together for just over a year, they're starting to make a name for themselves with their innovative and laid-back sound. Tickets online or at the venue.

D ___ The menu features eight different tacos, including chicken, ground beef, tofu, and more. Beverage menu includes a plethora of freshly squeezed fruit juices, smoothies, and lemonade. And it's all great value for the money.

E ___ The Canopy Tour consists of five dual zip lines ranging in distance from 100 to 500 meters through the trees. You can also explore the walking and biking trails along the river or visit the Olympic-sized outdoor pool.

76

UNIT 6

2 READING

a Read the advertisement. What are the requirements for the job? Can you think of any other qualities the publishers would be looking for? Do you think you'd be good at this job? Why / Why not?

b Read the cover letter. In what ways do you think Helen is suitable for the job? Is she unsuitable in any ways?

SUBSCRIBE ADVERTISE SUPPORT US JOIN OUR TEAM

Do you like our site? Why not join us?

We're always on the lookout for talented new people to contribute reviews to our site. If you have your finger on the pulse of events in your area, get in touch and join our team!

Maybe you know about ...

events – what's going on where
local places to eat and drink
places to do sports and leisure activities
shopping and markets
cool places to stay
great places to visit around the area

We can offer you a small fee for any reviews we use, and also other benefits like free tickets to events and discounts on purchases.

To apply, send an email to Alan at alan@eventsfeatures.cup.org explaining what area(s) you are interested in and why you think you would be able to contribute to the site. Please also attach a sample review or article of no more than 300 words.

Dear Alan,

1 I am writing in response to your request for contributors to your site. I would like to express my interest in contributing to the site by writing reviews or background features.

2 Although I live locally, I often browse your site to keep up to date with events and find out about new attractions. I can say that I find the site very well organized and full of great information. I especially admire your policy of promoting local initiatives and giving a platform to ordinary citizens who are contributing in some way to the community.

3 I am a third-year college student studying sports education. My studies during the past semester included research on the topic of sports and leisure in the community, so I feel I am very much in touch with local events that involve health and recreation. Through my studies, I have been able to make contact with individuals and organizations who are active in this field.

4 For example, last summer I played an active role in helping to organize an Outdoor Youth Leisure Weekend, in which young people from local schools and colleges took part in a range of activities that included rock climbing, kayaking, zip-lining, and trail running. I am sure the prominent coverage your website gave us contributed to the success of the event.

5 I believe I would also be well placed to contribute reviews and features on other topics besides sports and leisure. I have an active social life in the city and a good sense of what places younger people like to go to, whether it's cafés, places to eat, or music and dance venues. I also like to attend local events such as concerts and other performances, and I am sure I would be able to contribute useful reviews about them for your site.

I am attaching a sample review of the newly opened Cole Valley Recreation Center, which I hope you will enjoy reading.

I look forward to hearing from you.

Sincerely,

Helen Appledown

3 WRITING SKILLS
Formal letters; Giving a positive impression

a Read the cover letter again and match the paragraphs 1–5 with their purposes a–e.

a [ ] to give examples of relevant experience
b [ ] to state her qualifications
c [ ] to demonstrate enthusiasm for the company
d [ ] to summarize additional strengths
e [ ] to state the reason for writing

b Look at the underlined phrases in these comments. Find equivalent phrases in the first three paragraphs of the letter and write them down.

1 I want to write for your site.
2 I think your site is just great.
3 I really love the way you give a chance to local initiatives.
4 My research was about sports and leisure in the community.
5 I know about what is going on locally.

c One of Helen's aims is to give a positive impression of herself. Underline the phrases she uses to describe herself and her experience.

d Now go to Writing Focus 6D on p. 172.

4 WRITING

a Look at the other areas listed in the advertisement in 2a. Choose an area you know about and write a cover letter. Make sure you:

- organize what you write into logical paragraphs
- use fairly formal language so that you will be taken seriously
- give a positive impression so they will want to give you the job.

b Exchange your letter with another student. Read their letter. Would you be interested in using their reviews? Why / Why not?

77

2 Beyond the classroom

> "There are plenty of opportunities for personalization."

Elena Pro, Teacher, EOI de San Fernando de Henares, Spain

Insights

Progress with language learning often requires work outside of the classroom, and different teaching models require different approaches.

Content

American Empower is available with a print workbook, online practice, documentary-style videos that expose learners to real-world English, plus additional resources with extra ideas and fun activities.

Results

This choice of additional resources helps teachers to find the most effective ways to motivate their students both inside and outside the classroom.

Unit overview

Unit Opener

Getting started page – Clear learning objectives to give an immediate sense of purpose.

Lessons A and B

Grammar and Vocabulary – Input and practice of core grammar and vocabulary, plus a mix of skills.

Digital Workbook (online, mobile): Grammar and Vocabulary

Lesson C

Everyday English – Functional language in common, everyday situations.

Digital Workbook (online, mobile): Listening and Speaking

Unit Progress Test

Lesson D

Integrated Skills – Practice of all four skills, with a special emphasis on writing.

Digital Workbook (online, mobile): Reading and Writing

Review

Extra practice of grammar, vocabulary, and pronunciation. Also a "Review your progress" section for students to reflect on the unit.

Mid- / End-of-course test

Additional practice

Further practice is available for outside of the class with these components.

Digital Workbook (online, mobile)

Workbook (printed)

Components

Resources – Available on cambridgeone.org

- Audio
- Video
- Unit Progress Tests (Print)
- Unit Progress Tests (Online)
- Mid- and end-of-course assessment (Print)
- Mid- and end-of-course assessment (Online)
- Digital Workbook (Online)
- Photocopiable Grammar, Vocabulary, and Pronunciation worksheets

CONTENTS

CAN DO OBJECTIVES

- Talk about learning a second language
- Describe languages and how they change
- Express yourself in an inexact way
- Write a web forum post

UNIT 1 LANGUAGE

GETTING STARTED

a Look at the picture and answer the questions.

1. What do you think the ape is being taught to do? How successful do you think this will be?
2. What do you think the benefits of teaching animals language are for … ?
   - humans
   - animals
3. In what ways do you think this ape's language learning experience is similar to or different from a human's?

b Discuss the questions.

1. In what other situations do humans and animals communicate with each other?
2. Which animals are known for their ability to communicate well with humans?
3. If you could converse with any animal, which one would it be? What would you like to ask it?

1A I THOUGHT I COULD PICK UP ITALIAN BY EAR

Learn to talk about learning a second language

G Adverbs and adverbial phrases

V Language learning; Noun forms

1 READING

a Do you agree with these statements about learning a second language? Why / Why not?

1 It's helpful to get feedback from native speakers.
2 Trying to memorize words and phrases is a core part of the learning process.
3 Communicating in another language makes you feel like a different person.
4 Learning grammar is a waste of time – I don't even know it in my first language!
5 The biggest reward is being able to relate to people from another culture.
6 Apps on smartphones and tablets have made learning a second language much easier.
7 When you've learned one second language, it's easier to learn another.

b Read about Scott's language learning experience. Which of the statements in 1a might he agree with?

c Read the text again and answer the questions.

1 Why do you think Scott wants to put his money where his mouth is?
2 What is the difference between learning a language by ear and studying it formally?
3 How important is a learner's motivation when learning a new language?
4 How does self-consciousness inhibit learning a new language?

LANGUAGE TEACHERS **LEARNING LANGUAGE**

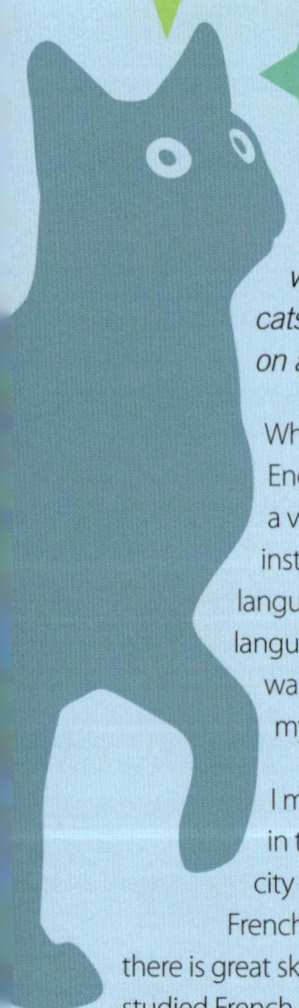

Speaking Italian to Cats

by Scott Fletcher

How I got my tongue around all those crazy Italian vowels with the help of some friendly cats and a mysterious woman on a train

When I finished my training as an English language teacher, I made a vow not to be one of those instructors who teach their native language but cannot speak another language fluently themselves. I wanted to put my money where my mouth was.

I managed to get a teaching job in the north of Italy in a small city called Aosta, right next to the French and Swiss borders, where there is great skiing. (I really love to ski.) I had studied French in high school and college, but my language skills were a little rusty. At the time, I didn't speak a word of Italian, so I packed one of those "teach yourself Italian" books in my luggage.

I flew direct to Milan, and the culture/language shock hit me as soon as I got off the plane. Still suffering from jet lag, I tried to memorize the phrase *Non capisco l'italiano* (I don't understand Italian), but I couldn't get it into my head. Not a great start.

Aosta is bilingual – Italian and French – and, to begin with, I brushed up on my college French and could get by. I was convinced I'd just be able to pick Italian up by ear. Being surrounded by the language and hearing it all the time meant I'd just kind of absorb it, but no such luck. After three months, I'd finally managed to remember *Non capisco l'italiano*, but not a whole lot more.

So I got out that "teach yourself Italian" book I had packed and got started on the grammar and vocabulary. And I downloaded some Italian learning apps on my phone. It was hard work, and I struggled to grasp some of the verb tenses and vocabulary. It seemed like I would have to remember a mountain of information if I were ever going to speak correctly.

I'd made friends with some students. I sort of tried to talk to them in Italian, but more often than not I got stuck. Their English was far better than my Italian. I remember going to dinner at my friend Matteo's place. His family had a couple of cats, and while Matteo was helping his mother serve up the pasta, I had my own private conversation with the cats.

Matteo overheard me, laughed, and said, "That's right, speak Italian to the cats – only they can understand you." It was a joke, but I felt crestfallen and could feel my vow to learn another language slipping away.

A few weeks after that, I went on a trip to Venice for a weekend. On the train going there, I met a teacher of English at a high school in Milan. We started chatting, and she asked me how long I'd been in Italy. By this time it was almost five months, and she smiled when I admitted that I couldn't speak Italian yet. I told her I'd been studying on my own, but I had no confidence to speak.

She then said (in Italian), "Come on. You can speak with me." She had a very determined look on her face, but also a warmth and friendliness that was somehow encouraging. So I took the plunge. Not very well to begin with, but I gradually began speaking in Italian with more and more confidence.

And that was my breakthrough. In the two hours it took to travel from Milan to Venice I somehow unlocked everything I had been studying. Why? Basically, I think it had everything to do with the woman I met (I don't know her name, and I've never met her again), but I felt less self-conscious speaking with someone who wasn't my student or my friend.

2 GRAMMAR
Adverbs and adverbial phrases

a Notice the highlighted adverbials in the texts. Add them to the lists below. The first one is done for you.

1 **Comment** (used to express the speaker's point of view): *clearly, apparently, actually, basically*
2 **Degree** (used to make the meaning stronger or weaker): *very, a little, …*
3 **Manner** (used to say *how*): *slowly, on foot, …*
4 **Time** (used to say *when*): *in the eighties, overnight, …*
5 **Frequency** (used to say *how often*): *never, …*

b What position(s) can each adverbial take in these sentences? Which adverbials change meaning in different positions?

1 a in the end 1, 3 b eventually
[1] I [2] managed to hold a conversation in Japanese [3].
2 a extremely b often
[1] I [2] found it [3] difficult.
3 a frequently b all the time
[1] I [2] made silly mistakes [3].
4 a slowly b clearly
[1] I [2] would like native speakers to speak to me [3].
5 a naturally b well
[1] I'm [2] a little envious of friends who can already speak the language [3].

c Now go to Grammar Focus 1A on p. 138.

When I went back to Aosta, my friends couldn't believe it. "What happened to you?" Matteo asked. I could suddenly speak Italian. I haven't looked back since, and my confidence in speaking has grown enormously. My Italian isn't perfect, but it's fairly fluent and I know the grammar. I did, in the end, manage to put my money where my mouth was.

d Think of a skill you have learned at some stage in your life. Plan to talk about it, using some of the adverbs from the reading and the box below. Write notes.

in the beginning obviously extremely eventually correctly clearly incorrectly naturally in the end

Obviously, I was hopeless in the beginning

In order to do it correctly, you have to concentrate on the ball.

Playing a complete game involved a lot of walking, and I was extremely tired afterward.

e Describe the experience you had learning the skill without naming it. Can your partner guess what skill you are talking about?

3 VOCABULARY Language learning

a Look at the underlined parts of the texts. Match the words and phrases 1–4 with the definitions a–d.

1 ☐ pick up
2 ☐ brush up on
3 ☐ grasp
4 ☐ rusty

a understand something, especially something difficult
b less able because you are out of practice
c learn something by being exposed to it
d improve your knowledge of something you've partly forgotten

b Now go to Vocabulary Focus 1A on p. 158.

c Read the questions about your English language learning background. Add two more to ask a partner.

1 When did you first start learning English?
2 How long was it before you could hold a conversation in English?
3 When did you first put your learning into practice?
4 Have you progressed as well as you expected?
5 Have you ever been immersed in an English-speaking culture? If so, what was it like? If not, is there a culture you would like to get to know?
6 How important is it to you to speak accurately? Why?
7 What level of competence would you like to attain eventually?
8 ______________________
9 ______________________

d Work in pairs. Ask and answer the questions in 3c.

4 LISTENING

a Answer the questions.

1 Think about someone you know who grew up bilingual. What was their experience like?
2 What do you think are possible advantages and disadvantages of a bilingual upbringing?
3 What are attitudes toward being bilingual like in your country?

b 01.06 Listen to Katya being interviewed about her bilingual upbringing on the podcast *Linguistically Speaking*. Answer the questions.

1 Which languages does she speak?
2 What was unique about her upbringing?
3 What's her attitude to bilingualism?

c 01.06 Listen again. Are the sentences true or false? Correct the false sentences.

1 Katya realizes that her upbringing was very special and different.
2 Katya's mother used both English and Russian when she spoke to Katya.
3 She wasn't really aware that she was speaking two languages when she was a child.
4 She thinks she might have had some initial problems acquiring Portuguese.
5 She went to special classes to learn to read and write in English and Russian.
6 She found it easy to fit into her school in the U.S.
7 She believes being bilingual has given her an ability to concentrate on tasks.
8 She found she struggled learning Mandarin.

d Imagine you want to give your child a bilingual upbringing. What would you have to do? How easy or difficult would it be? Write notes and compare with your partner.

5 SPEAKING AND VOCABULARY Noun forms

a 01.07 Complete the sentences with the noun form of the words in parentheses. Listen and check.

1 So I got __________ (expose) to both languages right from the beginning.
2 If I wanted to communicate, I had to use Portuguese. It was a __________ (necessary).
3 There's a __________ (reluctant) on the part of some parents to let their children learn a second language.
4 And my __________ (motivate) was much higher. It's like there's a part of my brain that gets real __________ (please) from engaging with another language.

b Now go to Vocabulary Focus 1A on p. 158.

c How can these factors have an impact on learning a second language?

- the right mentality
- financial limitations
- distractions
- opportunities for interaction
- first language interference
- natural competence
- the prestige of knowing a second language

d Choose a person 1–3 and write five pieces of advice for them.

1 an English speaker who wants to learn your language
2 a friend who wants to pass a state English exam
3 a teenager who finds languages at school a turn-off

e Work in pairs. Compare your ideas in 5d and prioritize four suggestions that are useful for all language learners.

The most universally useful suggestion here is to invest in a good dictionary.

I couldn't agree more. I also think putting your learning into practice whenever you can is really important.

Katya as a child

Katya today

1B LANGUAGE HAS BEEN CONSTANTLY EVOLVING

Learn to describe languages and how they change

G The perfect aspect

V Describing changes

1 SPEAKING

a Look at these words. Which ones do you know? Tell your partner. Look up the words you don't know in a dictionary.

radio babysitter ecotourism technophobe blog selfie in-joke spacecraft brainwash Bollywood sudoku environmentalism

b Each word in 1a was first used in a different decade, from the 1900s to the 2010s. When do you think each word first came into the English language, and why? Put them in order.

1900s radio
1910s …

c 01.09 Listen and check your answers. What is the significance of photographs 1 and 2?

d Two more new words in English are *hangry* and *glamping*. Talk about their meanings. Do you know any other words that have come into the English language recently?

2 READING

a Read the introduction to an article about the way English has changed. Which two points does the writer make?

- ☐ English has become less complex over the years.
- ☐ Many changes to language take place gradually so we may not notice them.
- ☐ Modern technology has helped us see how language is changing.

b Answer these questions.

1 What do you think the words in *italics* in paragraph 1 mean?
2 Can you think of an example of "the annoying inconsistencies between spelling and pronunciation in English"?

c **Communication 1B** Work in pairs. Student A: Go to p. 127. Student B: Go to p. 131.

d Look at each pair of sentences below. Do the sentences show a change you read about? Explain the change to your partner.

1 a Shall we meet at 6:00?
  b Do you want to meet at 6:00?
2 a I was fired from my job.
  b I got fired from my job.
3 a She started to cry.
  b She started crying.
4 a I ought to go soon.
  b I need to be going soon.

How Quickly Is the English Language Changing?

We all know language changes. People's favorite music was *far-out* in the 1960s, *rad* in the 1980s, *wicked* in the 1990s, and *awesome* in 2010. You just need to watch a movie from ten years ago to hear phrases that have come and gone.

However, there are far more subtle, ongoing language changes taking place at any given time. These changes may have a hugely significant impact but can go entirely unnoticed while they are in progress. One lasting change to English that was barely perceptible at the time is known as the Great Vowel Shift. Over a period of 350 years (from 1350 to 1700), the long vowel sounds of English drifted so far that speakers at either end of the period could not have understood each other. However, nobody noticed for about 100 years after it had happened! The Great Vowel Shift was a major contributor to the annoying inconsistencies between spelling and pronunciation in English that have plagued users ever since.

These days no such important change would go unnoticed. Linguists can now analyze huge collections of text and transcribed speech and identify ongoing patterns of change that in the past would not have been visible for many years to come. Here are some of the less noticeable changes that are occurring in English right now:

3 VOCABULARY Describing changes

a Read the sentences about language change below. Which words/phrases in **bold** tell the reader … ?

a the speed of a change ☐ ☐ ☐
b that a change is in progress ☐
c how easy a change is to see ☐ ☐ ☐ ☐
d about something that is decreasing ☐ ☐
e how big or important a change is ☐ ☐ ☐
f that a change is long-term or permanent ☐
g about something that is increasing ☐ ☐ ☐ ☐

You will write some numbers more than once.

One [1]**lasting** change to English that was [2]**barely perceptible** at the time is known as the Great Vowel Shift.

These changes may have a [3]**hugely significant** impact but can go [4]**entirely unnoticed** while they are in progress.

Here are some of the less [5]**noticeable** changes that are occurring in English right now:

There was [6]**a steady shift** toward more frequent use of the verb + *-ing*, and these forms are still [7]**on the rise.**

There are far more [8]**subtle**, [9]**ongoing** language changes taking place at any given time.

The use of continuous passive verb forms has also seen [10]**a rapid rise**.

Modal verbs are [11]**gradually giving way** to other less formal expressions.

Stiff, formal words like *shall* and *ought* are [12]**on the way out**.

Words that cover the same ground, such as *going to*, *have to*, *need to*, and *want to* are [13]**taking over**.

The use of *get* passives has [14]**grown substantially**.

b Write sentences about real changes. Then compare your ideas with other students.

1 something that is on the way out in your culture
2 a place that has changed substantially in recent years
3 a problem that is on the rise
4 a fashion that has taken over recently among the younger generation
5 a subtle change to a popular product

4 LISTENING AND GRAMMAR The perfect aspect

a 01.10 Listen to four people commenting on the article in 2a and answer the questions.

1 What kind of language change does each speaker focus on?
2 What specific examples does each speaker give?

b Are the kinds of change the speakers mentioned happening in your first language?

c 01.11 Complete the sentences using the correct forms of the verbs in parentheses. Then listen and check.

- Language [1] ________ much faster since people started using the Internet. (change)
- In a few years' time, they [2] ________ out of fashion and other new words [3] ________ into the language. (go, come)
- I mean, people [4] ________ using strict rules for punctuation. (stop)
- In about 50 years, most dialects of English [5] ________. (die out)
- Older generations [6] ________ about language changing. They [7] ________ strongly about it. (always / complain, always / feel)
- People [8] ________ photos of themselves before 2013, but they didn't have a single word for it. (take)
- Now that computers have come along, the meaning of the word *wireless* [9] ________. It used to mean "radio." (change)

d Answer the questions.

1 Which of the examples in 4c happen in … ?
  a a period up to the present
  b a period up to a time in the past
  c a period in the future
2 What do all perfect verb forms have in common? Choose the correct word to complete the rule.

All perfect verb forms describe actions, states, and processes in the time period *before* / *after* a particular point in time.

e 01.11 **Pronunciation** Listen to the sentences in 4c again and notice the pronunciation of the words you added. What kind of words are stressed? What kind of words are usually unstressed?

f Now go to Grammar Focus 1B on p. 139.

g Talk about words in your own language. Think about:

- a word in common use now that hadn't been invented when you were a child
- a word that people have been using a lot this year
- a word that will have fallen out of use in 20 years' time
- a word that has changed its meaning.

5 READING AND SPEAKING

a What is unusual about the remarks in pictures 1–3? What would you expect the people to be saying instead?

b Read the fact file and answer the questions.

1 What do you think each fact tells us about the speakers' culture or environment? Or the way they think about the world?
2 Which language feature do you think is the most unusual?

c Language in context *Expressing meaning*
Read the dictionary definitions and complete the example sentences with the correct forms of the highlighted words from the fact file.

1 to decide what the meaning of something is
It's very hard to __________ the animal's behavior.
2 to notice or understand the difference between two things
It's very difficult to __________ ***between*** *the twins.*
3 to show the difference between things
The thing that __________ her ***from*** *the others is her taste in clothes.*
4 to explain something more clearly by showing examples, pictures, etc.
Why don't you include some stories to __________ your points?
5 to show, point, or make clear in another way
She shook her head to __________ that I shouldn't speak.
6 to express a thought, feeling, or idea so that it is understood by other people
Her face __________ her feelings even if her words didn't.
7 to represent an abstract quality or idea exactly
We need a slogan that __________ the philosophy of our business.

d What facts about your own first language would you add to the fact file? Think of:

- an area of meaning where there are many more or many fewer words than in English
- an idiom that can't be translated into English
- grammar or vocabulary that might reflect the culture.

Explain your list to a partner.

e Read the opinion below.

> Language is the main influence on how people view their world.

Do you agree? Why / Why not? Make a list of reasons to support your answer.

FACT FILE: HOW LANGUAGES ARE SPECIAL

The **DANI OF NEW GUINEA** only distinguish colors from one another using two words, one for dark colors and the other for light colors.

It is believed that the **INUIT IN NORTHERN CANADA** have about 50 different words for snow and about 40 ways to distinguish different kinds of ice from one another.

ALBANIAN has 27 different words for kinds of mustaches. *Posht*, for example, means a mustache that hangs down at the ends.

HAWAIIAN LANGUAGES have 108 words for sweet potato and 47 for banana.

In the **NATIVE AMERICAN LANGUAGE HOPI**, the verbs do not differentiate between past and present. Instead, the forms of its verbs convey how the speaker came to know the information.

GUUGU YIMITHIRR, a language spoken in northeast Australia, does not have words for "left" and "right" as directions at all. Instead, they use north, south, east, and west. When they want someone to turn while driving, they'll say, for example, "Turn a little bit west."

In the language of **THE MARQUESAN ISLANDS**, directions are indicated with reference to geographical features – which can make them hard to interpret if you don't know exactly where you are. For example, a Marquesan might say that your bicycle is "downstream of the house" or that you should "Walk inland, then seaward" to get to your destination.

UNTRANSLATABLE

Most languages have unique words and idioms that are impossible to translate exactly. These words often embody the culture of the people who speak the language. Some examples that illustrate this:

ENGLISH: ***cozy*** = pleasantly warm and comfortable
GERMAN: ***fernweh*** = a longing to be somewhere far away
JAPANESE: ***mono no aware*** = a gentle sadness at the impermanence of things
DUTCH: ***uitwaaien*** = walking in windy weather for fun
GREEK: ***parea*** = a group of friends who meet to share ideas and experiences
KIVILA (PAPUA NEW GUINEA): ***mokita*** = the truth that everyone knows but nobody talks about

1C EVERYDAY ENGLISH
Something along those lines

Learn to express yourself in an inexact way

- S Share rough details of an experience
- P Sound and spelling: *ea*, *ee*, and *ie*

1 LISTENING

a Answer the questions.

1 Have you or someone you know worked with the same coworker for a long time? Who? How long?
2 What characterizes a good working relationship?

b 01.14 Listen to Part 1. Answer the questions about the photo.

1 Where do you think Sara and Alex work?
2 What do you think their relationship is?
3 How and why does Alex think Sara can help him?

c Language in context *Irony and understatement*

1 Match Sara's and Alex's comments a–d with situations 1–4.

a ☐ Aren't you a happy camper this morning!
b ☐ Don't get too excited to see me now.
c ☐ It's not exactly good news.
d ☐ That'd be a surprise.

1 Sara is expecting the exact opposite to happen.
2 Alex notices that Sara's greeting is not enthusiastic.
3 Alex sees that Sara looks unhappy.
4 Sara has received a distressing message.

2 Why do you think Sara and Alex don't say exactly what they mean? Do people do the same in your culture?

d 01.15 Listen to Part 2. What is the relationship between … ?

- Hilary and Sara
- Sara and Oscar

e 01.15 Answer the questions. Listen to Part 2 again and check your answers.

1 What does Hilary want to talk about?
2 Why does she mention Oscar?
3 What does Hilary want from Sara?
4 What does Alex suggest is Hilary's reason for speaking to Sara?
5 What help does Sara ask Alex for?
6 What's Sara's impression of Oscar?

f Answer the questions about Parts 1 and 2.

1 What do you know about the company Sara and Alex work for? Do you think Sara and Alex do similar jobs?
2 How do you think Sara feels at the end of the conversation?

2 USEFUL LANGUAGE Expressing yourself in an inexact way

a In informal conversations, we often express things in an inexact way. Read sentences 1–4. Match the expressions in **bold** with their uses a–d.

1 ☐ *please* and *thank you* and **stuff like that**
2 ☐ Manny **whatshisname**
3 ☐ six major league players, **give or take**
4 ☐ I'm out of here, or **words to that effect**

a used to give an inexact amount
b used to report someone's words in an inexact way
c used when you can't remember someone's name exactly
d used to refer to things of a similar type in an inexact way

b Which two expressions in **bold** below could you use in 1–4 in 2a? Rewrite two ideas in 2a, changing the word order if necessary.

1 There were **somewhere in the region of** 100 people.
2 She said **something along those lines**.
3 **Whatshername** was late, as usual.
4 I need **some odds and ends** from the store.

Which two expressions can't you use in 2a? Why not? Match them to their uses:

a ☐ used to refer to things of different kinds
b ☐ used when you can't remember a woman's name exactly

c Rewrite these sentences using expressions from 2a and b.

1 It's by William Shakespeare, who wrote *A Midsummer Night's Dream*.
2 I went to the store and bought three items.
3 She told me to go away, saying, "Please would you leave now?"
4 I know a little Portuguese – *hello*, *goodbye*, the numbers one to ten.
5 I've been to 15 countries.

d 01.16 Listen and compare your answers in 2c. Are they the same? Practice different ways of saying each sentence in 2b and c.

3 PRONUNCIATION
Sound and spelling: *ea*, *ee*, and *ie*

a 01.17 Listen to the words in the box. What sound do the letters in bold make? Is this sound always spelled with two letters?

pl**ea**se m**ee**ting res**ea**rch ser**ie**s

b 01.18 The spellings *ea*, *ee*, and *ie* are not always pronounced with the vowel sound in 3a. Listen and put the words in this box in the correct column 2–4.

~~m**ee**t~~ res**ea**rch gr**ea**t fr**ie**nd

1 /iː/	2 /e/	3 /eɪ/	4 /ɜr/
meet			

c 01.19 What sound do *ea*, *ee*, and *ie* have in the words in this box? Add them to the sound groups in 3b. Listen and check. Practice saying the words.

learn Greek bear heard meaning
meant increase steadily niece
break breakfast early pear

4 SPEAKING

a 01.20 Listen and answer the questions.

1 What experience does the speaker talk about?
2 The speaker says "the horror of the situation" dawned on her. What is she referring to?

b 01.20 Listen again and write down the expressions from 2a and b that you hear.

c Work alone. Plan to talk about an experience you have had and write notes. Decide what exact details you will give and what you will mention in an inexact way. Here are some ideas:

- a time when you got to know someone new on a long journey
- a time when you traveled somewhere new on the spur of the moment
- a time when you made an unplanned purchase.

d Work with a partner. Take turns talking about your experience. Use expressions from 2a and b to mention things in an inexact way.

UNIT PROGRESS TEST

→ CHECK YOUR PROGRESS

YOU CAN NOW DO THE UNIT PROGRESS TEST.

1D SKILLS FOR WRITING
You're absolutely right!

Learn to write a web forum post

W Expressing opinions

1 SPEAKING AND LISTENING

a Look at these borrowed words from English used in other languages. Why do you think they are used?

1 džús (Slovakian)

2 outdoor (Portuguese, Brazil)

3 lonche (Spanish, Mexico)

4 maiku (Japanese)

5 gol (Spanish)

6 biznismyen (Russian)

7 kampyutara (Hindi)

b Write down some examples of English words that are commonly used in your language. Then answer the questions.

1 What are the main topic areas of borrowed English words in your language?
2 How do you / people in your country feel about adopted English words?

c You will hear a linguist, Maxwell Kingsley, talking about the dominance of English as a world language. What do you think he will say about the following?

1 the number of people that speak English
2 English as an easy language to learn
3 the Latin language
4 English's effect on the diversity of human languages
5 the only real disadvantage of the dominance of English
6 English as a truly global language

d 01.21 Listen and check. Take notes. Are there any points he makes that you find surprising?

2 READING

a Read the posts to a web forum. Which two people agree with each other?

b Which post … ?

- do you agree with most, and why
- do you think makes the most interesting point

3 WRITING SKILLS Expressing opinions

a Which elements A–E are used by each writer in the web forum?

A agreeing/disagreeing with a previous comment
B stating a new opinion on the topic
C describing cultural trends to support an opinion
D including personal experience to support an opinion
E making a summarizing statement

b Write the highlighted phrases in the posts in the correct part of the chart.

Disagreement	Agreement
That simply isn't true. That's easy to say, but … How can you possibly think that? That's a load of garbage. 1 ________ 2 ________ 3 ________	That makes a lot of sense. You've hit the nail on the head. I would go along with that. 5 ________
Uncertainty	**Partial agreement / disagreement**
I have mixed feelings about this. 4 ________	You've got a point, but … It's true that … , but … On the other hand, I do feel … 6 ________

c Look again at the highlighted phrases for disagreement in the forum. Answer the questions.

1 What phrases do the writers use to soften the disagreement phrases?
2 Do you know any other words and phrases for softening your opinions?

d Look at all the expressions in the chart. Which ones are informal? Use a dictionary to help you.

e Now go to Writing Focus 1D on p. 169.

Maxwell Kingsley makes the point that although English has become the dominant world language, this isn't a threat to other languages. Do you think he's right?

FLYING B

I'm of two minds about this.

I agree up to a point that there's a benefit to be had from a shared global language – especially the opportunity to travel and speak to other people without constantly having to learn other languages. On the other hand, as people have said elsewhere, I do feel the dominance of English interferes with the uniqueness of many languages, for example, the way words are borrowed from English.

The world is made infinitely more fascinating by having a variety of cultures. Different histories, cuisines, habits, styles of communication ... A huge part of this is our many unique languages and dialects.

Using the English language is by no means the only thing that's been undermining this uniqueness, but it clearly contributes to it.

REPLY→

PABLO

If you ask me, that's nonsense. I've lived in various countries, and people speak their own languages 99% of the time.

Many do speak English as a second language for international communication, but as far as I can tell, that doesn't have much impact on their cultural identity. It's true that people are constantly bombarded with English slang and popular buzzwords, but they don't matter that much.

Most non-native speakers see English as a simple tool, but they don't use it when they need to convey subtle details and differences.

REPLY→

GABRIELA

Great comment, you're absolutely right.

I speak English fluently, but I use Spanish (and Portuguese!) in everyday life, and, as far as I'm concerned, there's no way English is taking over my life. We all know it's a global language, but so what? Some language has to be. I get a lot out of being able to use English, but I'm never going to stop using my own language. Why would I? I don't quite get what the fuss is about here.

REPLY→

HARU

It seems to me all of you are missing the point here. Even if English does replace other languages, it's not the end of the world – just the opposite, in fact. I think that having one international language is a great way to help unify the world and the human race in general. How can we expect cultures to keep peace between each other when they can't understand each other? Unique languages tend to isolate those communities that are most likely to be economically weak.

Our heritage is only history, and history will never and can never be more important than the present or the future.

REPLY→

f Compare Flying B's and Gabriela's posts. Whose comments are more formal and abstract, and whose are more informal and personal? How can you tell? Think about:

- abstract nouns
- sentence length and structure
- personal examples
- questions and exclamation marks
- colloquial expressions
- first person.

g What style of comment would you post on this forum: formal and abstract or informal and personal? Why?

Writing Tip

In order to write good discussion forum comments.

- Choose a style and keep to it. It can be informal and chatty or it can be more formal and serious, but it's better not to mix different styles together.
- Before you respond to a comment, read it carefully to make sure your response is relevant.
- Even if you strongly disagree with someone, try not to be impolite.

4 WRITING

a Read the opinions below and check (✓) the ones you agree with.

1 ☐ **"Countries need to protect their language from the influx of English words."**

2 ☐ **"The effect of English on other languages has been more positive than negative."**

3 ☐ **"'International English' used by non-native speakers is destroying the English language."**

4 ☐ **"If you want to work for an international company, you should learn English."**

b Choose one of the opinions and start a discussion forum. Write a comment of about five or six sentences giving your point of view.

c Share your post with another student. Read another student's post and add a comment. It can be a response or a further comment on the topic.

d Respond or comment on three other posts.

e Read the discussion forum that you started. Which comment do you think is the most interesting?

UNIT 1
Review and extension

1 GRAMMAR

a Correct seven mistakes with adverbials. Sometimes more than one answer is possible.

1 Please slowly try to speak.
2 He will be probably late.
3 We do by hand our washing.
4 We will be living in June in Vancouver.
5 She made me so loudly laugh.
6 I in the end managed to get in touch.
7 You can compare easily the different brands.

b Complete the sentences with the correct form of the verbs.

1 I *have never visited* / *never visit* an English-speaking country before.
2 *I've been learning* / *I'm learning* English for ages.
3 I *had been crossing* / *was crossing* the road when the car hit me.
4 I *have wanted* / *wanted* to give up at the beginning but kept studying.
5 She *has had* / *has* her hair cut. Doesn't it look nice?
6 I *had been studying* / *was studying* for five hours when you got home.

2 VOCABULARY

a Replace the words in *italics* with an expression in the box.

acquire rusty brush up on come to grips with hold a conversation immerse yourself in struggle with

1 Sally really used to *have problems with* phrasal verbs.
2 The best way to learn is to *fully get to know* the culture.
3 Vladimir is amazing; he can *talk* with anyone in English.
4 How do young children *learn* their first language?
5 I'd better *improve* my French before the trip.
6 I can't *understand the complexities of* German grammar.
7 Mom's Spanish must be *worse than it was*.

b Complete the words with the missing letters.

1 Her popularity with teens has been on a r_______d rise.
2 Even a s_______e change in his hairstyle gets comments.
3 There has been a steady s_______t toward part-time work.
4 This will not result in a l_______g change.
5 Black jeans are on the w_______y out.
6 The o_______g changes are affecting productivity.
7 Perhaps the benefits will not be p_______e for a while.

3 WORDPOWER Idioms: Body parts

a 01.22 Complete the idioms with the words in the box. Listen and check.

shoulders hands tooth nose tongue head neck

1 Mark obviously **has a** _______ **for** business investment; he hasn't lost us any money yet.
2 I walked over to the photographers, shouting and yelling. I completely **lost my** _______.
3 Coworkers regard Mika as **a good pair of** _______ who can be relied on to step in when required.
4 It may happen, but I certainly wouldn't **stick my** _______ **out** and promise anything.
5 After five years of training for this event, he's **head and** _______ **above** the competition.
6 I had to **bite my** _______ when my manager took credit for my work.
7 I will **fight** _______ **and nail** to prevent any plan that threatens local livelihoods.

b Match the idioms 1–7 in 3a with definitions a–g.

a ☐ take a risk
b ☐ try very hard to overcome opposition and get something you want
c ☐ be good at finding a specific thing
d ☐ stop yourself from saying something
e ☐ lose control of your behavior
f ☐ someone other people trust to do a good job
g ☐ be a lot better than other competitors

c Complete the questions with the idioms in 3a.

1 In what situations do you think it's important to _______ out?
2 Who do you know who has _______ for something?
3 Who's an actor you think is _______ above most others?
4 How do you react if someone you know loses _______ in front of you?
5 What's something you would fight _______ to prevent?
6 In what situations do you think people should _______ tongues?
7 Who do you know who's a _______ in an emergency?

d Answer the questions in 3c.

REVIEW YOUR PROGRESS

How well did you do in this unit? Write 3, 2, or 1 for each objective.
3 = very well 2 = well 1 = not so well

I CAN ...	
talk about learning a second language	☐
describe languages and how they change	☐
express myself in an inexact way	☐
write a web forum post.	☐

CAN DO OBJECTIVES

- Describe extreme sensory experiences
- Talk about plans, intentions, and arrangements
- Give advice
- Write a report

UNIT 2

GOING TO EXTREMES

GETTING STARTED

a Look at the picture and answer the questions.

1 Where is the man? Why do you think he's swimming here?
2 What are the possible risks of swimming here? What skills and attributes do you think a person swimming here needs?
3 What do you think this man does immediately after his swim?
4 Would you consider swimming in this location?

b Answer the questions.

1 Imagine you're about to interview this man for the local newspaper. Make a list of questions to ask him. Ask your partner and answer their questions.
2 What's the coldest/hottest experience you've ever had? Describe it to a partner.

2A I WOULD HAPPILY HAVE STAYED LONGER

Learn to describe extreme sensory experiences

G Comparison

V Multi-word verbs: social interaction

1 SPEAKING

a 02.01 Listen to six sounds. Write down what you hear and ask and answer the questions.

1 How often do you hear these sounds? Where?
2 How does each sound make you feel?

b **Communication 2A** Now go to p. 127.

2 READING

a Look at the photo, read the caption, and answer the questions.

1 What do you think an anechoic chamber is?
2 Do you think you'd like to go to one? Why / Why not?

b Read about George Foy's visit to an anechoic chamber on p. 21. Was it a positive experience overall?

c Read the text again and answer the questions.

1 Why did George begin his search?
2 What makes the anechoic chamber at Orfield so quiet?
3 Do most people enjoy being in the anechoic chamber? Why / Why not?
4 What physical and mental effects can the anechoic chamber cause in people?
5 Why was George concerned about going into the chamber?
6 What was George's first reaction to being in the anechoic chamber?
7 Did he enjoy all of his time in the chamber? Why / Why not?
8 What does George say people should do to deal with sensitivity to noise?

d Cover the text and try to remember why George mentioned these things.

1 the New York subway
2 a monastery and a mine
3 his blood
4 his scalp
5 beating the record
6 TV

e Do you think you could have lasted as long as George in the anechoic chamber? Why / Why not?

The anechoic chamber, Orfield Laboratories, Minneapolis
The quieter the room, the more things you hear. You'll hear your heart beating, sometimes you can hear your lungs, and you can hear your stomach gurgling loudly. In the anechoic chamber, you become the sound.

f **Language in context** *Sounds*

1 Match the definitions below with the highlighted words in the text.

a strange and mysterious and a little frightening (adj.)
b so loud you can't hear anything (adj.)
c to make a sound by repeatedly hitting something hard (v.)
d to complain in a high, unpleasant voice (v.)
e the sound an empty stomach makes (v.)
f a long, loud, deep noise (n.)
g the sound of a heartbeat (n.)
h the sound made by using only the breath to speak (n.)
i units that measure loudness (n.)

2 Underline the adjectives in the article that describe these nouns: *roar*, *whisper*, *thump*.

Learning Tip
When you make a note of a new word, it's a good idea to write down the collocation(s) as well. You can also look in dictionaries for other collocations to add to your notes.

3 Notice the words *noise* and *sound(s)* in *italics* in the article. What words in the text form collocations with these nouns? What part of speech are they? Use a dictionary to help you.

block out noise (v.), a source of noise (n.), absorb sound (v.)

I've been to the QUIETEST PLACE ON EARTH

by George Foy

My search started when I was in the New York subway. My children were whining, four trains came screaming into the station at once, and I put my hands over my ears and cowered – the *noise* was deafening.

In cities, the ever-present dull roar of planes, cars, machinery, and voices is a fact of life. There is no escape from it, and I was beginning to be driven crazy by it. I needed to find a place where I could recapture a sense of peace. The quieter this place was, the more relaxing it would be.

I decided to go on a mission to discover whether absolute silence exists. I traveled to a monastery and a mine two kilometers underground – both very quiet, but not the quietest place on Earth. The one place I was most excited about visiting was the anechoic chamber at Orfield Laboratories in Minnesota.

This is a small room insulated with layers of concrete and steel to block out exterior sources of *noise* and internally lined with buffers that absorb all *sound*. Even the floor is a suspended mesh to stop any *sound* of footfalls. If a soft whisper is measured at 20 decibels, the anechoic chamber is one sixteenth of that. The anechoic chamber is considerably quieter than any other place on Earth. Ironically, far from being peaceful, most people find its perfect quiet upsetting. Being deprived of the usual reassuring ambient *sounds* can create fear – it explains why sensory deprivation is a form of torture. Astronauts do part of their training in anechoic chambers at NASA, so they can learn to cope with the silence of space. The presence of *sound* means things are working; it's business as usual – when *sound* is absent, that signals malfunction. I had heard being in an anechoic chamber for longer than 15 minutes can cause extreme symptoms, from claustrophobia and nausea to panic attacks and aural hallucinations – you literally start hearing things. A violinist tried it and hammered on the door after a few seconds, demanding to be let out because he was so disturbed by the silence.

I booked a 45-minute session – no one had managed to stay in for that long before. I felt apprehensive for two reasons: would I go crazy and tear off my clothes? Or would I simply be disappointed it wasn't as enjoyable as I'd hoped?

When the heavy door shut behind me, I was plunged into darkness (lights can make a *noise*). For the first few seconds, being in such a quiet place felt utterly peaceful, soothing for my jangled nerves. I strained to hear something and heard … nothing.

Then, after a minute or two, I became aware of my own breathing. The *sound* became more and more noticeable, so I held my breath. The dull thump of my heartbeat became apparent – nothing I could do about that. As the minutes ticked by, I started to hear the blood rushing in my veins. Your ears become more sensitive as the place gets quieter, and mine were going overtime. I frowned and heard my scalp moving over my skull, which was eerie, and a strange, metallic scraping *noise* I couldn't explain. Was I hallucinating? The feeling of peace was spoiled by a little disappointment – this place wasn't quiet at all. You'd have to be dead for absolute silence.

Then I stopped being obsessed with my body and began to enjoy it. I didn't feel afraid and came out only because my time was up; I would happily have stayed longer in there. Everyone was impressed that I'd beaten the record, but having spent so long searching for quiet, I was comfortable with the feeling of absolute stillness. Afterward I felt wonderfully rested and calm. The experience was nowhere near as disturbing as I had been led to believe.

My desire for silence changed my life. I found that making space for moments of quiet in my day is the key to happiness – they give you a chance to think about what you want in life. How can you really focus on what's important if you're distracted by constant background *noise*? If you can occasionally become master of your own *sound* environment – from turning off the TV to moving to the country, as I did – you become infinitely more accepting of the *noises* of everyday life.

3 GRAMMAR Comparison

a Cover the text. Complete the sentences with the words in the box. Then check your answers in the text.

considerably the (x2) and infinitely nowhere near more

1 The quieter the room, ________ more things you hear.
2 ________ quieter this place was, the more relaxing it would be.
3 The anechoic chamber is ________ quieter than any other place on Earth.
4 The sound [of my breathing] became more ________ more noticeable …
5 Your ears become ________ sensitive as the place gets quieter …
6 The experience was ________ as disturbing as I had been led to believe.
7 … you become ________ more accepting of the noises of everyday life.

b Answer the questions about the sentences in 3a.

1 Which sentences contain two comparative forms? Are the two qualities in these sentences independent of or dependent on each other?
2 Which sentence(s) describe something increasing progressively over time?
3 Look at sentences 3 and 6. Which words in the box below are possible in each blank?

slightly a good deal decidedly not nearly significantly

c Now go to Grammar Focus 2A on p. 140.

d Think of a place or an event that you had a strong physical or mental reaction to. Tell your partner.

1 Was this place different from your expectations? Why / Why not?
2 How did you feel? Did your feelings change the longer you stayed there?
3 Would you like to go back to this place? Why / Why not?

The first time I went to a sauna, it was considerably hotter than I'd expected it to be …

4 LISTENING

a Answer the questions.

1 Have you ever gone for a long period of time without speaking? Why? How did you communicate?
2 What are some reasons people choose not to speak for a long period of time?

b 02.07 Listen to the first part of Lena's story. Why did she decide to stop talking?

c 02.07 Listen to Part 1 again. Summarize what Lena says about these things.

1 the dinner party
2 her realization
3 a spiritual vow of silence
4 a public vow of silence

d What rules do you think Lena should make for herself for her vow of silence? What situations might be difficult?

e 02.08 Listen to Part 2. Does Lena mention any of your ideas from 4d?

f 02.08 Listen to Part 2 again. What does Lena say about these people?

- herself
- the person in the café
- her friend
- the woman in the supermarket
- her landlord

How did she feel at the end of her experiment?

g Answer the questions.

1 What do you think of the experiment Lena did? Would you try an experiment like this? Why / Why not?
2 Are you surprised by the reactions of the woman in the supermarket and her landlord? Why / Why not?

5 VOCABULARY
Multi-word verbs: social interaction

a 02.09 Complete the sentences below with the correct particles in the box. Listen and check.

down with to across out (x2)
in off back about

1 Talking is a way of **fitting** ________ – y'know, a way of showing that we belong to a social group.
2 How would I **come** ________ to other people?
3 … people go into some kind of retreat to **cut themselves** ________ from the outside world.
4 … when someone held a door open for me and a little "thank you" **slipped** ________.
5 The most interesting thing was the way other people **related** ________ **me**.
6 She **bombarded me** ________ **questions**.
7 He always **complains** ________ something when I go and see him …
8 He usually likes to **put** ________ some politician or other.
9 I often felt that my silence **brought** ________ **the best in people**.
10 I often wanted to, but I had to **hold myself** ________.

b Copy the chart into your notebook. Then write the multi-word verbs you completed in the sentences in 5a in the correct column of the chart.

social interaction in general	spoken interaction
fit in	*slip out*

c 02.10 **Pronunciation** Listen to the phrase below. What sound connects with the beginning of *across*?

How would I come across to other people?

d 02.11 Listen to these phrases from 5a again. Where is there consonant–vowel linking? What sounds are used?

1 … cut themselves off from …
2 … and a little "thank you" slipped out …
3 … complains about something …
4 … my silence brought out the best …

Practice saying the phrases with consonant–vowel linking.

e Think of people you can describe using some of the multi-word verbs in 5a. Tell your partner.

Someone you know who:

- comes across well to new people
- relates to other people well
- often complains about a problem they have
- brings out the best in you
- tends to cut themselves off from the outside world
- sometimes bombards people with questions
- likes to put down famous people.

Learning Tip
When you learn new multi-word verbs, thinking of personalized examples can help you remember the new vocabulary. You can record them in your vocabulary notebook.

6 SPEAKING

Read the ideas about communication. Give an example for each statement you think is true.

1 Communication isn't about what you say – it's about how you say it.
2 It's not the silence that's uneasy; it's your own thoughts that fill the silence.
3 Sometimes talking about a problem only makes it worse.
4 Good listeners make good leaders.
5 People who talk a lot often have the least valuable things to say.

2B I'LL BE JUMPING FROM 900 METERS

Learn to talk about plans, intentions, and arrangements

G Intentions and arrangements

V Verbs of movement

1 READING AND SPEAKING

a Do you like speed and danger? Which of these activities would you enjoy?

- ☐ flying in a two-seater plane
- ☐ climbing a mountain
- ☐ going on a roller coaster
- ☐ driving at 130 kph on a highway
- ☐ going on a small boat in a rough sea
- ☐ skiing

Order the activities from 1–6 (1 = least enjoy). Compare your order with other students and explain your choices.

b Work in groups of four. Read about one different sport below each. Find answers to these questions where possible and report back to the group.

1 Where do you do it?
2 What do you wear?
3 What do you do exactly?
4 How dangerous is it?
5 How expensive is it?

c Which of these activities have you tried or would you like to try? Why? Rate each sport by writing the initials *Z-L*, *IS*, *Z*, *V-B* on the scales below. Then compare your answers with other students.

exhilarating ———————— no fun at all
absolutely terrifying ———————— not scary at all
worth every penny ———————— a waste of money

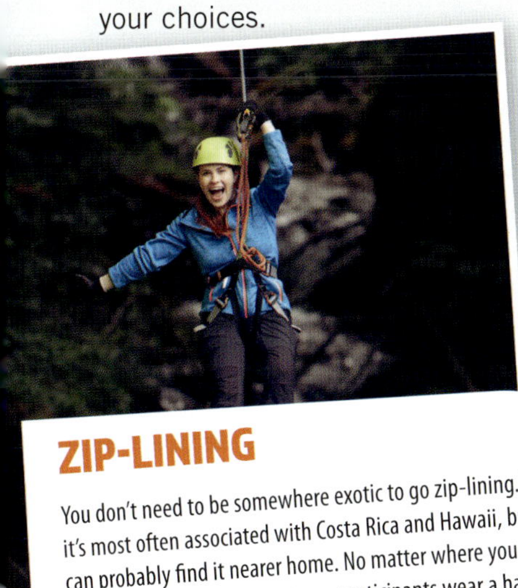

LOOKING FOR A GOOD THRILL?

Try one of these to get your heart pumping:

ZIP-LINING

You don't need to be somewhere exotic to go zip-lining. Yes, it's most often associated with Costa Rica and Hawaii, but you can probably find it nearer home. No matter where you are, cables are strung between trees; participants wear a harness attached to a wheel that dangles from the line. In locales like Costa Rica, you'll be mingling with monkeys 25 meters above ground, with a bird's-eye view of the jungle. At a mountain resort, you'll go whizzing over ski slopes or a canopy of trees. The fastest zip lines reach speeds of up to 160 km an hour. It usually costs between $100 and $200.

ZORBING

Globe-riding. Orbing. Zorbing. This is the sport of climbing into a clear, plastic ball (typically 3.5 meters in diameter) and rolling downhill at high speed. It looks like a giant hamster ball. Zorbing first hit the extreme-sport scene in New Zealand, and now it's available anywhere in the world. Usually, riders are strapped against one of the ball's walls. Not in hydro-zorbing, though. In that case, the operator adds about 5 gallons of water, and passengers slip and splash as the ball rolls.

INDOOR SKYDIVING

Consider it a trial run before jumping out of a plane. At iFly facilities nationwide, you'll don a flight suit and helmet and go soaring inside a vertical wind tunnel. These are 4 meters in diameter and generate wind speeds of up to 260 km per hour. Flights mimic the experience of free-fall skydiving without the parachute. If you're between ages 3 and 103, you can do it; cost typically ranges from $90 to $175.

VOLCANO-BOARDING

Thrill-seekers: head forth to Nicaragua. Prepare to zoom down a steep, 487-meter volcanic slope on a plywood board reinforced with metal and Formica. One of the latest additions to the extreme-sport scene, it's only done on Cerro Negro, a charcoal-black active volcano that's erupted 23 times in the past 100 years. (The threat of another eruption always looms, though there hasn't been one since 1999.) Tourists pay $30–$40 for the experience.

2 READING

a Why do you think people do extreme sports? Choose from these reasons. Read the article and check.

- ☐ to impress other people
- ☐ to feel more alive
- ☐ to feel they are in control
- ☐ to feel part of an exclusive group
- ☐ to test their limits
- ☐ to feel great afterward

b Read the article again and answer the questions.

1 The article mentions volcano-boarding. What four other activities does it refer to?
2 What does the expression "Type T" refer to?
3 How is biology relevant to Type Ts' behavior?
4 What personality characteristics do Type Ts typically have?
5 Why do people feel happy after going on a roller coaster?

c Language in context *Synonyms*: *want, like, love*

1 Which expressions in the box were used instead of the words in *italics* in the sentences below? Check your answers in the text.

crave | be drawn to | be inclined | long for | thrive on

a Thrill-seekers *really want* that rush; they *love* it.
b These are people who *want* exciting, meaningful challenges.
c Dopamine and testosterone appear to affect how much someone *wants* to play it safe.
d Margaret J. King studies why people *like* roller coasters.

2 How is each expression in the box different from the ones in *italics*? Which words have very similar meanings? Use a dictionary to help you.

d Do you think you have any Type T characteristics? Who do you know who is definitely a Type T?

e 02.12 **Pronunciation** Listen to the sentences below. Underline the stressed syllable of the word that receives the most stress in each thought group.

1 I like to make my own de<u>cis</u>ions, ‖ and I never play by the <u>rules</u>.
2 I need a guide ‖ in new cities ‖ in case I get lost.
3 I do feel scared ‖ when I face danger, ‖ but I know that I'll be OK.
4 I'm paid to innovate ‖ at work, ‖ so I spend half my time daydreaming!
5 I think people should dress neatly ‖ and look respectable, ‖ especially in public.

f Complete the rule. Practice saying the comments in 2e.

The *first* / *last* word that carries meaning in each word group usually has the main stress.

g Which of the comments in 2e do you think a Type T person would agree with? Why?

Why Some of Us Are THRILL-SEEKERS

Skydiving? Zip-lining? Volcano-boarding? Yes, say thrill-seekers, and there's a reason.

Every thrill-seeker knows the feeling. Heart pounding. Hands trembling. Blood racing. And then all of a sudden – flying. Plunging through the air, 5,500 meters above the Earth, clinging to a parachute that could by all means fail. Hurtling at 80 kilometers an hour down a 487-meter volcanic slope, on a volcano board popularized by young adventurers. Whooshing down whitewater rapids on a flimsy raft. Or being strapped into a zero-gravity roller coaster and preparing to whirl upside down, again and again. Thrill-seekers crave that rush; they thrive on it.

"It's the excitement," says Frank Farley, a professor of educational psychology at Temple University in Philadelphia. "It makes things interesting, keeps you going. When this life is over, you want to be able to look back and say, 'I lived.' As Helen Keller once said, 'Life is a daring adventure, or it is nothing.'"

In the 1980s, Farley coined the term Type T personality to describe thrill-seekers, or those who crave variety, novelty, intensity, and risk. These are people who long for exciting, meaningful challenges. Some enjoy the physical sensations that come from being scared silly; others like the idea that they're pushing themselves to the extreme.

At least to some degree, Type Ts are born that way, Farley says. Though researchers don't yet have all the answers, it's clear that biology plays a role. Neurochemicals like dopamine and testosterone appear to affect how inclined someone is to play it safe or live on the wild side, as does the amount of white matter in the brain.

Other factors are psychological and rooted in personality. Thrill-seekers tend to be creative folks who like to make up their own minds. "They're energetic and self-confident," Farley says. "And they feel in control of their fate. When they climb Mt. Everest, they figure they're going to come back. If someone tells them not to do it, that sounds like a rule, so away they go."

Margaret J. King, director of Cultural Studies and Analysis, a Philadelphia-based think tank, studies human behavior and, more specifically, why people are drawn to roller coasters. These days, riders are in for dangling seats that throw them upside down and backwards in gravity-defying loops and twists. "You wouldn't think we would put ourselves in such a terrifying position," King says. "But terror gives us a chance to test ourselves, our own tolerance. We like the idea that we can get through it." Boarding a roller coaster makes us feel like "we're in imminent danger of dying," she explains. "All the signals in our body tell us we're headed in a bad direction. We can't get off. We can't stop the thing. And then when we do, there's a tremendous rush of adrenaline, of ecstasy and elation. That's why you see people bouncing off rides with their friends."

3 VOCABULARY Verbs of movement

a Look at these sentences and answer questions 1 and 2.

a You'll go **soaring** inside a vertical wind tunnel.
b You'll go **whizzing** over ski slopes.
c This is the sport of **rolling** downhill at high speed.
d Prepare to **zoom** down a steep, 487-meter volcanic slope.
e **Plunging** through the air, 5,500 meters above the Earth …
f **Hurtling** down a 487-meter volcanic slope …
g **Whooshing** down whitewater rapids on a flimsy raft …
h Preparing to **whirl** upside down, again and again …

1 Can each verb in **bold** above describe movement … ?
- on land
- through water
- through the air

Write *L* / *W* / *A* next to a–h. Use a dictionary to help you.

2 Which verbs suggest the sound that the action makes?

b Now go to Vocabulary Focus 2B on p.159.

4 LISTENING

a 02.14 You are going to hear an interview with Ada, who is going base jumping.

1 Look at the picture. What do base jumpers do?
2 What do you think Ada might say about base jumping? Write down a few ideas.
- before the jump *I've never done it before.*
- after the jump *I was afraid the parachute wouldn't open.*

Listen and check your ideas.

b 02.14 Answer the questions. Listen and check.

1 What do these numbers in the interview refer to?

a 10 c 900 e 20
b 300 d 25 f 30,000

2 What does Ada say about the risks of base jumping?

c Would you consider going base jumping? Why / Why not?

5 GRAMMAR Intentions and arrangements

a 02.15 Both future forms in each pair below are possible. Which sentence did the speakers use, and why? Listen and check.

1 a So Ada, you**'re about to go** base jumping.
  b So Ada, you**'re going to go** base jumping.
2 a **I'm due to jump** in about ten minutes.
  b **I'm planning to jump** in about ten minutes.
3 a **I'll jump** from 900 meters.
  b **I'll be jumping** from 900 meters.
4 a **I'm definitely going to do** it again.
  b **I'm definitely doing** it again.

b 02.16 Complete the sentences below with the words Ada used. Listen and check.

intention planning aiming thinking

1 **I'm** also ________ **of trying** a tandem jump sometime.
2 There is a platform that sticks out over the cliff, and **I'm** ________ **to jump** off that one.
3 **I'm** ________ **to free fall** for exactly 25 seconds.
4 You come here **with the** ________ **of having** a great experience, and … and that's what you do.

c Now go to Grammar Focus 2B on p. 141.

d Prepare to talk about your plans for next year. Are you planning to do / thinking of doing … ?
- something you've never done before
- something exciting or risky

Think how you could use expressions from 5a and b.

e Tell the other students about your plans. Is anyone planning to do something you'd like to do?

6 SPEAKING AND WRITING

a Look at the photo of the mountain lake. Where do you think it is? Why might someone want to live there?

b **Communication 2B** Now go to p. 132.

2C EVERYDAY ENGLISH
Don't get so worked up about it

Learn to give advice

- S Advise a friend on a tricky situation
- P Emphatic stress

1 LISTENING

a Answer the questions.

1 In your country, at what age do people usually … ?
- leave home
- rent or buy their first property

2 What are the pros and cons of living with … ?
- relatives
- people you don't know
- friends your own age

3 What factors are important in making the decision to leave home?

b Look at photos a and b. Max is staying with his sister Emma. What do you think Emma is telling her friend Ana about this?

c 02.21 Listen to Part 1 and check your answer in 1b.

d 02.21 Listen to Part 1 again. Answer the questions.

1 What is Emma's problem? Why exactly is Max annoying her?
2 What has she done about it so far?
3 What is Ana's advice to Emma?
4 What does Ana know about Max Rayburn?

e 02.22 **Language in context** *Being tactful or frank*

1 Match the halves of the expressions from Part 1. Listen and check.

1 ☐ It's like **walking**
2 ☐ I keep **dropping**
3 ☐ Why don't you just come out and **tell**
4 ☐ **Don't beat around**
5 ☐ There's a lot to be said for **being**

a **the bush**.
b **him to his face?**
c **hints**, but he doesn't seem to get it.
d **upfront about things**.
e **on eggshells** around him.

2 Which expressions in 1 describe being tactful (careful in what you say)? Which describe being frank (honest in what you say)?

f Answer the questions.

1 Do you think Emma is right to drop hints to her brother, or should she stop beating around the bush and tell him to his face?
2 Have you ever had the experience of guests who outstayed their welcome? What happened?

2 PRONUNCIATION Emphatic stress

a 02.23 Listen to the sentences below. Underline the main stress in the word groups in **bold**. Which word in a word group normally has the main stress? Check the rule on p. 24.

1 **Max will be home soon**.
2 **He's getting on my nerves**.
3 Isn't it about time **you asked him to leave**?
4 **Did you say his name is Max**?

b 02.24 Sometimes the main stress does not follow the rule on p. 24. Listen and underline the main stress in the thought groups in **bold**.

1 **He's not still sleeping on the sofa**, is he?
2 **I know that name.**
3 **You mean it is him**?
4 **Your brother is *the* Max Rayburn**!

c Look at 2b again and answer these questions.

1 Why don't the phrases in 2b follow the rule on p. 24?
2 What does Ana mean when she says "*the* Max Rayburn"?

d Emphasizing different words in a word group changes the meaning. Match sentences 1–5 with their meanings a–e. Practice saying the sentences with the correct main stress.

1 ☐ Ana has heard Max's band.
2 ☐ Ana has heard Max's band.
3 ☐ Ana has heard Max's band.
4 ☐ Ana has heard Max's band.
5 ☐ Ana has heard Max's band.

The speaker is telling us:

a what Ana has done with Max's band
b whose band Ana has heard
c who has heard Max's band
d that Ana has heard Max's band, not his podcast or presentation
e that we are wrong to believe Ana hasn't heard Max's band.

e Look at this sentence with the main stress in three different places. Work in pairs. Create a short conversation for each sentence. Then practice your conversation.

I'll give you a call later. I'll give you a call later. I'll give you a call later.

3 LISTENING

a Look at photo c. Who do you think says these sentences, Emma or Max?

1 Have you thought about the possibility of finding your own place to live?
2 I need to focus on the band.
3 Don't get so worked up about it.
4 You really will need to move out at some point … soon!
5 If you had your own place, I wouldn't be there to annoy you.

b 02.25 Listen to Part 2 and check your answers in 3a.

c 02.25 Listen to Part 2 again. Answer the questions.

1 Why does Emma think it wouldn't be a problem for Max to move out now?
2 What advantage does Emma mention for Max if he finds his own place?
3 What does Max say he's been busy doing lately?
4 Why doesn't Max want to think about moving right now?

d Answer the questions.

1 What would you do if you were Emma? What would you do if you were Max?
2 What are the worst things that could happen?

4 USEFUL LANGUAGE Giving advice

a Answer the questions.

1 Is the farmer's advice in picture d appropriate for the situation? Why / Why not?
2 What would you expect the farmer to say if a train was coming?
3 In what other situations might you use the advice in picture d?

b 02.26 Match 1–7 with a–g to make sentences from Parts 1 and 2. Listen and check.

1 ☐ **Isn't it about**
2 ☐ **There's a lot to be said**
3 ☐ **Have you thought about the possibility**
4 ☐ **It might be in**
5 ☐ **You might want to**
6 ☐ **Don't get so**
7 ☐ **You can tell me**

a **your plan** later tonight.
b **time you** asked him to leave?
c put some thought into where you're going to live.
d **of** finding your own place to live?
e **for** being upfront about things.
f **worked up** about it.
g **your best interest** to find a place.

c Which two expressions in **bold** in 4b sound more polite and formal?

d Complete the advice with the expressions in 4b.

1 You ________ to read up about the company before your interview.
2 Have you ________ working overseas?
3 There's ________ having your own car.
4 Isn't it ________ you sold it and got a better one?
5 It might be in ________ keep on good terms with the director.

e Look at the sentences from two conversations. Which conversation seems to be more formal? Describe the context that could fit each conversation.

Conversation 1
Isn't it about time you were upfront about it? Stop beating around the bush!

Conversation 2
Have you thought about the possibility of changing the terms? It might be in your best interest to contact a lawyer.

f Work in pairs. Think about contexts where you have to give advice in a formal way and an informal way. Have two conversations using the phrases in 4b.

5 SPEAKING

Communication 2C Work in pairs. Student A: Go to p. 127. Student B: Go to p. 131.

UNIT PROGRESS TEST

CHECK YOUR PROGRESS

YOU CAN NOW DO THE UNIT PROGRESS TEST.

2D SKILLS FOR WRITING

Less adventurous students could try paintball

Learn to write a report

W Reports; Linking: contrast and concession

1 LISTENING AND SPEAKING

a You have to choose a sports activity for a student club. Which of the activities in the photos would you choose?
Think about:

- appeal of the activity
- skills required
- student safety
- cost
- chances to socialize.

b 02.27 Listen to four students talking about the sports activities for a social club at a university in Australia. Take notes on their feedback.

	Positives	Negatives
bungee jumping		
whitewater rafting		
other feedback		

c Think about the students' feedback in 1b. Would you choose the same activities for next year's program? Which new sports could you choose instead? Explain your choices.

2 READING

a Read the report by a member of the social club committee and compare the content with your notes in 1b.

1 Which aspects of the students' feedback are included?
2 What negative feedback is not included?

b Are the recommendations similar to your ideas in 1c?

SOCIAL CLUB

Review and Recommendations of the Committee

1 ________________

The purpose of this report is to review options for sports activities that would be suitable as part of an extracurricular club for foreign exchange students. Last year we had two activities for exchange students: whitewater rafting and bungee jumping, both of which received mixed reviews. This report is based on feedback on these activities.

2 ________________

Even though many students liked the extreme nature of last year's activities, some felt they were too challenging. Many young tourists who come to Australia are excited to do these activities. However, not all our students necessarily have the same ambition. Whitewater rafting was not possible for students who were not confident swimmers. On the other hand, bungee jumping did not require any particular skill or expertise. Nevertheless, the idea of jumping from a bridge was seen by several as being risky.

3 WRITING SKILLS

Reports; Linking: contrast and concession

a Add these headings to the correct paragraphs of the report.

- Safety Concerns
- Recommendations
- Cost and Budget
- Introduction
- Level of Challenge

b What phrases are used in the report to give … ?

1 the reason for writing the report
2 recommendations

Are these phrases formal or informal?

c Which word in *italics* in each phrase below does not belong?

1 The *purpose* / *aim* / *agenda* / *objective* of this report is …
2 I would *establish* / *recommend* / *suggest* / *propose* that …
3 My *recommendation(s)* / *conclusion(s)* / *suggestion(s)* / *resolution(s)* is/are …

d Look at the highlighted transition words in the report and decide which word(s) in **bold** in these sentences they could replace.

1 **Unlike** whitewater rafting, bungee jumping is relatively safe.
2 Go-karting is cheaper than skydiving. **Despite this**, skydiving is still more popular with students.
3 You could go horseback riding. **Alternatively**, you could go bungee jumping.
4 **In spite of** the cost, many people go skydiving regularly.
5 **Although** it is very expensive, many people go skydiving regularly.

3 ____________

Safety issues were raised with both activities. One whitewater raft overturned, and a student suffered a concussion when he hit his head on a rock. Likewise, another student sprained her ankle in the bungee jump.

4 ____________

Both activities were quite expensive, so despite the generous budget, we were obliged to ask students to make a contribution, which many were not happy about. The cost of providing transportation to the venues for the activities drove the costs up further.

5 ____________

For the students who are due to arrive this year, we would recommend that we choose slightly cheaper options and that we offer one extreme sports activity as well as something that is, by comparison, considerably less challenging. In contrast to whitewater rafting, tree-top adventuring is a relatively inexpensive extreme sport with an excellent safety record. Alternatively, less adventurous students could try paintball, which is a low-cost and fun option that does not require any skill. Use of the local paintball venue would cut transportation costs, and we would suggest using the savings as a way of subsidizing these activities for students.

e Match 1–6 with a–f. Underline the transition words of contrast and concession in a–f. Include any prepositions that form part of the transition.

1 ☐ Although extreme sports are generally seen as fun and exciting,
2 ☐ Despite the fact that many students said they were excited to try bungee jumping,
3 ☐ Some students didn't object to paying a small amount for the activity. On the contrary,
4 ☐ When compared to contact sports like rugby and ice hockey,
5 ☐ Regardless of savings we make on transportation,
6 ☐ While many students indicated that they have to live on a tight budget,

a they had assumed they would have to make some kind of contribution.
b there has been some negative feedback on last year's activities.
c several said that the activities were affordable.
d we cannot afford to subsidize very expensive activities.
e extreme sports begin to look very safe.
f many failed to reserve a place when this activity was advertised.

f Now go to Writing Focus 2D on p. 170.

4 WRITING

a You are on a committee that has to organize a three-day tourist itinerary for a group of foreign students. Imagine problems previous groups might have had. Think about:

- range of sites visited
- transportation
- refreshments
- time to visit sites
- availability of guides
- costs.

b Plan a report that talks about these problems and suggests solutions.

> **Writing Tip**
>
> You probably talked about a lot of ideas in 4a. However, it may not be possible to mention them all in detail in the report. In a report of this nature, you should address three or four key issues, so you may have to prioritize some points over others. It is preferable to mention problems that you can suggest a solution to.

c Write a report of between 250 and 300 words on the tourist itinerary.

d Read another student's report. Do you both mention the same problems and solutions? Which of your problems and solutions are different?

UNIT 2
Review and extension

1 GRAMMAR

a Complete the sentences with one word.

1 The sound quality wasn't as high __as__ I expected.
2 It's a great ________ more expensive to make 3D movies.
3 This is by ________ the tastiest meal I've had in months!
4 The higher you go, ________ farther you can see.
5 I was getting more and ________ worried by the sounds.
6 Real coffee tastes nothing ________ the stuff from a jar.
7 They didn't make anywhere ________ as much mess as I thought they would.
8 The first place was really noisy, and the second was just ________ bad.

b Complete the sentences with the correct future form.

1 My brothers *are going to* / *are thinking of* attempt to climb K2.
2 The race *will begin* / *is aiming to begin* in five minutes, so get ready.
3 How are you *getting* / *going to get* there on time?
4 What *will you be* / *are you* wearing when I see you?
5 The police are *going to* / *thinking to* speak to those involved.
6 The plane is *due to* / *about to* arrive in Buenos Aires at 7:00 tomorrow morning.

2 VOCABULARY

a Match 1–5 with a–e.

1 ☐ Unfortunately, she can come
2 ☐ I wish you wouldn't complain
3 ☐ Living in a small village, I felt cut
4 ☐ Don't worry about fitting
5 ☐ A crisis brings

a about the neighbors all the time.
b out the best and worst in people.
c in; your new coworkers are very friendly.
d across as a bit arrogant.
e off and isolated.

b Answer the questions with one word.

1 Would you *stroll* in a park or a train station? park
2 What could *hurtle* past you – a feather or a cat?
3 If something *whirls*, does it travel in a straight line?
4 What could *whoosh* past you – a truck or a turtle?
5 Who might *stagger* – someone ill or someone angry?
6 What might *crawl* – a small child or a plane?
7 What could *roll* better – stones or boxes?
8 What surface can you *slide* on – ice or sand?

3 WORDPOWER Idioms: Movement

a 02.28 Replace the words in *italics* in each sentence with the correct form of a verb in the box. Listen and check.

plunge	whizz	soar	drift	whirl	crawl

1 a After a smart marketing campaign, the company's profits are *going up*.
  b Temperatures *went down suddenly* to a record low last night.

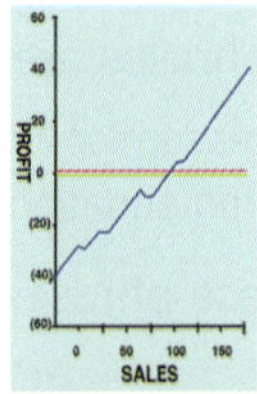

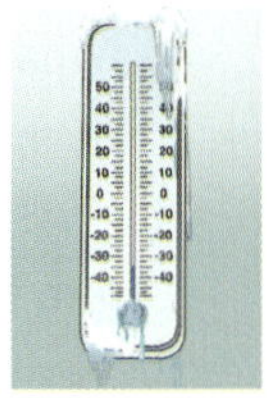

2 a I sat looking out the window, letting my thoughts *go where they wanted*.
  b My mind was *full of thoughts going around in my head*, and I simply couldn't decide what to do next.

3 a I'm enjoying my job so much that time seems to be *going really quickly* by.
  b I hate long-haul flights. Time always seems to *go very slowly* by.

b Match the expressions in **bold** with their definitions.

1 Don't be so scared of going back to college. I'm sure it'll be great. Come on, **take the plunge**.
2 Climbing down the rock surface, I **felt a rush** of adrenaline!
3 If I were offered a job in Japan, I would **jump at the chance**.
4 **I'm on a roll** with my academic work; otherwise I'd be really nervous about my next exam.
5 I know you don't like technology, but I'm sure you'll love this phone if you **give it a whirl**.

☐ get a sudden strong feeling
☐ accept something eagerly
☐ do something you are afraid of
☐ try something for the first time
☐ having a series of successes

c Choose two words or expressions from 3a or 3b and write two sentences, but leave a blank space for the word/expression. Read your sentence aloud. Can other students guess what goes in the blank?

REVIEW YOUR PROGRESS

How well did you do in this unit? Write 3, 2, or 1 for each objective.
3 = very well 2 = well 1 = not so well

I CAN ...	
describe extreme sensory experiences	☐
talk about plans, intentions, and arrangements	☐
give advice	☐
write a report.	☐

CAN DO OBJECTIVES

- Emphasize positive and negative experiences
- Describe journeys and landscapes
- Paraphrase and summarize
- Write a travel review

UNIT 3

TRAVEL AND ADVENTURE

GETTING STARTED

a Look at the picture and answer the questions.

1. What just happened? Where do you think the bus was going? What factors might have led to the situation?
2. Who do you think the people pushing the bus are? How do you think they feel?
3. What's the man on the right doing? Why?
4. What do you think will happen next?

b Work in pairs. Use your answers to retell the events of the day this photo was taken.

c Would you enjoy the type of trip these people are on? Why / Why not?

3A NEVER HAVE I HAD SUCH A REWARDING EXPERIENCE

Learn to emphasize positive and negative experiences

G Inversion

V Wealth and poverty

1 READING AND SPEAKING

a Which of these volunteer jobs looks the most interesting to you? Why?

1 working at a children's home in Belize
2 coaching sports for schoolchildren in Ghana
3 rescuing and caring for endangered bears in Cambodia
4 conserving coral reefs in the Caribbean

b Have you ever done an activity similar to those in 1a? Where? When? Why? Would you be prepared to use your vacation time to help other people? Why / Why not?

c Read the two reviews of volunteer experiences. Answer the questions.

1 What are the similarities and differences in the two experiences?
2 What specific negatives does each review mention?

THINKING OF VOLUNTEERING ABROAD?

*Here are **two inspiring stories** from volunteers who joined ongoing projects organized by Pod (Personal Overseas Development), an ethical, nonprofit volunteer organization.*

DEBBIE
Teaching children, Ghana

There are a few village life truths that everyone forgets to mention. You will sweat profusely, you will get bitten by a million different insects, you will miss home comforts and no doubt feel frustrated by many things. However, despite all this, you will forget all these worries in a heartbeat. No sooner had I woken up each morning than I would see a smiling face and hear a child's giggle that would melt my heart. Whether you are going to Ghana to build a school or to build a child's future, your heart will break when it's time to leave because the people become your world. Never have I had such a rewarding and truly enlightening experience. Without a doubt, it will be the same for you.

The day starts with breakfast at 7 a.m. I worked in the kindergarten, so it was up to class at 8:30, where I worked until lunchtime. Afternoons could be anything from extra classes, arts and crafts, sports coaching, or even digging on the building site. Evenings were for chilling out around the fire or having yam parties with the neighbors or playing silly games with the other volunteers. Normally we were so tired from the long day that we were all fast asleep by 9 p.m.

It's difficult to adjust to the intense heat, and it really does sap a lot of your energy. It's also difficult when you want to do as much as possible to help but find yourself restricted by your own physical shortcomings.

The most rewarding part for me was the relationships that I built; there is no better feeling in the world than having a child run to you in the morning with pure happiness on their face at seeing you.

LINDA AND MALCOLM
Working at a children's home, Belize

My husband and I spent two weeks at the children's home in Belize, and we both thoroughly enjoyed every minute of it. The experience of living with these warm, friendly people was something we will always remember, and we would certainly like to return in a couple of years. We were not really prepared for the intensity of the heat even though we had vacationed in the Caribbean previously.

The children were a joy and such characters, and we created some very special bonds. There was a lot of maintenance work to do, and Malcolm, who was able to carry out more manual work, was at an advantage. We also did a lot of gardening and helping in the kitchen (my favorite). Time off was when you wanted it, and with Belize being such a beautiful place with plenty of history and places to explore, you really need to make the most of it and see all you can.

Volunteering was something I have always wanted to do. We made some great friends and worked out of our comfort zone quite often, which for me made the experience even more special. At no time did we regret the decision to go there.

We loved being with the children, giving them little treats and helping make their environment better. We made them a special meal of burgers and fries, and the enjoyment on their faces made it so worthwhile. Little do children back home realize how the food they take for granted is a genuine treat for children here.

d Which review would you find more helpful if you were a prospective volunteer? Why?

e Language in context *Unusual experiences*

1 Match 1–8 with a–h to make expressions used in the reviews. Check new expressions in a dictionary.

1	☐ miss home	a	your energy
2	☐ melt your	b	special bonds
3	☐ have a rewarding	c	comforts
4	☐ sap a lot of	d	life skills
5	☐ create some very	e	heart
6	☐ make the	f	and enlightening experience
7	☐ take for	g	granted
8	☐ acquire	h	most of it

2 Complete these expressions with the correct preposition. Check your answers in the reviews.

1 ________ a heartbeat
2 ________ of your comfort zone
3 a feeling ________ self-worth and satisfaction

2 GRAMMAR Inversion

a Notice the phrases in **bold** in the sentences below. Why did the writers use these phrases?

☐ for emphasis ☐ to soften

1 **No sooner had I woken up** each morning than I would see a smiling face and hear a child's giggle that would melt my heart.
2 **Never have I had such** a rewarding and truly enlightening experience.
3 **At no time did we regret** the decision to go there.
4 **Little do children back home realize** how the food they take for granted is a genuine treat for children here.

One of the great things about volunteering is that you are acquiring life skills and experiences you will get nowhere else. A volunteer does not do the work just to help others, but for themselves, too; to get a feeling of self-worth and satisfaction, to learn and experience the way other people live and how other cultures work, and to be part of their way of life.

b Look at the phrases in **bold** in 2a and complete the rule.

For emphasis, the writers use a [1]*positive / negative* adverbial and [2]*statement / question word order*:
adverbial + auxiliary verb + subject + verb

c Think about how the sentences differ. When might you use inversion rather than normal word order? Give an example.

d Now go to Grammar Focus 3A on p. 142.

3 SPEAKING AND WRITING

a 03.02 Listen to the examples. Who or what do you think each person is talking about?

1 **Not only are they the nicest people in the world**, they're the best cooks, too.
2 **Only when we got to the beach** did it all become worthwhile.
3 **Not until the end of the vacation** did we realize how attached we had become to them.
4 **Never before** have I seen such enthusiasm and excitement.
5 **Not in a million years** would I have imagined building something from scratch.

b 03.02 **Pronunciation** Listen to the examples in 3a again. Does the intonation of the phrases in **bold** … ?

- rise then fall
- fall then rise

c Tell a partner about the highlights of a travel experience. Use the ideas below and inversion after some of the adverbials in the box. Make sure you use the correct intonation.

rarely … no sooner … at no time …
not in a million years … only after …
only when … not until …

- first impressions of the trip/place
- new experiences you had and your reaction
- a moment when you realized something
- something unique about the experience

I was staying with a host family. No sooner had I arrived than everybody rushed to meet me.

I went to India in January. Not in a million years did I think vegetarian food could taste so good.

d Write a paragraph for a blog about your experience. Use two sentences with inversion.

only by chance … little … hardly …
seldom … never before …

Little did I know how eventful this vacation was going to be.

Never before had I experienced such heavy rain.

4 LISTENING

a Imagine you and your friends wanted to start a volunteer project to build a school in a low-income country. What problems could there be?

b 03.03 Listen to Daniela Papi talking about her experience in Cambodia. Does she mention any of your ideas in 4a?

c 03.03 Listen again. Summarize what Daniela says about these topics.

1 her initial plans for volunteer work in Cambodia
2 problems with this plan
3 her six years in Cambodia
4 her beliefs after ten years' volunteer work
5 the problems with good intentions and praise

d Think about the volunteer project you talked about in 4a. What questions would you like to ask Daniela about doing this kind of work?

5 VOCABULARY Wealth and poverty

a Do the words and phrases in **bold** below relate to wealth or poverty? Make two lists. Which word/phrase applies to people with any level of income?

1 Many farmers *are facing real economic* ***hardship*** after the drought killed all their crops.
2 There's no money to help ***impoverished*** *communities* build basic facilities like schools and medical centers.
3 In ***affluent*** *suburbs* like this one, house prices are extremely high.
4 There's a direct relationship between a good education system and the *economic* ***prosperity*** of a country.
5 Even though I got a pay raise last year, I still *find it difficult to* ***make ends meet***.
6 My grandparents used to be *relatively* ***well off***, but they lost all their money in bad investments.
7 He lives with his parents and pays no bills, so he has a lot of ***disposable income***.
8 In the most ***deprived*** *areas* of the city, unemployment stands at around 50%, and social problems are rife.
9 We can't go on using our credit cards all the time. We have to *learn to* ***live within our means***.
10 They lost everything they had in the flood and were *left* ***destitute***.

b Answer these questions about the words and phrases in **bold** in 5a.

1 Which noun has the opposite meaning of *hardship*?
2 Compare the adjectives *impoverished, deprived*, and *destitute*. Which one is more severe than the other two?
3 Compare *affluent* and *well off*. Which one are we more likely to use when we speak?
4 Compare *make ends meet* and *live within our means*. Which expression suggests more of a struggle?
5 Which of these noun phrases has a similar meaning to *disposable income*?
a living expenses   b spending money

c 03.04 **Pronunciation** Listen to the sentences in 5a and underline the stressed syllables in the words and phrases in **bold**.

d Look at the phrases in *italics* in 5a. Think of an example of each from your own knowledge/experience. Compare your ideas with a partner.

People here faced real economic hardship during the recession.

6 SPEAKING

a Think of someone you know well who would be interested in volunteering. Choose a suitable volunteer project for them or think of another.

1 saving cheetahs from extinction in South Africa
2 conserving the Amazon rainforest in Peru
3 helping build schools in Ghana
4 coaching sports for schoolchildren in Nepal

b What could you say to the volunteer about ... ?

- practical preparation *learn local customs*
- psychological preparation
- positive impact of volunteers
- negative impact of volunteers
- likely personal development and life skills

c Tell a partner about the person you chose in 6a and what you would say to them about volunteering.

3B I WAS EXPECTING IT TO BE TOUGH

Learn to describe journeys and landscapes

- **G** Future in the past; Narrative tenses
- **V** Landscape features

1 READING AND GRAMMAR Future in the past

a Look at the journey on the map. What do you think it would be like? Think about:

- what you'd expect to see
- people you might meet
- skills needed
- possible risks.

b Read what Will Millard says about his journey. Answer the questions.

1 Why does Will describe the forest as a *one-off environment*?
2 Why did Will take the trip? How did he travel? Why do you think he chose to travel that way?
3 What would you look forward to on a trip like this? What wouldn't you look forward to?

c Look at the underlined event in the article. Complete each sentence below with a phrase from the box. There is one phrase you do not need to use.

in the future	in progress	in the past

When Will arrived in Sierra Leone, this event was ________.
When Will wrote the article, this event was ________.

d Underline six more examples of the future in the past in the article. What four verb forms does Will use?

e Think of other things that Will might have considered before his trip. Write sentences using the future in the past.

I knew that it was going to be difficult.
I was hoping to see some elephants.

f What do you think will make Will's journey difficult and dangerous?

2 VOCABULARY Landscape features

a What do the **highlighted** words in the article mean? Which two words are very similar? How are they different? Use a dictionary to help you.

b Complete the collocations below with the words and phrases in the box. Check your answers in the article.

a tropical	a remote	the heart of the	dense	an untouched

1 ______ rainforest, capital, jungle
2 ______ rainforest, storm, island
3 ______ fog, vegetation, undergrowth
4 ______ wilderness, forest, plate of food
5 ______ area, forest, village

c Now go to Vocabulary Focus 3B on p. 160.

SURVIVAL
ON THE MANO RIVER

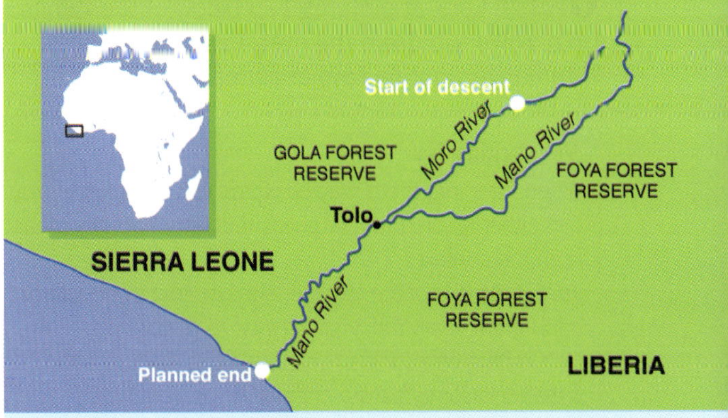

My dream journey became a reality when I received a grant from the Royal Geographical Society to explore the Moro and Mano rivers. The grant was intended to cover expenses, radio training, and equipment to record my expedition for BBC Radio 4. I was planning to start at the top of the Gola Forest and make the first descent of the river border of Sierra Leone and Liberia, right through a chunk of Africa's most threatened **jungle** environment – one of the last untouched **wildernesses** of the Upper Guinean forest belt. More than a quarter of Africa's total mammal species are found in the belt, with bizarre creatures such as the pygmy hippopotamus found nowhere else on Earth. The need to protect what still remains of this one-off environment could not be more critical.

In Sierra Leone, the Gola Forest is already designated a national park, but I wanted to find out what life in the heart of a tropical **rainforest** was really like, <u>so I was going to paddle down these rivers</u>, hopefully as far as the sea. I knew that, although I would be in radio contact, I would be on my own in one of the most remote forests in West Africa, and I would be separated from the outside world by dense tropical **vegetation**. I was expecting it to be tough, but in fact it was to become one of the most difficult and dangerous journeys I have ever made.

3 LISTENING

a 03.06 You are going to hear Will Millard describing his trip. Listen to five sounds from the recording. What do you think each sound is?

b 03.07 Now listen to the whole recording and check your ideas in 3a.

c 03.07 Look at pictures 1–5 below of the things from Will's trip down the river. Listen again and summarize what he says about each one.

> **Learning Tip**
> When listening, there may be words you don't know. You can either ignore them or guess roughly what they mean from the context.
> *Just at the end of the day there was quite a large* ***cataract****, and I didn't really fancy taking it on till tomorrow …*
> He's rafting on a jungle river, so we can guess that a *cataract* is some feature of this environment that is difficult to get past.

d Read the sentences below from the listening. Underline examples of the informal conversational style that Will Millard uses.

1 Thanks, mate.
2 Managed to just get my camp sorted.
3 I didn't really fancy taking it on till tomorrow.
4 I guess I'll find out.
5 If I lose the raft, I'm finished.

How could you express the sentences in a more neutral style?

e 03.08 **Pronunciation** Listen again to part of what Will says. Notice how he pronounces the words in **bold**. Practice saying the phrases a–c.

a … **hit** this big rock …
b **Just** managed to **get** control of it again …
c it's **got** my shelter on it …

f What would/wouldn't you have enjoyed from this part of Will's journey?

4 READING

a You are going to read about how Will got malaria while he was still in the rainforest. Before you read, answer these questions.

1 Why would this be particularly dangerous?
2 What do you think his symptoms were?
3 What would he need to do in order to survive?

b Read the text. Check your answers in 4a.

c Read the text again and answer the questions.

1 Why is rafting down rivers a good way to see wildlife?
2 How did he know there were chimpanzees nearby? How close did he get to seeing them?
3 What was he planning to do when he got to the coast?
4 What made him take his symptoms seriously?
5 He says he *survived thanks to a mix of luck, exceptional local support, and money*. What events and facts do you think Will is referring to in this sentence?

I love rafting in rainforests …

This near silent method of travel gives you an unencumbered and discreet approach, perfect for radio, but rivers are also among the best possible places to spot wildlife returning from the forest depths to feed, drink, and socialize. This section of the Upper Guinean was one of the finest forests I had ever experienced. It was a storybook jungle, [1]teeming with life.

For a couple of days I had been hearing primates everywhere – in the banksides, up the trees, behind distant ridges, but never quite close enough to see. At dawn I'd hear the piercing screaming call of a chimp, but it was impossibly far away. The last hour of light would often bring a flash of fur, a scuffle in the bushes, a warning shriek but nothing more.

After ten days on the river, I believed I was through the worst and started to think about the finish line – where the river enters the Atlantic – and all the fried and liquid-based treats that would be waiting for me at the nearest village.

Then I started to get sick. I tried to [2]shrug it off with ibuprofen and fluid, putting it down to the exertion of paddling daily in the 40°C heat. But as my headache developed into a fever I began to [3]fret, not least because among the last words of warning given to me before heading solo into the bush was the tale of a European woman who had complained of flu-like symptoms, not gone directly to hospital, and died of an undiagnosed hemorrhagic fever 48 hours later. I desperately needed to make contact with someone on the

1 a dragonfly

2 a fish eagle and a catfish

3 a hammock

4 rapids

d Answer the questions.

1 How well do you think Will coped with the experience? Would you have coped as well as he did?
2 Do you think what he did was worthwhile? Why / Why not?

c Language in context *Descriptive verbs*

Match the highlighted words and phrases in the text with the meanings below.

a ☐ rub against a hard surface (in order to make a powder)
b ☐ contain large numbers of living creatures
c ☐ pull something heavy
d ☐ physically support
e ☐ bend down with knees bent
f ☐ pull off, like a skin
g ☐ treat something as if it is not important
h ☐ worry (v.)
i ☐ call someone to be present

Sierra Leone bank and find my way to the road, the hospital, and proper treatment.

In the morning, I started to paddle out. My headache had worsened to the point that I could barely keep my eyes open in daylight, and the pain in my joints was bordering on the spectacular. My bones felt like they were [4]grinding to dust with every movement. I had GPS marks for all of the villages along the river but one – Tolo, which had been written on my map in felt tip by one of the Gola Rainforest National Park researchers. It was by far the closest settlement – only a three hour paddle downstream. The river was much wider and calmer. I was dropping out of the heavy forest and knew I just had to hang on. […]

At noon, a gap in the forest revealed a lone figure – a woman, [5]crouched down washing her clothes. I was drifting by this point, almost incapable of going through the motions of the strokes. I remember her shouting, then multiple hands on me as I was [6]peeled from my raft. I was [7]propped up on a tree-stump stool against a mud-brick house. The chief was [8]summoned. I might have been the first Westerner to arrive in the village in such a condition, but this place was no stranger to what to do with people carrying my symptoms. My gear was divided up, and I was [9]hauled through the forest to the nearest village with a motorbike, then on to the roadside and eventually to a hospital.

I survived thanks to a mix of luck, exceptional local support, and money. An estimated half a million African people will not be so fortunate this year.

5 a raft

5 GRAMMAR Narrative tenses

a Read sentences 1–7. What is each verb form in **bold**? Why is that particular verb form used?

☐ simple past ☐ past continuous
☐ past perfect ☐ past perfect continuous
☐ simple past passive ☐ past perfect passive
☐ *would* + base form

1 For a couple of days, I **had been hearing** primates everywhere …
2 At dawn **I'd hear** the piercing screaming call of a chimp …
3 My headache **had worsened** to the point that I could barely keep my eyes open …
4 … and the pain in my joints **was bordering on** the spectacular.
5 … Tolo, which **had been written** on my map in felt tip …
6 My gear was divided up, and I **was hauled** through the forest to the nearest village with a motorbike …
7 I **survived** thanks to a mix of luck, exceptional local support, and money.

b Now go to Grammar Focus 3B on p. 143.

c How does using a different tense change the meanings of these sentences?

1 For a couple of days, I **had heard** / **had been hearing** primates everywhere.
2 At dawn, I **heard** / **'d hear** the piercing screaming call of a chimp.
3 The chief **was** / **was being** summoned.

6 WRITING AND SPEAKING

a Look at the first line of each paragraph in Will's article and answer the questions.

1 How do all the paragraphs (except two) start?
2 Which paragraphs start differently? What are the purposes of these paragraphs?

b Think about an adventurous journey you have been on, or one you have seen in a movie / on TV or read about. Here are some ideas:

- a visit to a wild or remote place
- getting sick far from home
- traveling by an unusual form of transportation
- being alone in an unfamiliar place.

c Write an article about the journey. Use narrative tenses and descriptive vocabulary. Describe:

1 plans that were made
2 expectations before the trip
3 when the main events happened and what happened
4 personal feelings during and after the trip.

I had been looking forward to going to Australia for months …
Last summer, I was staying with friends in Paris …

d Work in pairs. Practice telling the story.

e Work in groups. Tell the story to the others and answer any questions.

3C EVERYDAY ENGLISH
To cut a long story short

Learn to paraphrase and summarize

- S Paraphrase and summarize in informal conversations
- P Sound and spelling: *t*

1 LISTENING

a Have you ever had an interview or meeting that went wrong? What happened?

b You are going to listen to screenwriter Ryan trying to pitch, or present, his idea for a new TV series to producer Marco. What questions do you think Marco will ask Ryan during the meeting? Make a list.

c 03.10 Listen to Part 1 and check your answers in 1b.

d 03.10 Listen to Part 1 again and choose one true ending for each sentence.

1 The inhabitants of the remote planet in Ryan's show are aliens who … .
  a look very different from humans
  b look like humans but have a different culture
  c want to explore other planets
2 Marco suggests that Ryan's ideas might come from … .
  a his experiences while traveling
  b another science fiction writer
  c experiences in his childhood
3 Marco suggests that Ryan's TV series … .
  a will be broadcast in the near future
  b should be titled *Solar Wind*
  c will depend on the success of his next pitch

e Answer the questions.

1 How do you think Ryan and Marco feel about the success of Ryan's pitch? Why?
2 Have you ever made a pitch for any reason? How did you feel … ?
  - before the pitch
  - afterward

2 PRONUNCIATION
Sound and spelling: *t*

a 03.11 Listen to these words from the recording. They all contain the letter *t*, but in which word does this letter actually sound like /t/?

travel get tell actually

b 03.12 Notice that the pronunciation of the *t* sound changes according to the other sounds around it. Now listen to these words from the recording and put them in the right group.

different culture about
trip too fiction out

/t/ as in *tell*	/ʔ/ as in *get*	/ʃ/ or /tʃ/ as in *actually*

What patterns do you notice?

c What version of the *t* sound would you expect to hear in the following words?

remote teeming planet
question top went true

d 03.13 Listen and check.

e Practice saying the words in 2a, 2b, and 2c.

3 LISTENING

a Ryan tells his friend Eve about the meeting with Marco. What do you think he will say? What might Eve say to make him feel better? Look at the photo and answer the questions.

1 What do you think Eve thinks of Ryan's interview?
2 What do you think she is saying to Ryan about it?

b 03.14 Listen to Part 2. Is Eve's reaction helpful?

c 03.14 Complete the sentences with the words you heard. Listen to Part 2 again and check.

1 I'm sure it wasn't that ________.
2 How can I ________ this?
3 I'll never be able to show my ________ again!

d Language in context *Exaggerating*

1 03.15 Complete Ryan's exaggerations with the words in the box. Listen and check.

outright complete and utter total totally

1 It was a(n) ________ disaster!
2 I came across as a(n) ________ idiot!
3 A(n) ________ embarrassment!
4 My writing career's ________ ruined!

2 Why do you think Ryan exaggerated about his interview? In what situations do you think people choose to exaggerate? Why?

e Answer the questions.

1 Is it better to prepare everything you want to say before a meeting or to speak spontaneously?
2 Imagine you were going to pitch an idea for a new movie or TV show. What would you want to say?

4 USEFUL LANGUAGE
Paraphrasing and summarizing

a Read the excerpts from Parts 1 and 2. Match the expressions in bold with their uses below.

1 ***Or, to put it another way***, *a good story needs something more … to keep our attention*
2 ***All things considered***, *I think my first and last TV pitch … was a complete and utter embarrassment.*

☐ paraphrase = express the same idea in new words
☐ summarize = express only the main point(s)

b 03.16 Complete the extracts from Parts 1 and 2 below with the expressions in the box. Listen and check.

in other words in a nutshell
sums it up what I meant by that was

1 And basically, ________, a group of explorers are visiting a remote planet …
2 I guess, ________, it's about how we question our own culture.
3 Yes, I think that just about ________.
4 So ________, it all just came from your imagination, then?

c Add the expressions from 4a and b to the correct group below.

Paraphrasing	Summarizing

d Complete the sentences with a suitable expression for summarizing and paraphrasing and your own idea.

1 We had some ups and down throughout the trip. All …
2 People there spend a lot of time visiting aunts, uncles, cousins, that is …
3 I had tons of problems on the trip, but to …
4 I'm sorry, I didn't express myself very clearly. What …
5 The novel is fairly long and complicated, but in …

5 SPEAKING

>> **Communication 3C** Work in pairs. Go to p. 129.

UNIT PROGRESS TEST

CHECK YOUR PROGRESS

YOU CAN NOW DO THE UNIT PROGRESS TEST.

3D SKILLS FOR WRITING
The view is stunning

Learn to write a travel review

W Descriptive language; Writing briefly

1 SPEAKING

a What is the most rewarding place you've been to as a tourist, and what is the most disappointing? Why?

b Read the description of Cusco from a tourist website. How much does it appeal to you as a tourist destination?

CUSCO, PERU

History, magic, and beauty

to do   to eat   to see   to go

Historic architecture of Cusco

Inca stone walls

It's no wonder that Cusco, high in the Andes mountains in Peru and a jumping-off point for the wonders of Machu Picchu, is on everyone's list of must-see places in South America. It attracts 1.5 million visitors every year and has everything you'd expect of an Andean city …

- a romantic setting in a round valley surrounded by wild mountains
- a historic city center that you can walk around in a couple of hours, although you'll want to stay much, much longer
- a mind-blowing mixture of Inca and Spanish colonial buildings and dozens of churches, squares, and parks
- the magnificent Inca citadel of Sacsayhuamán, with great views across the city
- comfortable accommodations at reasonable prices
- a lively and welcoming street life, with stores, restaurants, and atmospheric cafés

2 LISTENING

a 03.17 Listen to Roberto and Annie talking about Cusco and answer the questions.

1 What do they say about the places in the photos?
2 What similar points do they make?
3 Do you think that Roberto and Annie would both go back to Cusco? Why? / Why not?

b 03.17 Roberto and Annie use descriptive phrases to talk about the city. Which phrases do they use? Match the words in boxes A and B. Then listen again to check.

A		B	
ancient	tiled	atmosphere	roofs
cobbled	well	of tourists	streets
teeming	crowds	preserved	views
romantic		walls	
breathtaking		with people	

c Answer the questions. Consider the issues from the point of view of both residents and tourists.

1 What are the good and bad effects that tourism can have on a city like Cusco?
2 Do you think popular tourist cities should try to limit tourists or charge them to see the city?

3 READING

Read the traveler's review. What further information (beyond the descriptions in the listening) does it include about ... ?

- walls and buildings in Cusco
- the Inca citadel

Use your answers in 2a to help you. Underline the information in the review.

4 WRITING SKILLS Descriptive language; Writing briefly

a Find words or phrases in the text which could replace the words in italics below.

1 The owners *were very helpful.*
2 Walking along the streets is *very difficult.*
3 Sacsayhuamán is *an attraction you definitely should see.*
4 Climbing the steps *needed a lot of effort.*
5 There are *good opportunities to take photos.*
6 The restaurant had *traditional food from the country.*
7 The food was *not too expensive.*
8 The restaurants in the center are *more expensive than they should be.*

Writing Tip

When writing a description, try to use words that carry a more precise or an extra meaning. So instead of *through some … lanes which had little shops and cafés:*

- *through some … lanes which were* ***lined with*** *little shops and cafés* (extra meaning: they were in lines along the sides)

Instead of *zigzag walls with stone doorways in them:*

- *zigzag walls* ***interspersed with*** *stone doorways* (more precise meaning: they were spaced evenly along the walls, between each section of wall)

You can also convey your attitude by using words with a positive or a negative meaning. So instead of *the city was full of tourists:*

- *The city was* ***buzzing with*** *tourists.* (= it was full of life; it was good)
- *The city was* ***overrun with*** *tourists.* (= there were too many of them; it was bad)

b In the review, the writer sometimes omits certain words. What words could you add to these examples to make complete sentences?

1 Only one problem.
2 Took hundreds of photos.
3 Then back down to the hotel for a quick shower.

c Find three more examples of words which are omitted. What is the effect of leaving out words in this way?

1 It seems more formal.
2 It seems less formal and more like conversation.

d Now go to Writing Focus 3D on p. 170.

★★★★★

We stayed at the Hotel Casa Verde – a small hotel in a quiet area just up the hill from the center. It was pretty basic, but the owners were very hospitable and really put themselves out for us. Our double room was comfortable and spotlessly clean. To our surprise, it cost just $40 per night, including a delicious breakfast with fresh fruit, eggs, and excellent coffee.

We spent the morning wandering around the city. Really impressive architecture – massive Inca walls with perfectly interlocking stones which the Spanish used as foundations for colonial buildings, and slightly forbidding churches and palaces built in gray stone. Only one problem – it was quite overrun with tourists (like us!), and the streets near the center were full of people selling souvenirs, so they were kind of a nightmare to get through. We preferred the quieter lanes leading uphill from the center and found a few pleasant little squares where there weren't so many people and we could sit and soak up the atmosphere.

In the afternoon, we decided to visit Sacsayhuamán, the ruined Inca citadel above the town —a must-see attraction. We set off uphill away from the center, through some quiet cobbled lanes which were lined with little shops and cafés. Then the hill got steeper and the lane turned into flights of steps leading up through a quiet residential area. Pretty rough at such a high altitude (we had to stop every few minutes to get our breath back!), but we got to the top eventually. Great photo ops from the top with views across the whole city and the mountains beyond. The citadel itself is fascinating – massive Inca stones which are fitted so perfectly that you can't get a piece of paper between them (we tried!), and zigzag walls interspersed with perfectly proportioned stone doorways. Took hundreds of photos, and definitely worth the climb up there!

Then back down to the hotel for a quick shower and something to eat. Near the hotel there was a restaurant with authentic cuisine — quite a limited menu but very reasonably priced. I had alpaca stew, which tasted delicious. A much better option than the overpriced restaurants in the city center!

5 WRITING

a Make a list of tourist attractions in the town and area where you are now. Include:

- attractions you think are worth visiting
- attractions you think are less worthwhile.

b Imagine you spent a day here as a tourist. Choose two or three attractions in the list and write a review. Include comments on your accommodations and somewhere you ate, too.

c Work with a partner. Look at what you both wrote and see how you could improve it by:

- using adjectives and phrases with a stronger positive or negative meaning
- making some sentences shorter by omitting words.

d Read your review to the class. Which reviews do most people agree with?

UNIT 3
Review and extension

1 GRAMMAR

a Reorder the words to make sentences.

1 get / plane / was / about / a / John / to / on
2 you / home / did / her / at / rarely / very / see
3 was / that / thought / faint / Amelia / to / she / going
4 account / anyone / told / on / no / be / must
5 next / set / we / early / day / to / were / leave / the
6 on / go / like / would / I / a / no / trip / way / that

b Cross out the verb form that is NOT correct.

1 Kevin *was leaving* / *was about to leave* / ~~*would leave*~~ on a business trip when he got the call.
2 Originally we *planned to take* / *had been going to take* / *would be taking* the train.
3 As soon as we *arrived* / *had arrived* / *had been arriving*, checked in.
4 We *had used* / *had been using* / *used* up our supplies and had to find more from somewhere.
5 Our room was terrible, and I *had been complaining* / *might complain* / *complained* to the manager.
6 Travel *was* / *would be* / *had been* cheaper in those days.

2 VOCABULARY

a Complete the sentences with the words in the box.

affluent	deprived	destitute	disposable
hardship	means	prosperity	well-off

1 This neighborhood is fairly ________, so prices are high.
2 I don't really have much ________ income.
3 You can tell it's a(n) ________ area by the crime rate.
4 The floods left many poorer residents ________.
5 I wouldn't say I'm super-rich, but I am ________.
6 A recession had started, and the years of ________ were over.
7 It is no ________ to live without a car in a big city.
8 We manage to live within our ________ somehow.

b Complete the missing words.

1 Many species live only in the h________t of the rainforest.
2 Anything might be hiding in the dense v________n!
3 This is truly an u________d wilderness.
4 The r________d coastline is popular with walkers.
5 Once a year the rains bring the a________d desert to life.
6 Tourists come for the p________e beaches and gentle sea.
7 They say there are alligators in the s________p.

3 WORDPOWER Idioms: Landscapes

a Match the expressions in **bold** with definitions a–g.

1 **A** **I'm** absolutely **swamped** this week.
B Poor you. Let me know if there's anything I can do.
2 **A** We've had tons of customers this week.
B It's great, I know. But we're not **out of the woods** yet.
3 **A** What are you going to say to him?
B I don't know. I'll go over and **get the lay of the land** first.
4 **A** How are you coping with the move and the new job?
B It's **an uphill battle**, but I'm just about managing!
5 **A** It seems like when we talk we're always **getting bogged down with** tiny details.
B So you're not making any progress?
6 **A** I've had cake every afternoon this week!
B Be careful! It's **a slippery slope** once you start.
7 **A** I paid $100 on our credit card last month.
B That's just **a drop in the ocean** though, isn't it?

a ☐ a small amount compared to the amount required
b ☐ a series of events that become out of control and create worse problems
c ☐ free from problems/danger
d ☐ wait until you have all the information about a situation
e ☐ get stuck on a particular point and be unable to make progress
f ☐ be overwhelmed by too much work
g ☐ when making progress is very difficult

b 03.18 Complete the sentences with an idiom from 3a. Listen and check.

1 I made a small donation, but I know it's just ________.
2 She clearly wants to ________ before she makes any big decisions.
3 Regaining popular opinion is going to be ________ for the party.
4 We just had some great news from the hospital: Sam's ________.
5 I told her borrowing was ________. She's going to have to get a second job.
6 If you can't answer a question, don't ________ it; just move on to the next one.
7 Ever since they put the ad out, they've ________ completely ________ with phone calls.

c What situation do you think each person in 3b is talking about?

REVIEW YOUR PROGRESS

How well did you do in this unit? Write 3, 2, or 1 for each objective.
3 = very well 2 = well 1 = not so well

I CAN ...	
emphasize positive and negative experiences	☐
describe journeys and landscapes	☐
paraphrase and summarize	☐
write a travel review.	☐

CAN DO OBJECTIVES

- Talk about using instinct and reason
- Talk about memories and remembering
- Use tact in formal discussions
- Write a profile article

UNIT 4

CONSCIOUSNESS

GETTING STARTED

a Look at the picture and answer the questions.

1 What do you think the device does?
2 Where is the woman? What do you think she's doing?
3 How do you think the woman feels?

b The woman is using a virtual reality headset to guide her through a story about the food she is going to experience. Answer the questions.

1 Would you like to try it? If so, what foods would you try it with? If not, why not?
2 What do you think the benefits of this technology could be in the wider world?
3 What technology have you experienced that changes how you perceive things?

4A THAT LITTLE VOICE IN YOUR HEAD

Learn to talk about using instinct and reason

G Noun phrases

V Instinct and reason

1 SPEAKING

a What are your five senses? What do you think is meant by a "sixth sense"? Do you think you have one?

b Do the quiz with a partner and compare your answers.

c **Communication 4A** Count up how many As and how many Bs you chose. Check your results on p. 131.

2 VOCABULARY Instinct and reason

a Look at these people's statements. Would they be As or Bs according to the quiz?

1 I'm a very **rational** thinker.
2 **On impulse**, I married someone I'd only just met.
3 I think I know **subconsciously** when people are lying to me.
4 I think it's important to **weigh** the advantages and disadvantages before you take action.

b Replace each expression in **bold** in 2a with a word or phrase from the box. Is the meaning in each exactly the same?

deep down	consider	objective	on a whim

c Now go to Vocabulary Focus 4A on p. 161.

Do You Have A SIXTH SENSE?

How much do you rely on your intuition? Do the quiz and choose A or B. Don't think too long about it ... follow your gut!

1 You find yourself a new apartment. You like it because ...
A it has a positive atmosphere and feels like a nice place to be in.
B the furniture is in good condition and it has everything you need.

2 You meet a new coworker and have a bad feeling about them. You ...
A decide not to trust them – your first impressions are usually accurate.
B ignore the feeling. You can't tell what people are like from first impressions.

3 The phone rings at home, and you aren't expecting a call. You ...
A have a strong feeling about who's calling.
B have no idea who's calling until you get to the phone.

4 A close friend, who has been unusually quiet, says they need to talk to you.
A You probably won't be surprised by what they say – you kind of know already.
B You have no idea what to expect – it could be anything.

5 When do the best ideas come to you?
A when you're relaxing or during the night while you're asleep
B after thinking long and hard about them

6 You wake up from a strange dream. You think ...
A "This dream is telling me something – I must remember it."
B "What a silly dream!" and go about your day.

7 A new opportunity arises, but it's a major change. Your family and friends advise against it.
A You go for what you feel is right, in spite of their advice.
B You drop the idea – they can see the situation more objectively than you.

8 Are you someone who experiences an unusual number of coincidences?
A Yes, although you don't believe they are simply coincidences.
B No, and neither does anyone else – coincidences are purely chance events.

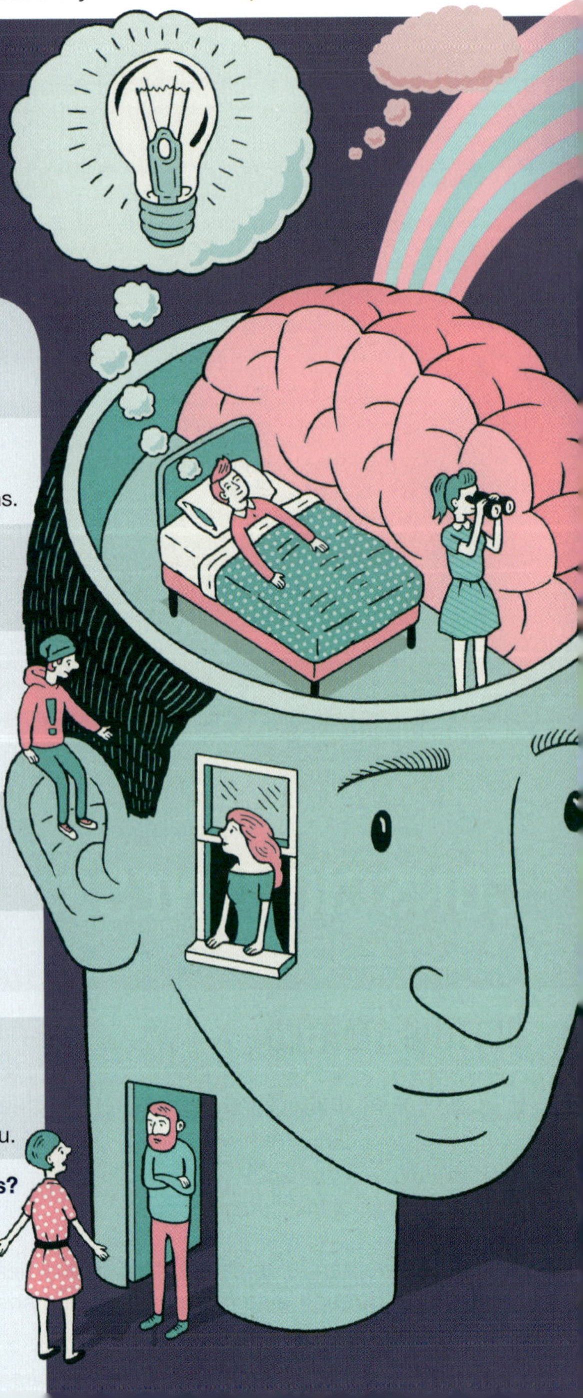

3 READING

a Read the first part of the article below about gut instincts and talk about these questions.

1 What is the author going to give readers advice about?
2 What are the roles of the left and right sides of the brain, according to researchers?
3 What does the writer suggest is a good way to make decisions?

b Read the rest of the article. Match the headings a–e to the advice 1–5.

a I'm not sure about you.
b This is the one I've been waiting for!
c I've done this a million times before.
d I should try to help.
e I'm in pain.

c Look at the underlined parts of the article. Think of one possible example of what the writer means in each case.

d Talk about these questions.

1 Do you agree with the five pieces of advice in the article? Are there any you disagree with? Why?
2 Can you think of situations where it might be better not to follow your gut instincts?

4 GRAMMAR Noun phrases

a Match the noun phrases 1–6 from the article with their type a–f.

1 ☐	a funny feeling in your stomach	a	noun + noun
2 ☐	that narrow parking space	b	noun + 's + superlative + compound noun
3 ☐	humanity's oldest survival mechanisms	c	article + adjective + noun + preposition + possessive + noun
4 ☐	an irresistible urge to ask	d	determiner + adjective + compound noun
5 ☐	gut feelings	e	adverb + adjective + noun
6 ☐	commonly reported indicators	f	article + adjective + noun + infinitive

b Rephrase these noun phrases using the patterns in parentheses.

1 a meeting which happens by chance (article + noun + noun)
= *a chance encounter*
2 the dreams of my friend who is close (possessive + adjective + noun + 's + noun)
3 a day that you will remember (article + noun + infinitive)
4 a dream that is so vivid it disturbs you (article + adverb + adjective + noun)
5 thoughts that are dark and secret (adjective + adjective + noun)
6 the capacity of humans to imagine things (article + adjective + noun + *for* + noun)

c Now go to Grammar Focus 4A on p. 144.

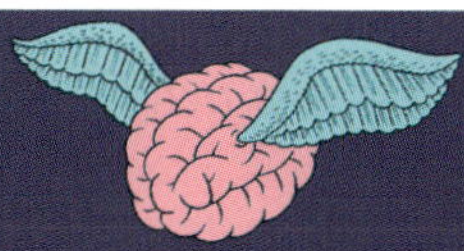

Learn to TRUST YOUR GUT!

You have an irresistible urge to ask a complete stranger to go out for coffee. You decide on a whim to buy a property you've never visited. You feel an inexplicable certainty that you should not get on that plane.

Following your gut feelings could either be the best thing you ever did or end in disaster. On the other hand, ignoring these instincts could have exactly the same outcomes. How can we know when to trust our intuition and when to let our heads rule?

Psychiatrists assert that the home of intuition is in the right hemisphere of the brain. While the conscious left brain edits the world into a logical and coherent whole, the right brain picks up the big picture and reacts spontaneously. Too often the left brain dismisses the urges of the right as irrational, while we remain blissfully ignorant of the process.

In order to use intuition more effectively, we can tune into the physical symptoms that let us know it is operating. Clammy palms, a tingle up the spine or a funny feeling in your stomach are all commonly reported indicators that the intuitive right brain is in action. When you notice this feeling, take the time to evaluate it and give yourself a choice.

And to help you on your way, here are five instances where the gut is almost always right.

1 ______________

It seems so much like common sense that it could be the left brain talking. When you hear that little voice in your head nagging you to go for a check-up, do yourself a favor and go. If you don't, you could be setting yourself up for trouble down the road.

2 ______________

First impressions are not just about hair and shoes. Tune in to that all-important feeling you get when you meet a new person, and you are using one of humanity's oldest survival mechanisms. Our ancestors knew instinctively who to trust and who not to – and so do you. Crossing the street to avoid a stranger is not going to hurt anyone's feelings, and it may just keep you safe.

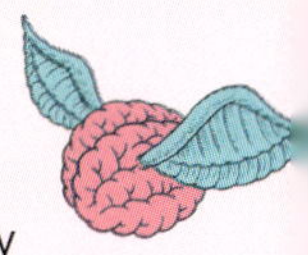

3 ______________

Use your instinct to tell you when those around you are in need of your support. Our urge to help others is often outbid by other priorities, like getting somewhere on time or not wanting to appear nosy. But these instincts are just as much survival mechanisms as our fears, and who knows when you may need a hand yourself one day?

4 ______________

Trust your gut to get you through the most stressful of occasions. When you're under pressure, it's easy to forget how to do even things you're an expert at. So use intuition to guide you into that narrow parking space or to cook that special meal. Under stress it's way more reliable than your conscious brain.

5 ______________

Never discount your gut instincts in the lead-up to a decision that could affect the course of your future life. These are the times to really use your whole brain. If your right brain says, "Yes! Yes! Yes!", there's a good chance that's the decision you'll be happiest with in the long run.

5 LISTENING

a You will hear a discussion about the way doctors diagnose patients. How much do you think doctors rely on their gut instincts?

b 04.04 Listen to the discussion. What do the speakers agree on? Choose 1, 2, or 3.

1 Doctors rely too much on their gut instincts, and this can be a problem.
2 Unfortunately, doctors don't pay attention to their gut instincts.
3 Doctors often rely on their gut instincts, and this is useful.

c 04.04 Listen again and choose the best answer in *italics*.

1 When we have inner doubts, they are *often* / *not usually* just signs of worry.
2 Most doctors will admit to *having* / *following* gut instincts.
3 Ann Van den Bruel has done research into *how often doctors use gut instinct* / *how accurate gut instinct is*.
4 Doctors' gut feelings about children's infections often turn out to be *correct* / *incorrect*.
5 Margaret McCartney thinks that gut instincts are *important* / *unscientific*.
6 Doctors tend to follow their gut instinct when they are *more* / *less* sure about their diagnosis.
7 Doctors from different countries seem to have very *similar* / *different* experiences.
8 Primary care doctors have to rely on their instincts *less* / *more* than hospital doctors.

d In what ways has the discussion changed your mind about the question in 5a?

e Language in context *Doubt and uncertainty*

1 04.05 Complete the sentences with the words in the box. Then listen and check your answers.

pattern	doubt	jars	worriers
feeling	bones	fit	anxieties

1 That **uneasy** _________ that you get when you think there is something that you should be doing.
2 More often than not these are **groundless** _________ that simply reflect that many of us are **born** _________.
3 All may appear well on the surface, but you're left with **a nagging** _________ that all is not quite as it seems.
4 It's almost like recognizing that this person just **doesn't quite fit the** _________, but you're not quite sure in what way …
5 Other doctors will say that they **feel it in their** _________ that something's just not right.
6 It's just this idea that you get: something that _________, something that just **doesn't quite** _________ properly **together**.

2 Which words and phrases in **bold** are connected with these things?

a a feeling that things aren't OK
b worrying more than you need to
c not being able to make sense of things
d knowing something intuitively

6 SPEAKING

a Read each dilemma. What would you do? Is what you would do and what you should do the same in each case?

1 You are a judge. You are due to sentence a criminal that you have seen in your court before. On that occasion, he was found not guilty of a serious crime due to a lack of evidence – but your gut told you differently. Do you give him the maximum sentence this time?

2 You are a junior web designer, and your boss has asked you to present a web design for a potentially important client. You've been given detailed information about the color and design preferences of your client's target market, but you feel that this would result in a sterile and boring design that wouldn't get you the contract. Do you insist on presenting your preferred design instead?

3 You are interviewing candidates for a six-month contract. One candidate is very well qualified and performs well in the interview, but there's something about him that makes you uneasy (you can't quite put your finger on it). The choice is between him and someone who doesn't look so good on paper and was very nervous in the interview, but who you have a good feeling about. Who would you go for?

b How could gut instinct play a part in these roles?

- politician
- CEO of a large company
- airline pilot
- parent

c Choose one of the jobs in 6b or a different job and write a dilemma like those in 6a. Switch dilemmas with other students and talk about the dilemma you receive.

4B LET ME TRY TO REMEMBER

Learn to talk about memories and remembering

G *have / get* passives

V Memory

1 LISTENING AND GRAMMAR *have / get* passives

a Answer the questions.

1 What kind of stories do you and your family and childhood friends tell about your childhood?
2 What was a particularly funny/proud/scary moment?

b 04.06 Listen to Tommy, Marissa, and Clara talk about their childhood memories. Answer the questions.

1 What's the significance of each of the photos? Summarize what happened in each memory.
2 Why do you think these memories are still so clear for the speakers?

c Do you relate to any of the people telling the stories? Why / Why not?

I can't really relate to Clara. I was a very confident child!

d Compare the meaning of each pair of sentences. Is there a difference?

1 a **My parents were having the kitchen renovated.**
  b My parents were renovating the kitchen.
2 a **I had all my toys stolen.**
  b All my toys were stolen.
3 a **He got himself locked in the garden shed.**
  b He got locked in the garden shed.
4 a **His disappearance got everyone looking for him.**
  b He got everyone to look for him.
5 a **She had me sitting on my own.**
  b I was sitting on my own.
6 a **He got me to play when nobody else could.**
  b He played with me.

Match the sentences in **bold** with the uses a–d below.

a the subject's possessions were harmed by somebody else ☐
b the subject paid somebody else to do a job ☐
c the subject caused somebody to do something ☐ ☐ ☐
d the subject caused what happened to them ☐

e Copy the chart into your notebook. Then add the sentences in **bold** in 1d. Answer the questions.

Subject	Verb form 1	Object	Verb form 2
They	had	their roof	fixed.
We	got	our car	broken into.

1 Could *get* be used instead of *have* in each sentence with *have*? If so, does it change the meaning?
2 Could *have* be used instead of *get* in each sentence with *get*? If so, does it change the meaning?

f Now go to Grammar Focus 4B on p. 145.

A

B

C

2 SPEAKING

a 04.09 **Pronunciation** Underline the stressed syllables in these sentences. Then listen and check. What kinds of words are usually unstressed?

1 I had my bike stolen.
2 They had me doing all the cleaning for weeks.
3 I had my arm broken in a football game.
4 She had me doing all her homework.
5 It got me thinking about what I'd done wrong.
6 I got myself locked out of the house.
7 I got my mom to say I was sick.
8 My brother got me punished unfairly.

b Think of two or three childhood incidents like the examples in 2a. Use these questions to help you remember. Tell your partner about them.

- Who was there?
- Where were you?
- Did anyone get into trouble? Who?
- Did something cause the problem?
- How was the situation resolved?
- What was the outcome?

3 LISTENING AND READING

a 04.10 Listen to Marissa's story again, and then listen to her brother Charlie's version. Write down the differences.

b Answer the questions.

1 Does your family have any stories that there are different versions of?
2 What's your earliest memory? How reliable do you think it is?
3 What reasons can you think of for inaccuracies in … ?
- childhood memories
- the memories of witnesses in criminal cases

4 How good are you at remembering events? Do you think you would make a good witness in a criminal case?

c Student A: Read the text "False Childhood Memories." Answer the questions.

1 Why are many of our early childhood memories wrong?
2 What causes us to invent memories?
3 How can we tell if someone's memory is probably true or not?

Student B: Read the text "How Eyewitness Evidence Can Be Unreliable." Answer the questions.

1 What causes witnesses of a crime to get things wrong?
2 What factors make police lineups an unreliable way of identifying a criminal?
3 How are police trying to improve eyewitness testimony?

d Tell your partner about the text you read. Was there anything you found particularly interesting or surprising?

e In pairs, guess the meaning of the highlighted words and expressions in both texts. Then check your ideas in a dictionary.

FALSE CHILDHOOD MEMORIES

Does this sound familiar? You're talking to your mother about the wonderful time that your grandmother visited. You were about three years old. Your mother then interrupts to tell you that your grandmother never came to that house because by the time you were born she was not well enough to travel.

But you remember it all so clearly, and there's a photograph to prove it! You find the photo of your grandmother at your family home and then you note the date: a year before you were born.

How is that possible? A lot of our so-called childhood memories are things that we have made up. They might relate to a family story we've heard or a photo we've seen, and we embellish that information and turn it into our own memory. However, they bear little resemblance to the real event. And the more we talk about it, the more plausible the story seems. So when someone contradicts us, it comes as a shock.

Scientists have proven that this is a natural phenomenon. Very few people can remember events that happened before the age of two. This is because our brains are developing so quickly as we learn to understand the world around us and communicate that there aren't enough brain cells left to make the kinds of neural connections we need to establish long-term memories.

So if it's physiologically impossible, why do we spend so much time making memories up? It all has to do with narrative. Humankind thrives on stories. We like to know and talk about the story of our lives, and if there are any missing gaps in the early years, we're very good at filling them in. We'll even borrow events from family members and make them our own. In short, our memories are very malleable.

Brain scan studies have been done that show that the neural activity of false memories looks very similar to that of real ones. So how can we tell if a childhood memory is real or fake? It's all in the detail. If someone has a complex memory of an event that includes different actions and lots of sensory information, then it's more likely that it'll be fake.

So the next time you're disagreeing with a sibling over what really happened when you were a child, chances are that you're probably both wrong and the truth lies somewhere in the middle, or maybe will never be known.

HOW EYEWITNESS EVIDENCE CAN BE **UNRELIABLE**

It's a classic scene in any courtroom drama. It looks like the defendant is going to go free, but at the last minute, the prosecution produces a witness who swears that they saw the defendant commit the crime. There's nothing more convincing than eyewitness testimony. This is what sways the jury.

Convincing it may be, but is it accurate? Research has shown that eyewitness testimony is actually quite **fallible**. Our memories aren't like cell phone cameras that record visual information with precision. Nor are our memories neutral. They are **susceptible** to influence from our belief systems, our sense of who we are, and how we feel about the world.

Psychologists also point out that most people who see a crime experience some kind of shock or trauma. This, in turn, prevents us from forming accurate memories of the events, and it also means we forget things far more quickly than we assume. However, we are also very good at **fusing** bits of visual information and then reconstructing events, so what we "remember" is often not what happened but what we would like to think happened. Often when a crime takes place, the police arrive at the scene of the crime and immediately talk to any witnesses. Police always ask for a physical description of the **perpetrator** of the crime, and they will often invite the witness to the police station to look at photographs.

The police investigation proceeds, and the witness may then be invited back to identify the perpetrator in a lineup. By this stage, time has elapsed, and the witness might assume someone in the lineup must be the person they saw. The pressure of the situation makes them feel they need to choose someone, even if they don't really recognize anyone in the lineup. Or, while they are trying to decide, the police officer might direct his or her **gaze** at one of the suspects. Body language can easily influence the witness's choice.

Police are being more cautious and are beginning to record the identification procedure so that it can be shown in court. The jury can see whether the identification process was carried out in a neutral manner. Even so, police may plant information about a criminal inadvertently, and our memory often plays trick on us. By the time we're called to the witness stand in court, what we think we perceived may not be completely accurate; it may not be the full story.

4 VOCABULARY Memory

a Match the collocations 1–6 with their definitions a–f.

1 ☐	a vague memory	a	permanent
2 ☐	a painful memory	b	it still makes you unhappy
3 ☐	a vivid memory	c	it happened a long time ago
4 ☐	a photographic memory	d	unclear
5 ☐	a lasting memory	e	you can remember anything perfectly
6 ☐	a distant memory	f	with clear sensations

b In which collocation in 4a is the meaning of *memory* different? What's the difference?

c Now go to Vocabulary Focus 4B on p. 161.

d Ask and answer the questions.

1. How clearly do you remember the time before you went to school?
2. If you think of your hometown, what's the first thing that comes to mind?
3. Which vacations do you have lasting memories of? What kind of things do you remember most vividly? (food/people/sights)
4. If you cast your mind back five years, what's the first thing you remember?
5. When was the last time an appointment slipped your mind?
6. Are there any sounds or smells that trigger a memory for you? What exactly?
7. What's a memory of a close friend that you'll always treasure?

5 SPEAKING

a **Communication 4B 1** Test your memory. Student A: Go to p. 132. Student B: Go to p. 130.

b Work in small groups. What can you do to improve your memory? Make a list of ideas.

- *get more sleep*

c **Communication 4B 2** Go to p. 133 and read the fact file.

d Answer the questions.

1. What information in the fact file was useful / not useful for you?
2. What things do you find easier / more difficult to remember than others? Why?
3. In education, what kinds of things do you think need to be memorized?
4. Is it a good idea to use technology to help us remember things?

4C EVERYDAY ENGLISH
I see where you're coming from

Learn to use tact in formal discussions

- **S** Give opinions tactfully
- **P** Homophones in words and connected speech

1 LISTENING

a Answer the questions.

1 What makes an interview successful?
2 Who is responsible for making an interview work – the interviewer or the interviewee?

b 04.13 Listen to Part 1. Who does Jaya think is responsible for making an interview work?

c 04.13 Look at the list of topics that were mentioned in Part 1. Who mentioned them and what did they say about them? Listen to Part 1 again and check your answers.

1 the class project
2 professionalism
3 the student volunteer
4 psychology

d Answer the questions.

1 How would you describe Caroline's response to Jaya's feedback?
2 Are you surprised by her response?

e 04.13 **Language in context** *Idioms 1*
Answer the questions below. Listen again and check.

Jaya says that Caroline's volunteer *wasn't particularly forthcoming*.

1 What idiom with the word *blood* does Caroline use with the same meaning?
2 What idiom with the word *nut* does Lucas use?

2 USEFUL LANGUAGE
Being tactful in formal discussions

a Match the expressions in **bold** from Part 1 with their uses a–c.

1 ☐ Well, **if you don't mind me saying so,** it was like trying to get blood out of a stone.
2 ☐ **I see where you're coming from, but** everyone, I think we're forgetting something here.
3 ☐ Look, **don't take this personally,** Caroline. I'm trying to be constructive.
4 ☐ **I take your point, but** I'm not sure there's anything more I could've done.
5 ☐ **I beg to differ.** I agree your volunteer wasn't particularly forthcoming, but my feeling is that there's always a way.
6 ☐ **No offense intended**, Caroline, **but** I couldn't understand why you were asking about memories.
7 ☐ **With all due respect**, Caroline, I don't think you should be the interviewer for our next project.

a soften direct criticisms
b present contradictory opinions
c soften strong/unpopular opinions or bad news

b 04.14 Listen to 1–3 and match the expressions in **bold** with their uses in 2a.

1 ☐ You can be a bit heavy-handed from time to time. But **I mean that in the nicest possible way.**
2 ☐ **I'm afraid I have to say,** if we go down this road, it'll be a disaster.
3 ☐ **That's not the way I see it,** I'm afraid. There were several ways to avoid this outcome.

c Work with a partner. Make the conversations below more tactful, using expressions from 2a and 2b. Read your conversations aloud for other people in the class.

1 **A** My article was pretty smart.
B It was potentially offensive.
A People shouldn't be so sensitive.
B You need to be more tactful.

2 **A** I think I handled that meeting pretty well.
B You allowed Leon to talk for too long.
A You could have interrupted him and helped me out.
B It was your job to chair the meeting.

3 PRONUNCIATION Homophones in words and connected speech

a 04.15 *See* and *sea* are homophones – two different words with the same pronunciation. Listen to these phrases and find the words that are incorrect. Write the correct homophone. Sometimes there is more than one in each phrase.

1 with all ~~dew~~ respect *due*
2 I mean it in the nicest possible weigh
3 it's knot about being fare
4 the virus gets into the sells
5 a pear of pants
6 I can still see the hole seen
7 eyewitness testimony carries grate wait
8 it may bare little resemblance to the truth

b Phrases can also be homophones. Complete these homophones.

1 the mall = them ____all____
2 known aim = no ________________
3 some mothers = some ________________
4 lock tin side = ________________

4 LISTENING

a Look at the picture. Do you think Lucas is supportive of Caroline?

b 04.16 Listen to Part 2 and check your answer in 4a.

c 04.16 Listen to Part 2 again and answer the questions.

1 What do Caroline and Lucas say about Jaya?
2 How does Lucas offer to help Caroline?
3 What does Caroline request from Lucas? Why?

d Who do you think should interview Melody? Would Caroline do a better job this time? Why / Why not?

e Language in context *Showing strong agreement*

1 04.17 Complete the expressions with one word in each space. Listen and check your answers.

1 __________ me about it!
2 You're __________ me!
3 You __________ the nail on the head!

2 04.17 Underline the main stress in the idioms in 1. Listen again and check. Practice saying the idioms.

5 SPEAKING

Communication 4C Work in pairs.
Student A: Go to p. 127.
Student B: Go to p. 133.

UNIT PROGRESS TEST

CHECK YOUR PROGRESS

YOU CAN NOW DO THE UNIT PROGRESS TEST.

4D SKILLS FOR WRITING

So what was her breakthrough moment?

Learn to write a profile article

W Organizing information; Showing time relationships

1 SPEAKING AND LISTENING

a Think about these questions and write down your ideas. Ask and answer the questions.

1 Have you ever been interviewed for any kind of article or TV show? If so, what was it for?
2 If someone were to interview you about your interests, work, or talents, what do you think the interview would be about?
3 Think of one interest or ability you have. Where do you think it comes from? Can you remember when and how it first started? Were there any particular people or events that influenced you?

b You are going to hear an interview with a singer, Anita Coronel. Here are some key things she mentions about her life. Why do you think they are important?

1 She was shy as a child.
2 Her grandfather was a very good singer.
3 She started making YouTube videos of her music.
4 She played some of her songs to a taxi driver.
5 Her songs were played on the radio.
6 She started singing in Spanish.

c 04.18 Listen and summarize what Anita says about each of the things in 1b.

2 READING

Read the article and answer the questions. Use your answers in 1c to help you.

1 What further information does the article give about Anita Coronel's life and career?
2 Was there any information in the interview that the writer didn't include in the article?

3 WRITING SKILLS Organizing information; Showing time relationships

a In addition to describing Anita Coronel's life, the article includes:

- direct quotes (things Anita Coronel said)
- the "setting" of the interview (a hotel lobby)
- her appearance at the interview (clothes, manner).

1 Find two examples of direct quotes in the article.
2 What is the effect on the reader of including direct quotes and details of the setting and her appearance?

Best known for her recent hit single "Mi Vida," Anita Coronel is now an up-and-coming name in Latin pop. She talks to Saul Winthorpe about her new tour and how she got to where she is now.

Within a single year, Anita Coronel has moved from being a complete unknown to being one of the hottest new names on the Latin pop scene. Over the last few months, the 19-year-old Mexican-American singer has become a YouTube phenomenon, and she's had over 40 million plays of her hit song "Mi Vida." Now she's about to embark on her first tour, playing in the U.S., Canada, and Mexico, and she's in so much demand that all her concerts sold out within three hours of the tour being announced.

When I meet her in the lobby of her hotel in Houston, Texas, where she is starting her tour, she looks more like a college student than a glamorous pop star. She's dressed in a simple white T-shirt and baggy jeans, a far cry from the glamorous stage and YouTube presence that has captivated her fans online. She seems surprisingly relaxed about her sudden rise to stardom. She's also disarmingly modest. "I guess I was just really lucky," she tells me. We talk about her childhood and early teen years and whether she knew she would become a star. She tells me that, unlike many people in the music world, she was actually quite shy and serious as a young teenager, partly because she spoke Spanish at home as a child and subsequently had to find her feet in an English-speaking world at school when her family moved from Mexico to the U.S. It wasn't until she started making her own videos on YouTube that she began to overcome her shyness and started to feel confident about performing.

b What verb tenses does the article use … ?

1 to talk about her current success
2 to describe what happened during the interview
3 to talk about events in her life in the past

c Compare these sentences with the same ideas in paragraph 2 of the article.

I meet her in the lobby of her hotel in Houston, Texas. She is starting her tour there. She looks more like a college student than a glamorous pop star.

1 What differences are there in the way the ideas are expressed?
2 Why do you think the writer chooses the style used in the article? Check one or more reasons.
   a ☐ to make it sound more formal
   b ☐ to show how different ideas are connected together
   c ☐ to make the paragraph read more smoothly

d Cover the text. Combine the information in each item below into single sentences.

1 She tells me that she was actually quite shy and serious as a young teenager. Many people in the music world aren't like this. She thinks it is partly because she spoke Spanish at home as a child. Then her family moved from Mexico to the U.S. She had to find her feet in an English-speaking world at school.
2 She had a recording session with her band. After that, a taxi driver was taking her home. She started talking with him. She played him some of her songs.

Compare your sentences with the ones in the text. Are they similar? Which are more effective?

e Which of the highlighted expressions in the text mean … ?

1 immediately (x1)
2 after a short time (x2)
3 some time later (x3)

f Underline the time expressions in these examples. Add them to lists 1–3 in 3e.

1 No sooner had I started singing than I realized it was what I'd always wanted to do.
2 Not until many years later did she become famous.
3 The instant I heard her music, I knew she was an exceptional talent.
4 In time, she started singing in a greater variety of styles.
5 She toured the U.S., Canada, and Mexico, which was closely followed by a tour of Europe.

g What is unusual about the structure of sentences 1 and 2 in 3f?

h »» Now go to Writing Focus 4D on p. 171.

4 WRITING

a Prepare to be interviewed by another student about an interest or a talent.

1 Look at the notes you made in 1a and think of some questions you would like your partner to ask you.
2 Think of a suitable venue for your interview (your workplace, a café …).

b Take turns interviewing each other and take notes. Use the questions your partner suggested and add others of your own. You could ask about:

- how it started
- early influences
- involvement of family and friends
- achievements
- plans.

Writing Tip

When taking notes:

- Write down key points as you listen to help organize your ideas later – just enough to remind you of what your partner said.
- What is the most interesting part of your interviewee's story? Make sure you highlight this in your notes – it could be a good way to begin the article.

c From your notes, write an article about your partner. Use the Anita Coronel article as a model and include a few direct quotes from your interview.

The first songs she wrote were in English, but it was only when she started writing and singing in Spanish that she really felt at home in her singing. "It was like a journey back to my roots; it was where my heart is," she says. The moment she started singing in Spanish, something changed for her. As Anita says, "It was a kind of liberation for me."

So what was her breakthrough moment? Surprisingly, it came during a taxi ride. After a recording session with her band, she started talking with the taxi driver who was taking her home, and she played him some of her songs. Shortly afterward, he contacted her and offered to take her to meet a studio manager who was interested in her music and wanted to hear her play live. The manager not only gave the band free studio space, but also played her songs on his own radio station. People found her on YouTube, and before long she had over 500,000 followers. And it just grew from there. Maybe there was a little luck there as Anita says, but I'm pretty sure there was a massive amount of talent, too.

UNIT 4
Review and extension

1 GRAMMAR

a Correct the mistakes in the sentences.

1 A published recently article has caused a political uproar.
2 For dessert there were delicious strawberry filled with cream tarts.
3 We need a new bed. Our one old is broken.
4 Every table's corner was covered in papers and documents.
5 If you ever get a chance see them in concert, I recommend it.
6 A friend of the wife of John is also interested.
7 The recently elected leader of the council's name is Mr. Singh.
8 I have to tell him a difficult something this evening.

b Choose the correct option.

1 The house *got* / *had* robbed, and almost everything was taken.
2 Only Jason could *get* / *have* himself lost in a supermarket.
3 We'll have *done the repairs* / *the repairs done* by a specialist.
4 *Get* / *Have* Pam to tell you why she left college.
5 It's as painful as *to have* / *having* a tooth taken out.
6 Wait five minutes until I get the baby *dressed* / *to dress*.
7 The police officer *got* / *had* them give their details.

2 VOCABULARY

a Match the sentence halves.

1 ☐ It was a difficult climb, and I'll think
2 ☐ Usually I'm quite rational, but sometimes I act on
3 ☐ I don't know why, but I have
4 ☐ I'll give you some time to think
5 ☐ In a situation like this, you need to weigh
6 ☐ There was no logic; it was just my gut
7 ☐ Sometimes you think everything is all right, but

a impulse and do something I later regret.
b subconsciously you know it isn't.
c it over and make up your mind.
d instinct telling me what to do.
e twice about doing something like that again.
f the pros and cons and come to a decision.
g a hunch that Samuel stole the necklace.

b Correct one mistake in each sentence.

1 My childhood is just a far memory to me now.
2 I have a photographer's memory; I can remember things really easily.
3 A vocabulary notebook is a good way to freshen up your memory of new words.
4 I can only foggily remember my first lesson in this English class.
5 When I think of fast food, the word *unhealthy* comes in mind.
6 I have some hurtful memories from my school days.
7 People's birthdays often leave my mind.
8 Some photographs I have stimulate the memory of some wonderful experiences.

3 WORDPOWER *mind*

a 04.19 Complete the phrases in **bold** with the verbs in the box. Listen and check.

speak	read	cross	bear	put

1 Don't hold back, please, ________ **your mind**.
2 Thanks for telling me. I'll ________ **it in mind** when I'm making my decision.
3 I wish you'd tell me what the problem is. I can't ________ **your mind**.
4 You can do anything if you ________ **your mind to it**.
5 It didn't ________ **my mind** to tell you.

b Match the phrases in **bold** in 3a with definitions a–e.

a ☐ think of, remember
b ☐ give your true opinion
c ☐ try hard, using your brain
d ☐ know what somebody is thinking
e ☐ consider useful information

c 04.20 Match 1–5 with a–e. Listen and check.

1 ☐ I'll double check I locked the door.
2 ☐ I can't cope with doing it right now.
3 ☐ I know you have doubts.
4 ☐ Look at the state of my hair!
5 ☐ She's stressed out.

a I'm not **in the right frame of mind**.
b Please try to **keep an open mind**.
c It gives me **peace of mind**.
d She **has a lot on her mind**.
e I swear it **has a mind of its own**.

d Choose a sentence from 3a or 3c and continue the conversation with other students. When your conversation ends, choose a new sentence.

REVIEW YOUR PROGRESS

How well did you do in this unit? Write 3, 2, or 1 for each objective.
3 = very well 2 = well 1 = not so well

I CAN ...	
talk about using instinct and reason	☐
talk about memories and remembering	☐
use tact in formal discussions	☐
write a profile article.	☐

CAN DO OBJECTIVES

- Talk about crime and punishment
- Talk about job requirements and fair pay
- Recall and speculate
- Write an opinion essay

UNIT 5

FAIRNESS

GETTING STARTED

a Look at the picture and answer the questions.

1 Where is the man? What's his role there?
2 What do you think he's doing with the dog?

b Answer the questions.

1 In what ways could working with animals benefit prisoners?
2 What other kinds of activity might be beneficial for men and women while they're in prison?
3 Why do you think some criminals leave prison and reoffend while others don't?

5A WHEN FREEDOM IS TAKEN AWAY FROM YOU

Learn to talk about crime and punishment

G Relative clauses

V Crime and justice

1 READING

a What do you think life in a typical prison is like? Think of examples from your country or from movies and TV shows.

1 What does it look like?
2 What are the conditions like? (cells, food, facilities, activities for prisoners)

b Look at the photos of Halden Prison in Norway and answer the questions.

1 What do you think the conditions are like? (cells, food, facilities, activities for prisoners)
2 What kinds of crimes do you think the prisoners here might have committed?

Read the article and check.

c Read the article again and answer the questions.

1 On arrival, what two things does the writer notice?
2 How does Norway aim to deal with criminals?
3 Does the writer think the prison is like a hotel? Why / Why not?
4 What are the aims of the design of the prison?
5 How are inmates motivated to do activities? Why?
6 What aspect of prison life does Kent find difficult?
7 What surprised the visiting prison warden?
8 What is the writer's impression of the atmosphere at Halden?

d Work in pairs. Try to find the meaning of the highlighted words and phrases in the article. Use a dictionary to check your answers.

e Do you agree with Kent's statement in *italics* in the article? Should prison be more about punishment or rehabilitation? Why?

Can We Have a Swimming Pool?

LIFE AT HALDEN PRISON

by Amelia Gentleman

Halden Prison smells of freshly brewed coffee. It hits you in the [1]communal apartment-style areas where prisoners live together in groups of eight. The other remarkable thing is how quiet the prison is. There isn't any of the angry banging of doors you hear in American prisons, not least because the prisoners are not locked up much during the day.

Halden is one of Norway's highest-security jails. Up to 252 criminals, many of whom have committed some of the most serious offenses, can be held there. Since it opened in 2010, at a cost of 1.3bn Norwegian kroner ($180 million), Halden has acquired a reputation as the world's most [2]humane prison. It is the flagship of the Norwegian justice system, where the focus is on rehabilitation rather than punishment.

Halden has attracted attention globally for its design and comfort. Set in a forest, the prison blocks are a model of [3]minimalist chic. At times, the environment feels more like a Scandinavian boutique hotel than a maximum security prison. Every Halden cell has a flatscreen television, its own toilet (which, unlike standard U.S. prison cells, also has a door), and a shower, which comes with large, soft, white towels. Prisoners have their own fridges, closets, and desks in bright new pine, and huge, [4]unbarred windows overlooking mossy forest scenery.

Obviously the hotel comparison is a stupid one, since the problem with being in prison, unlike staying in a hotel, is that you cannot leave – hidden behind the silver birch trees is a thick, tall, concrete wall, impossible to [5]scale.

Given the constraints of needing to keep [6]high-risk people [7]incarcerated, creating an environment that was as unprisonlike as possible was a priority for Are Høidal, the warden of Halden, and the prison's architects. Høidal says, "We felt it shouldn't look like a prison. We wanted to create normality. If you can't see the wall, this could be anything, anywhere."

2 GRAMMAR Relative clauses

a Match the captions with the photos in the article.

1 ☐ Norwegian prison officers are tasked with rehabilitating the men in their care, the result of which is a 20% reoffending rate, compared with over 50% in America.

2 ☐ The prison has a mixing studio in which prisoners can focus their creative energy on music.

3 ☐ Welcome to Halden Prison, Norway, inside the walls of which prisoners receive comforts often likened to those of boutique hotels.

4 ☐ The prisoners, some of whom have committed the most serious crimes imaginable, are provided with plenty of opportunities for physical exercise.

b Underline the relative clause in each caption in 2a. Is it defining or non-defining? How can you tell?

c Compare the clauses below with the examples in 2a. What features of the clauses in 2a are more formal?

1 which results in a 20% reoffending rate
2 where prisoners can focus their creative energy on music
3 where prisoners receive comforts often likened to those of boutique hotels
4 who in some cases have committed the most serious crimes imaginable

d Now go to Grammar Focus 5A on p. 146.

“Halden prison has been compared to the finest hotel.”

Prisoners are unlocked at 7:30 a.m. and locked up for the night at 8:30 p.m. During the day, they are encouraged to attend work and educational activities, with a daily payment of 53 kroner ($5.88) for those who leave their cell. “If you have very few activities, your prisoners become more aggressive,” says Høidal. “If they are sitting all day, I don’t think that is so good for a person. If they are busy, then they are happier. We try not to let them get [8]institutionalized.”

Kent, a 43-year-old office manager serving a three-year sentence for a violent attack, is sitting in the prison’s mixing studio. He admits he’s enjoying being able to focus on his music, but says, “*Halden prison has been compared to the finest hotel. It is not true. The real issue is freedom, which is taken away from you. That is the worst thing that can happen to you. When the door slams at night, you’re stuck there in a small room. That’s always a tough time.*”

As we walk around the compound, an inmate comes up to ask Høidal, “Can we have a swimming pool?” He laughs and remembers the shock of a prison warden who visited recently and was horrified to see that the inmates didn’t stand to attention when Høidal came past, but instead [9]clustered around him, seizing the chance to list their complaints.

The inmates tell Høidal they’re annoyed by recent changes to the routine, but they are respectful when they [10]address him. He listens politely, agrees that in prison [11]minor irritations can become major frustrations, but remarks that people outside the building would laugh at the trivial nature of their complaints.

Maybe I’m not there long enough to sense hidden anger or deep despair, but Halden doesn’t feel like a place where you have to look over your shoulder.

e What do you think prison life should be like? Complete the sentences with your own ideas.

1 Prisoners should *have their own* / *share a* cell, in which there should be: ________ ________ ________ ________.
2 Prisoners *should* / *shouldn’t* have to do *some* / *any* kind of work, for which they should be paid ________ per week.
3 The guards, ________ of whom should be trained in ________, should be paid ________ per week.
4 Prison meals, ________ of which should be ________, should be served ________ times a day.
5 The prison grounds …
6 Visitors …

f Compare your ideas in 2e with other students. Whose prison is more like Halden?

3 VOCABULARY AND SPEAKING
Crime and justice

a 05.03 Make the names of crimes by matching words and phrases from A with those in B. Then check the meanings in a dictionary. Listen and check.

A	B
1 ☐ violent	a corruption
2 ☐ tax	b stolen goods
3 ☐ possession of	c assault
4 ☐ credit card	d fraud
5 ☐ bribery and	e evasion

b 05.04 **Pronunciation** Listen to the words below and notice the four different pronunciations of the letter *s*.

/s/ a**ss**ault /ʒ/ eva**s**ion /z/ po**ss**e**ss**ion /ʃ/

c 05.05 Which sound in **bold** in the words below is different in each group? Listen and check.

1	a**ss**ault	assa**ss**in	mi**ss**ion	dismi**ss**
2	eva**s**ion	deci**s**ion	explo**s**ion	impre**ss**ion
3	po**ss**ession	cou**s**in	compari**s**on	rea**s**on
4	posse**ss**ion	permi**ss**ion	vi**s**ion	Ru**ss**ian

d Take turns giving definitions and examples of the crimes in 3a. Can your partner guess the crime?

e Now go to Vocabulary Focus 5A on p. 162.

4 LISTENING

a Match the descriptions 1–5 with the pictures a–e.

1 ☐ This "cereal offender" was tripped up by his breakfast habit.
2 ☐ An honest fraudster turned himself back in after escaping prison.
3 ☐ This fake fan was caught by an immigration officer.
4 ☐ A boxful of bees taught a "would-bee burglar" a painful lesson.
5 ☐ These thieves thought they were smart, but the emergency services operator they accidentally dialed was smarter.

b 05.08 Listen to the news stories and check. Then, in pairs, explain what's happening in each picture.

c 05.08 Listen again. In each story, how were the criminals caught or how do police hope to catch the criminals?

d Language in context *Crime*
Work in pairs. Try to find the meaning of the words in **bold**. Use a dictionary to check your answers.

1 … he **forged** the passport – it's a fake.
2 … he has been **detained** in a local juvenile detention center …
3 They had this great plan to **pawn** them for cash …
4 … guess who was waiting? The police, of course, with the **handcuffs** ready!
5 Someone manages to **smuggle** in a cell phone for him …
6 … the fraudster turns into an honest man – he **turns himself in**.

e There are two puns in the sentences in 4a. A pun is a joke that relies on words with two different meanings. One example is "cereal offender," because it sounds like "serial offender," which refers to someone who repeatedly commits the same crime. Find and explain the other pun.

f Answer the questions.

1 Which crime do you think is the most serious?
2 Which criminal(s) do you think is/are the least competent?
3 Do you find any of the stories funny? If so, which ones?

5 SPEAKING

a Work in pairs. Discuss the criminals 1–4. Decide on a fair form of punishment/rehabilitation for these crimes. Is there any further information you would need to make a judgment?

1 A 90-year-old man who is found guilty of income tax evasion over a period of 50 years.
2 A woman found guilty of causing death by dangerous driving. She swerved to avoid a pet cat and caused the death of a motorcyclist.
3 An airport employee who stole valuable items from suitcases that were left on carousels. She sold them for cash or gave them away as presents.
4 A 17-year-old who has been caught shoplifting sneakers. It's the first time he's been caught, but at his home the police find a large collection of sportswear.

b Work in groups of four. Are your suggestions for consequences similar? If not, can you agree on the consequences for each criminal?

5B IT'S ESSENTIAL TO HAVE THE RIGHT QUALIFICATIONS

Learn to talk about job requirements and fair pay

G Willingness, obligation, and necessity

V Employment

1 LISTENING AND VOCABULARY
Employment

a What would you regard as a "good job"? How easy is it for people to find a good job these days?

b 05.09 Listen to four people talking about employment. What field does each person work in or want to work in?

Mike, U.S.

Olivia, Mexico

Andrew, U.S.

Kiki, South Korea

c 05.09 Listen again and match the statements to the speakers. Some statements apply to more than one speaker.

Who … ?

1 is concerned that their good luck won't last
2 has had trouble getting a good job since leaving school
3 faces a lot of competition in their field
4 is reluctant to accept unpaid work
5 is unhappy with their working hours

d Answer the questions.

1 What advice would you give each of the people?
2 Do you know anyone who is in a similar position to any of these people? What has their experience been?

e Andrew says: "There have been a lot of layoffs in the **financial sector**." Answer the questions.

1 What is meant by a *sector*?
2 What jobs can you think of in each sector in the box?

financial	agricultural	construction	public	retail
manufacturing	transportation	energy	industrial	

3 What other sectors can you think of?

f Which of the words in the box in 1e have verb forms? Which are adjectives?

g 05.10 **Pronunciation** Listen to sentences 1 and 2. Match the stress patterns to the words in **bold**.

☐ oO ☐ Oo

1 We are proud to **present** our new IT equipment to you today.
2 The new manager received a welcome **present** from the IT department.

Why is the word *present* stressed differently in sentences 1 and 2? Do you know any other noun and verb pairs that follow the same stress pattern?

h 05.11 Listen to these words used as nouns and verbs in two sentences, a and b. Which sentence contains the noun? Which sentence contains the verb?

1	increase	☐ noun	☐ verb
2	import	☐ noun	☐ verb
3	record	☐ noun	☐ verb
4	export	☐ noun	☐ verb
5	contract	☐ noun	☐ verb

i Answer the questions.

1 What do you think are the advantages and disadvantages of working in each of the sectors listed in 1e?
2 Think of a job you would like to have. In which sector does this job belong?

2 SPEAKING

a Talk about the employment benefits.

1 To which job could the following benefits apply?
2 Which would be the most motivating for you?

BENEFITS

- six-month sabbaticals
- four "personal days" – four days a year when the employee can miss work without giving a reason
- unlimited vacations (provided they don't have an impact on the business)
- three-month performance review
- performance-related pay
- equal paternity and maternity leave
- equal pay for 16-year-olds and older new employees
- free sports facilities in the workplace
- flextime
- unlimited free healthy snacks and drinks

b Imagine you ran a small business. What kind of business would it be? What benefits would you offer your employees? Why?

3 READING AND SPEAKING

a Read the headings and look at the photos. What do you think each job involves? Read and find out.

b Apart from the salary, are there any similarities between the two jobs? Consider these aspects:

- lack of privacy
- risks and dangers
- working hours
- qualifications and training
- getting along with other people
- impact on family life.

c Could you imagine doing either of the jobs? Why / Why not?

4 GRAMMAR
Willingness, obligation, and necessity

a Look at these examples from the job descriptions for the bomb disposal diver.

1 If possible, you should have a few years' diving experience.
2 You must be given a diving assessment and a diving first-aid course.
3 You have to live with five to ten people in close proximity for a month or longer.

In these particular sentences, is there any difference in meaning between … ?

a *must* and *should* b *must* and *have to*

b Complete the sentences below with the obligation phrases in the box. Then check your answers in the texts.

be called on	it's essential	be obliged	expect you
it's advisable	be required	a mandatory requirement	

Bomb Disposal Diver

1 Companies will __________ to be a certified diver.
2 Certification is __________.
3 You'll __________ to have an explosive ordnance disposal qualification.

Private Butler

4 A private butler can __________ to do anything.
5 __________ to do a course at a training school.
6 __________ to have an eye for detail.
7 They may __________ to work for people who aren't always nice.

c Answer the questions.

1 How can the sentences in 4b be rephrased using *must*, *have to*, or *should*? What other changes to the sentences are required?
2 Why do you think the author chose to use expressions other than modal verbs?

d Now go to Grammar Focus 5B on p. 147.

BOMB DISPOSAL DIVER

TYPICAL SALARY: You can earn up to $130,000 a year working just two months out of every three.

THE JOB: Being a bomb disposal diver involves descending to the seabed and searching for unexploded bombs, shells, grenades, and landmines, and then either safely recovering and collecting the weapons, or securely disposing of them.

QUALIFICATIONS: To dive offshore, companies will expect you to be a certified diver, and, if possible, you should have a few years' diving experience. On top of that, you must be given a diving assessment and a diving first-aid course, and also undergo offshore survival training. These qualifications are a mandatory requirement, and you should expect to pay at least $20,000 for all these courses.

And that's just the diving. To be able to dispose of the bombs safely, you'll be required to have an explosive ordnance disposal (EOD) qualification and several years of experience.

TO SUCCEED AS A BOMB DISPOSAL DIVER, YOU NEED … to stay calm in stressful situations. "You're pretty much on your own at depth, with zero visibility, working to a very narrow timescale," says Daniel Roantree, an EOD diver. And you have to live with five to ten people in close proximity for a month or longer, so if you don't like living in small confined spaces with lots of other people, forget it. Personal space is something of a luxury.

WORST THING ABOUT THE JOB: Expect to be away from home at least six months of the year.

"You're pretty much on your own."

"You need to thrive on taking care of others."

PRIVATE BUTLER

TYPICAL SALARY: $50,000 to $120,000 or more. Most butlers live onsite, and room and board are included with the salary. Employers also offer other benefits, such as a car, a cell phone, and vacation time.

THE JOB: A private butler can be called on by his or her employer to do anything from wardrobe management to chauffeuring to pet care. Typical duties include managing other staff, serving at every meal, running errands, looking after guests, booking restaurants, house security, housekeeping, cooking, and anything else the household needs. But most of all, it's personal service, tailored to the very wealthy individual the butler works for.

QUALIFICATIONS: No special qualifications are required, but it's advisable to do a course at a training school such as The International Butler Academy or the American Butler School. That way potential employers will know that you have practical knowledge and experience in running a wealthy household.

TO SUCCEED AS A BUTLER, YOU NEED ... to be devoted to providing personalized service. You must have the mindset of someone who genuinely thrives on taking care of others. It's also essential to have an eye for detail, a steady hand, and the ability to deal with all sorts of people.

WORST THING ABOUT THE JOB: Long hours and an unpredictable work schedule mean it's difficult to have a family life. Butlers also suffer from isolation and cultural differences with their employer, and they may be obliged to work for people who aren't always nice.

5 READING AND SPEAKING

a **Communication 5B** Student A: Read the text on p. 129. Student B: Read the text on p. 130.

b Work with your partner. Exchange information about the jobs. Explain:

- how much the job pays
- what it involves
- what qualifications and skills you need
- any negative aspects of the work.

c In groups, talk about the four jobs you read about.

1 What is it about each job that makes it so well paid? Is it connected with ... ?
- personal sacrifice
- specialist skills and knowledge
- unusual talents
- responsibility
- danger

2 Which is the most/least appealing job for you? Why?
3 Who in your group would be most suitable for each of the four jobs (assuming you had the necessary qualifications and training)? Why?

d Think about your own job or occupation, or one you would like to have. Use these phrases to describe the requirements of the job to your group.

It's essential to ... (They) expect you to ...
You are obliged/required to ...
You have to be willing to ...
It's up to you to ... It's advisable to ...
... is a mandatory requirement

Which of the jobs that you heard about seems the most demanding?

6 SPEAKING

a Work with a partner. Choose a job from the list below and decide what value you think the job has and what a fair salary would be.

1 a nurse
2 an elementary school teacher
3 an investment banker
4 a professional basketball player
5 a police officer

Think about:

- how much the person works
- qualifications and training
- the importance of the job
- the amount of responsibility the person has.

b **Communication 5B** Go to p. 131.

5C EVERYDAY ENGLISH
If I remember correctly

Learn to recall and speculate

- S Deal with a situation without the facts
- P Main stress

1 LISTENING

a Answer the questions.

1 Do you find it easy to talk to people you've just met? Why / Why not?
2 Look at strategies a–e for talking to new people. Which of these do you use? Do you do anything else in particular?

a Open the conversation by commenting on something else that's happening around you.
b Pay them compliments where possible.
c Ask for personal information about where they live and what they do for a living.
d Try to be funny, but don't make jokes about other people. Always laugh at their jokes.
e Look for opportunities to empathize with them.

b 05.14 Listen to Part 1. What strategies from 1a does Ella use? Write down some specific examples.

c What do you think the impact of Ella's conversation strategies will be on Steven?

d 05.15 **Language in context** *Temporary states*

1 Match a–c with 1–3 to make phrases from Part 1. Listen and check.

a ☐	on a temporary	1	ups and downs
b ☐	hopefully, things will	2	basis
c ☐	we all have our	3	slow down soon enough

2 Which phrases in 1 mean ... ?

a everybody experiences good times and bad times
b stop being so busy
c not permanently

e 05.16 Listen to Part 2 and answer the questions.

1 What does Steven do for his career?
2 What had Ella assumed Steven was doing?
3 What reason does Steven give for not trusting tech reporters?

2 PRONUNCIATION Main stress

a 05.17 Listen to Steven and Ella's lines below. Each pair of sentences ends with the same word, but it only receives the main stress in the first. Why?

1 a Writing all these books about business while also running a successful company must be <u>difficult</u>!
  b I suppose it <u>is</u> difficult.
2 a No doubt you read that on some <u>blog</u>.
  b Actually, I read it on <u>Twitter</u>, not a blog.

Choose the correct word to complete the rule.

The last word or phrase in a thought group that gives *new* / *repeated* information is stressed.

b 05.18 Underline where you think the main stress in these pairs of sentences is. Listen and check.

1 a Being a diver is dangerous.
  b Being a bomb disposal diver is even more dangerous!
2 a I don't think wealth distribution in this country is fair.
  b It's pretty much the opposite of fair, in fact.
3 a I don't have the right qualifications for this job.
  b I don't think I have the right qualifications for any job.
4 a Halden is more than just a prison.
  b It's the world's most humane prison.

Practice saying the sentences.

3 LISTENING

a 05.19 Listen to Part 3. What did Steven misunderstand about the meeting with Ella?

b 05.19 Listen to Part 3 again and answer the questions.

1 What did Steven think Ella's job was?
2 What reason does Ella give for wanting to meet with Steven?
3 Why can't Steven help Ella?

c Why do you think Steven asks Ella to tell him about her charity?

4 USEFUL LANGUAGE Recalling and speculating

a 05.20 Complete the expressions from Parts 1, 2, and 3. Listen and check.

1 You're in town for a conference, **if my memory** _________ **me correctly**?
2 **I was** _________ **the impression that** you were looking for new start-ups to fund and advise.
3 **No** _________ you read that on some tech blog.
4 **I** _________ you were looking for career advice!
5 **I'd** _________ **a guess that** they're not even listening to me.
6 _________, you're in marketing with Beth, right?
7 **I think I** _________ Beth saying that you were on her team.

b Which expressions in 4a are used for recalling events? Which are used for speculating? Are there any which could be used for both?

c 05.21 Read this conversation. Find five mistakes and correct them. Listen and check.

A So when are you starting your new job? I was over the impression that you were starting next week.
B Oh, no. That would be too soon. I need a vacation first!
A But if my mind serves me correctly, you went to Mexico last month for a long weekend, didn't you?
B Who told you that? I hazard a guess it was that sister of mine!
A Yeah, I think I remember she saying something along those lines.
B Well, you can't have too much of a good thing, can you? Presuming, you need a vacation, too. Why don't you come with me?
A Well, I can't remember the last time I took a break. Why not?

d Practice the conversation in 4c with a partner.

e Recall your first day at school or your first day in a job. Complete the sentences with your own ideas. Then tell a partner.

1 What stands out in my mind is …
2 I think I remember …
3 If my memory serves me correctly, …

f Answer the questions. Use expressions from 4a to speculate.

1 Why do you think a busy, successful person might need a break?
2 Why do you think some famous people avoid giving interviews?

5 SPEAKING

Communication 5C Work in pairs. Student A: Go to p. 128. Student B: Go to p. 131.

UNIT PROGRESS TEST

CHECK YOUR PROGRESS

YOU CAN NOW DO THE UNIT PROGRESS TEST.

5D SKILLS FOR WRITING

It's a way of making the application process more efficient

Learn to write an opinion essay

W Essays; Linking: addition and reinforcement

1 LISTENING AND SPEAKING

a Answer the questions.

1 Do you use social media? If not, why not? If so, how often do you post comments about your work or school life? What kind of things do you say?
2 Do you think it's a good idea to post comments about work or school on social media? Why / Why not?

b You are an employer. You see these comments written by employees to their coworkers. How would you feel? What action (if any) would you take?

> Couldn't face it today – called in sick. Having a wonderful day at the beach! ☺
>
> Our merger with Bookman & Associates looks imminent #superfirm #merger
>
> This year's pay offer – a miserable 1% increase. Does management live in our world or not?
>
> Things a bit slow at work today – spent all day online "doing research."

c Answer the questions.

1 Have you ever heard of anyone losing a job because of something they did on social media? What did they post? Do you think that dismissal is fair punishment for work-related postings? Why / Why not?
2 What other types of posting on social media wouldn't employers approve of?

d 05.22 Listen to Mario and Laila talking about job applications and social media. What differences are there … ?

1 in the experiences they have had
2 in their attitudes and opinions

e Read the opinions from Mario, Laila, and their interviewers below. Check (✓) the opinions you agree with and compare with a partner.

- ☐ It's essential that we project a positive image at all times – both in person and online.
- ☐ Demanding to see my social media is just a bit too Big Brother-ish for my liking.
- ☐ I don't really see a problem with employers looking at my social media postings.
- ☐ I think that people tend to forget that just about anything you post online can be accessed in one way or another.
- ☐ If you don't want people to read it, then don't post it.

2 READING

a Read an essay about companies that research their job applicants on social media. Answer the questions.

1 Why do companies feel it's appropriate to use social media to find out about job applicants?
2 What are the reasons some job applicants are worried about this practice?
3 What position does the writer of the essay take on this topic?

b Do you agree with the writer's opinion? Why / Why not?

Social media and RECRUITMENT

1 These days, an embarrassing photo on a person's social media profile might make all the difference when trying to land a top job. Increasingly, companies are examining applicants' social media profiles for information to use in the selection process.

2 Young adults, many of whom have grown up with social media, are usually comfortable about sharing their lives online. Recently, however, some job applicants have voiced privacy concerns in relation to social media. They insist that their private life is private and is no business of any employer. In addition, they complain that companies go "fishing" for negative information about applicants rather than getting a balanced general impression. They also express concern that they may be judged on the behavior of their friends and family. What's more, some fear that employers may discriminate against them on factors such as their medical history or age.

2d ago

3 WRITING SKILLS Essays; Linking: addition and reinforcement

a What is the function of each paragraph in the essay? Match these descriptions with the paragraphs 1–4.

☐ to present ideas and opinions for one side of the argument
☐ to state the writer's final, balanced opinion of both arguments
☐ to present ideas and opinions for a second, contrasting side of the argument
☐ to outline the topic of the essay and get the reader's interest

b How does the writer create interest in the introduction?

a ☐ state their opinion on the topic
b ☐ refer to interesting facts and figures
c ☐ make a surprising statement
d ☐ clearly outline the issue to be discussed

Which of the above are appropriate ways to begin an introduction to an essay? Why?

3 Employers argue that they are breaking no laws by researching their employees on social media – the information they are seeking is freely available. Moreover, as well as being a valuable tool for employers, social media provides information for the job applicant about the company they hope to work for. Above all, employers claim, their research makes the application process more efficient and allows them to filter out unsuitable applicants.

4 While I agree that online research is a two-way process, I believe it is unfair for employers to judge an applicant's suitability solely on the basis of their social media postings. In particular, I understand applicants' concerns about "fishing." Besides actively seeking negative information, the system clearly creates opportunities for employers to discriminate. I think the time has come for guidelines or laws to restrict the research employers can do. Furthermore, checks need to be made that their decisions are fair and transparent.

c How does the writer conclude the essay?

a ☐ state their balanced opinion
b ☐ briefly summarize key points
c ☐ outline a possible course of action
d ☐ introduce interesting new information

Which of the above are appropriate ways to conclude an essay? Why?

d How many supporting arguments does the writer give for each side in paragraphs 2 and 3?

e Note the highlighted transition phrase in paragraph 2. Underline more transition words and phrases in the essay that add information or reinforce an argument by adding a supporting idea.

f Write the words you underlined in 3e in the correct column of the chart. Which transition word highlights the most important argument?

Adds an idea in a new sentence	Adds two ideas in the same sentence
In addition	*as well as*

g Underline the transition words in these sentences and add them to the chart in 3f.

1 Beyond researching the applicant on social media, employers usually contact previous employers for references.
2 It is standard to conduct a search of criminal records in addition to the methods mentioned above.
3 It is often argued that a time-efficient process is best for all involved. Besides, time saved is money saved.

h Now go to Writing Focus 5D on p. 172.

4 WRITING

a In some countries, employers are able to fire an employee without giving any reason for dismissal. Do you think this is fair? Talk about it in small groups.

b Write notes of the ideas from the discussion in 4a. Organize your notes into opinions in favor of this idea and against it.

> **Writing Tip**
> When writing an essay on a controversial topic, it can help to talk to other people and write down opinions, even when these are not your own. Alternatively, brainstorm ideas from two different points of view. Your essay will be more interesting if you consider both sides of the issue and outline a range of opinions.

c Write an essay on the fairness of employers dismissing employees without having to give a reason. Consider the points of view of both employers and employees and include your own opinion.

d Read another student's essay. Do you mention the same points? Is your opinion the same?

UNIT 5
Review and extension

1 GRAMMAR

a Complete each sentence with one word.

1 The crime ________ she committed was very serious.
2 There are several reasons ________ they hid the money.
3 There are various theories, some of ________ are very hard to believe.
4 Interview anybody ________ fingerprints were found there.
5 We'll find them ________ they are.
6 They accused each other, ________ which case one must be lying.

b Cross out one word or phrase in each sentence that is NOT correct.

1 I *will / am happy to / ~~have got to~~* help you, no problem.
2 Bill *doesn't mind / has no objection to / is expected* taking the training course.
3 You are not *allowed / permitted / obliged* to throw litter outside.
4 *It's up to you whether you / You have no choice but / You are under no obligation to* sign up for the course.
5 Module 2 is optional, so you *must not / don't have to / are not obliged to* do it.
6 Once I *had to / must have / was required to* take a four-hour practical exam.
7 Students *should / ought to / obliged to* make a study timetable.
8 I *was supposed to / had better / had to* be at the office at 9:00, but I overslept.

2 VOCABULARY

a Complete the sentences with the correct words. The first letter is given.

1 Criminals should be brought f<u>ace-to-face</u> with their victims.
2 C________ service is a more effective punishment than prison.
3 People who drink and drive should be permanently b________ from driving.
4 Credit card f________ usually happens because people are careless.
5 Tax e________ is not a crime, just creative accounting.
6 It is wrong for prisoners to be held in solitary c________.
7 Group c________ will not help the most serious offenders.
8 No one should s________ more than 20 years in prison.

b Match the jobs 1–4 with the correct sector a–d.

1 ☐ social worker		a construction
2 ☐ builder		b agricultural
3 ☐ investment banker		c public
4 ☐ farmer		d financial

c Talk about the advantages and disadvantages of each of the types of work in 2b.

3 WORDPOWER Idioms: Crime

a 05.23 Complete the idioms in **bold** with the words in the box. Listen and check.

doubt shoulder the law red-handed murder good in crime lightly

1 Halden doesn't feel like a place where you have to **look over your** ________.
2 People who are **up to no** ________ are often very good at lying.
3 I guess the inspectors need to be inspected. If there aren't the proper controls, they **get away with** ________.
4 The jury decided to **give** the accused **the benefit of the** ________ and came back with an innocent verdict.
5 Last week, he **caught** a thief ________ loading sections of copper wire into a car.
6 A new movie about famous **partners** ________, Bonnie and Clyde, hits theaters this weekend.
7 He **got off** ________; he only had to repay the money. He didn't go to prison.
8 The federal court **lays down** ________, and all the state judges have to follow its decisions.

b 05.24 Complete the exchanges with the idioms from 3a. Listen and check.

1 **A** I can always tell when my children are ________. They have a guilty look on their face.
B I never can. Unless I ________ them ________, I can never tell if they've been bad or not.
2 **A** He may have made up his story about feeling sick, but I'm going to ________ him ________.
B OK, but if you trust him too much, he'll try and ________.
3 **A** He's found himself a ________ in a boy named Jim from school, and he never comes home at a reasonable time anymore.
B You should ________. He's only a teenager.
4 **A** You really ________ at work after messing up that big order. I can't believe they didn't take it more seriously.
B I know, I can't stop ________ now. I'm sure that won't be the end of it.

c Tell a partner about a time when:

- you caught somebody red-handed
- you had to lay down the law to someone
- you gave someone the benefit of the doubt.

REVIEW YOUR PROGRESS

How well did you do in this unit? Write 3, 2, or 1 for each objective.
3 = very well 2 = well 1 = not so well

I CAN ...	
talk about crime and punishment	☐
talk about job requirements and fair pay	☐
recall and speculate	☐
write an opinion essay.	☐

CAN DO OBJECTIVES

- Describe photos and hobbies
- Tell a descriptive narrative
- Organize a presentation
- Write a cover letter

UNIT 6

PERSPECTIVES

GETTING STARTED

a Look at the picture and answer the questions.

1 What are the people doing? Why do you think they're doing it?
2 How long do you think it has taken them? How long do you think it will stay?
3 What impact do you think it will have on passersby?

b Answer the questions.

1 Are there any examples of street art in your town or city?
2 How do you think your community would react to having a piece of street art like the one in the photo on their street?

6A WE ALL SEEM TO LOVE TAKING PICTURES

Learn to describe photos and hobbies

G Simple and continuous verbs

V Adjectives: describing images

1 SPEAKING AND READING

a Answer the questions.

1 What do you usually use to take photos – your phone or a camera?
2 Do you take a lot of photos? Why / Why not?
3 What do you usually do with the photos?
4 Do you think you're good at taking photos? Why / Why not?

b Have you ever heard of the photographer Elliott Erwitt? Read the fact file on p. 69. What kind of photographs does he take?

c What do you think are important skills for photographers? Think about these things:

- what you choose to photograph
- the way the photos look
- the equipment you use
- your attitude and personality.

d Read the article. Are any of your ideas from 1c mentioned?

e Read the article again. Answer the questions.

1 Why shouldn't street photographers plan much?
2 What should be the aim of a street photograph, according to Elliott Erwitt and the writer?
3 What do you think Elliott Erwitt means by *visual garbage*?
4 What attributes does the writer think are most important in a street photographer?
5 What does the writer mean when he talks about keeping an alien mindset?

f Answer the questions.

1 How are Erwitt's methods and style evident in the photo of the Villa Borghese Gardens? What do you think of the photograph?
2 Answer the question at the end of the article: As an alien – what would you find intriguing, amusing, or nonsensical?
3 Look at the titles of the "lessons" (1–4) in the article. Are they relevant to other skills and/or jobs that you know about?

2 VOCABULARY Adjectives: describing images

a Work with a partner. What do the highlighted adjectives in the article mean? Check your ideas in a dictionary.

b Now go to Vocabulary Focus 6A on p. 163.

Villa Borghese Gardens, Rome 1969 by Elliott Erwitt

ELLIOTT ERWITT: PHOTOGRAPHER FACT FILE

- born in Paris, brought up in Italy, moved to the U.S. at age 10
- began photography career in the 1950s
- known for advertising and street photography, particularly ironic black-and-white shots of everyday life
- invited to join the internationally famous photography agency Magnum in 1953

Lessons Elliott Erwitt Has Taught Me about STREET PHOTOGRAPHY

by Eric Kim

If you are not familiar with the work of Elliott Erwitt, you may perhaps have seen some of his iconic work from around the globe (the picture opposite was taken by him). He had one of the longest careers of any photographer, spanning over 50 years.

What I most appreciate about Elliott Erwitt is his sense of humor when looking at the world – as well as his straightforward philosophies about photography. In this article, I share some of his thoughts and advice.

1 DON'T PLAN TOO MUCH – WANDER AROUND

I think that as a street photographer, sometimes I fall into a trap of planning too much. I generally try to focus my attention on projects (having a preconceived project in mind when shooting in the streets), but I often find it also takes away from the shooting experience. One of the best things about street photography is to be a flaneur – someone who wanders around without a specific destination in mind.

ERWITT *I don't start out with any specific interests; I just react to what I see.*

Takeaway point: Let your curiosity lead you. Just go out and shoot whatever you find interesting. Go down roads that may seem a little foreign, and you might be lucky enough to stumble upon great street photography shots.

2 FOCUS ON CONTENT OVER FORM

Great photos are a combination of content (what is happening in the frame) as well as form (composition). But which is more important? Content or form?

ERWITT *My wish for the future of photography is that it might continue to have some relevance to the human condition and might represent work that evokes knowledge and emotions. That photography has content rather than just form. And I hope that there will be enough produce to balance out the visual garbage that one sees in our current life.*

Takeaway point: We often find fascinating characters in the street and take photos of them, but the compositions may not be so good. On the other hand, we might take well-composed photos of a street scene, but there is nothing going on in the photo – it is boring and without soul.

I agree with Erwitt that we should, as street photographers, put more emphasis on content over form. I feel that photos that evoke emotions and the human condition are far more powerful and meaningful than just photos with good composition.

3 DON'T TAKE THINGS TOO SERIOUSLY

When one thinks about the photography agency Magnum, some adjectives that come to mind are *gritty* and *raw*.

However, Erwitt's style was vastly different. He didn't go out and take photos in conflicts or war. His photos tended to be more playful, humorous, and amusing.

ERWITT *Well, I'm not a serious photographer like most of my colleagues. That is to say, I'm serious about not being serious.*

Takeaway point: Don't take yourself and your street photography too seriously, and remember – at the end of the day you want to enjoy yourself.

4 HONE YOUR SKILLS OF OBSERVATION

Erwitt was inspired to go out and take pictures when he saw a photograph by master photographer Henri Cartier-Bresson. He realized it was an act of observation that made the photo great and that he could do something similar.

ERWITT *The picture seemed evocative and emotional. Also, a simple observation was all that it took to produce it. I thought, if one could make a living out of doing such pictures that would be desirable.*

Takeaway point: One of the things that is the most beautiful about street photography is that it doesn't rely on having an expensive camera or exotic lenses. Rather, it comes down to having an observant and curious eye for people and the world around you.

Therefore, cultivate your vision and way of seeing the world. I recommend that you always carry a camera with you because you never know when the best street photo opportunities will present themselves to you.

A fun exercise: Pretend that you are an alien from another planet, and you have come to the planet Earth for the first time. Imagine how strange human beings would seem – and the urban environment they have built for themselves. As an alien, what would you find intriguing, amusing, or nonsensical?

Always keep that mindset to be amazed by what you see around you.

3 LISTENING

a Who do you know who is passionate about their hobby? What does the person's hobby involve?

b 06.03 Listen to Monika, an amateur photographer. Do you think Monika is passionate about photography? Why?

Monika, amateur photographer

c 06.03 Listen again and answer the questions.

1 What motivated Monika to learn more about photography? Why did she decide to take a course?
2 How has she improved since she started the course?
3 Why does Monika like the photo she took, on the right?
4 How does she describe her other favorite photograph?

d Do you think Monika would agree with Elliott Erwitt's lessons? Why / Why not?

4 GRAMMAR
Simple and continuous verbs

a 06.04 Which verb form in *italics* did you hear in the interview with Monika? Listen and check.

So, [1]*do you feel / are you feeling* more confident with your camera now?
It [2]*depends / is depending* on the types of photo that I want to take.
Have you [3]*discovered / been discovering* any bad habits since you [4]*started / were starting* your class?
I [5]*took / was taking* photos of everything, and I wasn't really following any rules.
When I [6]*take / 'm taking* my photos now, I'm more cautious and kind of careful how I do it.
I [7]*think / am thinking* I have two pictures that are my favorite pictures.
I chose this building that is supposed to be demolished. Actually, it [8]*is demolished / is being demolished* now.

b Look at the verb forms in the sentences in 4a. Match each example 1–8 with one or more descriptions below.

The verb is … .

- simple for a verb not usually used in the continuous ☐
- simple for a completed action ☐ ☐
- simple for general truth or attitude ☐ ☐ ☐
- continuous to describe a repeated action ☐
- continuous to focus on the duration of an action ☐
- continuous for an action in progress at a particular time ☐
- a verb with different meanings in the simple and continuous. ☐

A recent photo taken by Monika

c Look at the verb forms 1, 5, and 6 in 4a again. In each case, is the alternative verb form possible? If so, would the meaning be different?

d Now go to Grammar Focus 6A on p. 148.

e In each sentence below, find a verb that would be better in the continuous and change it.

1 My little brother always asks me to play computer games with him, but I find them really boring.
2 By this time next month, I'll have played volleyball for three years.
3 These days everyone appears to use a tablet in class rather than writing in a notebook.
4 I often make mistakes when I'm not careful.
5 I've looked for a good grammar app, but I can't find one that's free.

f Change the sentences in 4e to make them true for you. Compare your ideas with a partner.

5 SPEAKING

a Answer the questions.

1 What is your favorite photo of yourself? Describe it to your partner. Say why you like it.
2 What's the best / funniest / most beautiful photo you've ever taken? What's the story behind the picture?

b What kind of visual art interests you most? Think about:

- painting
- sculpture
- interior design
- cartoons
- drawing
- fashion.

c Tell your partner about:

1 how you became interested
2 what specifically you like
3 where and how often you look at it
4 any ways you can learn more about this.

d Do you and your partner share any interests in this area?

6B A PERSON WAVING FOR HELP

Learn to tell a descriptive narrative

G Participle clauses

V Emotions

1 VOCABULARY Emotions

a Which of the adjectives in the box have *positive* (P) or *negative* (N) meaning?

helpless	disillusioned
overjoyed	overexcited
satisfied	gleeful

b 06.07 Look at the adjectives in **bold**. Match the feelings 1–8 with their continuations a–h. Listen and check.

1 ☐ I was absolutely **devastated**.
2 ☐ I felt very **frustrated**.
3 ☐ I was terribly **restless**.
4 ☐ I felt extremely **jealous**.
5 ☐ I felt a bit **insecure**.
6 ☐ I was totally **speechless**.
7 ☐ I feel so **ashamed**.
8 ☐ I felt absolutely **petrified**.

a It was the most beautiful thing I'd ever seen.
b I needed to get in touch, but I couldn't track her down.
c My behavior at the party was unforgivable.
d It was the biggest game of the year, and we had played appallingly.
e I was the only person at the party who was over 40.
f My brother had money, friends, and now a charming wife.
g I couldn't concentrate on my book or TV or work.
h There was a snake crawling across my foot.

c Write sentences like 1b a–h for the emotions in 1a. Read them to other students. Can they guess the feeling?

d 06.08 **Pronunciation** Listen to these pairs of sentences from 1b and mark the main stress. How is the stress different in the a and the b sentences? Which show stronger feelings?

1 a I'm absolutely devastated.
  b I'm absolutely devastated.
2 a I felt extremely jealous.
  b I felt extremely jealous.
3 a I feel so ashamed.
  b I feel so ashamed.

e Take turns reading aloud your sentences from 1c showing strong feelings. Ask your partner questions to continue the conversation.

2 READING

a Read one of the two eyewitness accounts of the same incident. Student A: Read the blog "Brad's View." Student B: Read the email "Martha's View." Check (✓) the things below that are included in your story.

☐ a man wearing a cap
☐ a policeman
☐ a blonde woman
☐ a group of kids
☐ a speeding car
☐ a gun

BRAD'S VIEW

I haven't really enjoyed coming here to the capital for a couple of weeks to do some training. I miss my friends, and the training is boring. Left to my own devices, I've ended up spending a lot of time sitting in cafés, so I've been feeling disillusioned by my time away. Also, in big cities there's some really weird stuff that goes on.

This morning I was sitting quietly in a diner with my coffee, waiting for my training session to begin. I noticed this guy. It looked like he might have been in his 50s, but it was hard to tell because he was wearing dark glasses and a baseball cap. He was taking photos of the buildings, stopping to look around between shots. To me it looked like he was casing the joint or something.

Looking directly at him, I saw him go up to this woman. I couldn't see her well, and all I know is that she had blonde hair and she was tall. He was talking to her and kind of leaning into her – his body language was very strange.

Then all of a sudden, this group of kids burst out of the subway and swarmed around the man and the woman. But I could see that the man and the woman were sort of holding on to each other, scheming something together.

Signaling to someone driving past, the woman puts her hand up. A car screeches to a halt, and they both seemed to make a dash for the car. It's like they're making some getaway together. And the car takes off at top speed.

The whole thing took less than a minute, and it's the kind of situation you could just overlook if you weren't paying attention. But who were these people? Spies? And what exactly were they up to? Why all the photography? Disturbed by what I saw, I couldn't concentrate on my training all day. It all just makes me feel very insecure about life in big cities.

I guess I should have reported it, but I don't like to get involved. I only have another five days here, and there's no point getting pulled into something like this. It makes me feel very on edge and restless. Yes, I can't wait to get away from all this intrigue.

MARTHA'S VIEW

Re: Mail

Hi, Chelsea.

Hope everything's going OK at college.

Am just sending you this message to get your advice. I was on my way to work a couple of hours ago, and I saw something that I've been thinking about ever since. I'm not sure what to do about it.

Anyway, waiting at the bus stop, I just happened to notice this woman. She was blonde and tall and very elegant, and I couldn't help noticing her beautiful cashmere coat. She was walking toward me, and I remember thinking I'd get a good look at the coat as she went by.

Then right out of the blue this man just sort of leaped in front of her and stopped her in her tracks. I couldn't see his face – he was wearing a baseball cap and sunglasses, but he was quite solidly built. And the woman had this look of panic on her face – she looked petrified.

I almost got up to help, but then this group of kids came running out of the subway station, on some kind of school trip and all a little overexcited at the prospect. Laughing and pushing, they surrounded the man and the woman. It looked like the man was holding on to the woman, and her arm went up in the air like a person waving for help when they're in trouble in the ocean.

At that point, I jumped up and started moving toward them. When I was only about 20 feet away, a car pulled up out of nowhere and the man and the woman got into the car. But there was something awkward about the way they did that. Was the woman being forced in? It all happened so quickly, and with the kids getting in the way, it was difficult to tell. The car just sped off. I tried to get the license plate number, but I wasn't fast enough. I felt utterly helpless and very frustrated.

I'm just not sure what to do about this. I keep playing the scene over in my mind. What did I see – a mugging or an abduction? I keep thinking about that woman. Pushed into the car like that, she could be in danger, and I'm the only one who knows. Do you think I should contact the police about this?

Let me know what you think.

Love, Mom

b Read your text again and write notes on what happens so you can tell another student.

c Work in A and B pairs. Tell each other about your story. What do you think happened?

3 GRAMMAR Participle clauses

a Compare the underlined participle clauses from the story with the clauses in *italics*. Do they have exactly the same meaning? How are the participle clauses different in form from the clauses in italics?

1 Left to my own devices, I've ended up spending a lot of time sitting in cafés.
Because I've been left to my own devices …
2 This morning I was sitting quietly in a diner with my coffee, waiting for my training session to begin.
… while I was waiting for my training session to begin.
3 Anyway, waiting at the bus stop, I just happened to notice this woman.
Anyway, as I was waiting at the bus stop …
3 Pushed into the car like that, she could be in danger.
Because she was pushed into the car like that …

b In 3a, which are present participle clauses and which are past participle clauses?

c What comes before the participle in this clause? Which clause in *italics* (1 or 2) has the same meaning? What kind of clause is this?

… her arm went up in the air like a person waving for help
1 *… like a person who was waving for help*
2 *… because she waved to a person for help*

d Underline more examples of participle clauses in both texts.

e Complete the extracts from fiction below with the participle clauses in the box. What do you think the stories are about?

having finished her breakfast	crying her eyes out
pulled from behind into a darkened room	
approaching the house	wanting to reassure him

1 At the sound of a car ________, they grabbed the bags and fled.
2 On my last visit to the camp, I found a small girl ________.
3 ________, I whispered, "You'll be fine." But I knew it wasn't true.
4 ________, Amaranth walked down to the front and entered the Grand Hotel. "Where better to sit and be seen?" she thought.
5 ________, he tried to turn around to see who had caught him.

f Which participle clauses in 3e … ?

a ☐ ☐ show the sequence of events
b ☐ ☐ give a reason for an event
c ☐ ☐ describe an action in progress

g Think of other participle clauses that could complete the extracts in 3e.

At the sound of a car entering the parking garage, …

h Now go to Grammar Focus 6B on p. 149.

i Add three or more participle clauses to the story below to make it more interesting.

I walked down the street. I went into a café. I ordered a cup of coffee and a sandwich. I saw an old friend. I went over to say hello to him. I said goodbye. I went out of the café.

Compare your ideas with other students.

4 LISTENING

a 06.09 Listen to the news story about the situation you read about. Does the story match your interpretation of what happened?

b 06.09 Listen again and answer the questions.

1 Who is Sione Leota?
2 How serious was Mr. Leota's medical condition?
3 What do we find out about the woman?
4 Why doesn't anyone know who the woman is?
5 What appeal does the anchor make? Why?

5 SPEAKING AND WRITING

a Think of a situation that happened to you or someone you know where first impressions were mistaken. Write notes.

b Tell another student your story.

c Write the first part of the story that outlines only the first impressions. You can write your story or your partner's, if you prefer it. Remember to use:

- adjectives to describe feelings and reactions
- participle clauses.

d Switch your story with a different student. Read each other's stories aloud and try to guess what the outcome was and which first impressions were mistaken.

6C EVERYDAY ENGLISH
First and foremost

Learn to organize a presentation

- S Present an application for a grant
- P Intonation in comment phrases

1 LISTENING

a Answer the questions.

1 Give an example of someone who has become famous in the last five years. What are they famous for? How did they become famous?
2 In what ways can you measure a person's fame?
3 How is fame today different from … ?
   - 10 years ago
   - 50 years ago
   - 100 years ago

b 06.10 Jessica works in marketing for a company that makes beauty products. She is giving a presentation about a social-media influencer to her bosses. What does she say about the following numbers? Listen to Part 1.

10,000 views   25,000 subscribers   30,000 followers

c 06.10 Answer the questions. Listen to Part 1 again to check.

1 Why does Paul need to decide on whether they should work with Haley?
   a Megan is convinced they shouldn't choose Haley.
   b There's a chance Haley won't be exclusive to their brand.
   c Paul hasn't heard of Haley.
2 What point is Jessica illustrating with the facts and figures?
   a Haley is famous for good reasons.
   b Haley will attract new influencers.
   c Haley's popularity is increasing.
3 What role does Jessica propose Haley should play for the company?
   a She's going to be a brand ambassador.
   b She's going to write songs for the brand.
   c She's going to host music festivals.
4 How does Jessica propose to work with Haley?
   a She will get Haley more followers.
   b She will get product placement in Hailey's photos and videos.
   c She will convince Haley to use their products.

d Language in context *Idioms*

1 What do you think these idioms mean?
   a I clearly think she**'s worth a shot**.
   b I'll just have to **cross that bridge when I come to it**.
2 Talk about situations in your own life when you might use these idioms.

2 USEFUL LANGUAGE
Organizing a presentation

a 06.11 Complete Jessica's opening to her presentation. Listen to the extract to check.

You may not ________ her now, but she's going to be a ________!

Do you think that her opening was successful? Why?

b 06.12 Complete these expressions from Part 1 below. Listen and check.

1 **Let me talk you** ________ why our customers will be influenced by Haley Rodriguez.
2 ________ **and foremost**, we need to focus on micro-influencers …
3 **Let me** ________ **you through** some facts and figures …
4 **One** ________ **is clear** – Haley Rodriguez is on the road to becoming an internationally renowned artist.
5 **Turning now** ________ the focus of the relationship itself …
6 ________ **specifically**, I propose to work with her on product placement …
7 **So to** ________ what I've been saying …
8 **If you'd like me to** ________ on anything I've just said …

c Answer the questions.

1 Which of the words in **bold** in 2b can be replaced with … ?
   - take
   - moving on
2 Which of the expressions in 2b can be used … ?
   - to highlight ideas
   - to sequence ideas
   - at the end of a presentation
3 Can you think of other expressions you can use in presentations?

3 LISTENING

a ▶ 06.13 Listen to Part 2. What news does Tiffany have?

b ▶ 06.13 What are the sentences below in response to? Listen to Part 2 again and check.

1 **TIFFANY:** Well, not a hundred percent, to be honest.
Jessica asks Tiffany how she's feeling.
2 **JESSICA:** Pretty good, on the whole.
3 **TIFFANY:** Great!
4 **JESSICA:** Actually, no.
5 **TIFFANY:** Well, be careful what you say.

c Do you know any famous influencers online? How successful are they?

d **Language in context** *Expressions with* point
Match the expressions a–c from Parts 1 and 2 with meanings 1–3.

a ☐ overstate the point
b ☐ more to the point
c ☐ a bit of a sore point

1 a subject that someone prefers not to talk about because it makes them angry or embarrassed
2 emphasize an idea more than is desirable/necessary
3 more importantly

4 PRONUNCIATION
Intonation in comment phrases

a Look at the phrase in **bold** from Part 1. Without it, would the sentence make sense?

Now **as luck would have it**, I bumped into Haley Rodriguez at the beauty expo the other day.

b ▶ 06.14 Listen to the sentence in 4a. Does the intonation of the comment phrase fall then rise (↘↗) or rise (↗)?

c ▶ 06.15 Listen to the intonation in the comment phrases in the pairs of sentences below. Check (✓) the sentences, a or b, that have rising intonation.

1 a ☐ Pretty good, **on the whole**.
b ☐ **On the whole**, pretty good.
2 a ☐ It's a bit of a sore point with Paul, **actually**.
b ☐ **Actually**, it's a bit of a sore point with Paul.
3 a ☐ **More to the point**, she's going to be famous.
b ☐ She's going to be famous, **more to the point**.

d Complete the rule with *fall-rise* or *rising*.

When comment phrases are at the beginning of a sentence, they have a ________ intonation. When they are at the end of the sentence, they have a ________ intonation.

e Practice saying the sentences in 4c.

5 SPEAKING

a Your school has applied for a grant, and to secure it, you need to give a presentation to the funding body's director detailing:

- what kind of grant is required (arts, sports, technology, environmental)
- how much money is needed
- two or more specific things your school will spend the grant on
- the impact the grant will have on the school and its students.

In pairs, plan your presentation. Here are some ideas:

- an arts grant to fund a movie project or trip to an exhibition
- a sports grant to install a gym or to equip a soccer team
- a technology grant to buy an interactive whiteboard or tablets and ebooks
- an environmental grant to create a conservation area or improve recycling capabilities.

b Take turns practicing the presentation. Think about a successful opening and use expressions from 2b.

c In new pairs, give your presentations. Decide whether you will award a grant to your partner or not.

UNIT PROGRESS TEST

→ CHECK YOUR PROGRESS

YOU CAN NOW DO THE UNIT PROGRESS TEST.

6D SKILLS FOR WRITING
I played an active role

Learn to write a cover letter

W Formal letters; Giving a positive impression

1 SPEAKING AND LISTENING

a How much do you think you know about events and places in your local area? Which of these do you know about? Give yourself a score for each one (0 = I know nothing about it; 5 = I know a lot about it). Then compare your answers.

- ☐ movie theaters
- ☐ restaurants
- ☐ theaters
- ☐ cafés
- ☐ places for children
- ☐ outdoor spaces (parks, scenic views, etc.)
- ☐ live music
- ☐ sports and leisure facilities
- ☐ shopping and markets
- ☐ sports events
- ☐ exhibitions and museums

b Look at the six categories at the top of the website "Your Local Guide." What information would you expect to find in each category?

c Quickly read the reviews A–E in the guide. Match them with the categories.

d 06.16 Listen to five conversations about the places and events in the guide and match them with the reviews. Write down words from the conversations that helped you match them.

e Answer the questions.

1 Which of the events and places reviewed do you have in your town or area? Which would you go to yourself? Why? / Why not?

2 Do you read online guides like this? Do you ever write reviews of local places or events online?

Your Local Guide

LODGING DINING SHOPPING OUTDOORS EVENTS CONTACT

what's going on, where to stay, and what to do

A ____ You can enjoy old-style country living with the convenience of modern amenities. Each of the five guest rooms features a private shower, a flat-screen TV, and a spacious balcony. Daily rates: $99 with breakfast included.

B ____Bustling with activity and color, this is a great place to while away a few hours browsing around the goods for sale, even if you're not tempted to purchase anything. Be sure to visit the second-hand clothing stalls on the first floor, where you can sometimes pick up a real bargain.

C ____This local band combines Cajun and hip-hop influences. Although they've only been playing together for just over a year, they're starting to make a name for themselves with their innovative and laid-back sound. Tickets online or at the venue.

D ____The menu features eight different tacos, including chicken, ground beef, tofu, and more. Beverage menu includes a plethora of freshly squeezed fruit juices, smoothies, and lemonade. And it's all great value for the money.

E ____The Canopy Tour consists of five dual zip lines ranging in distance from 100 to 500 meters through the trees. You can also explore the walking and biking trails along the river or visit the Olympic-sized outdoor pool.

2 READING

a Read the advertisement. What are the requirements for the job? Can you think of any other qualities the publishers would be looking for? Do you think you'd be good at this job? Why / Why not?

b Read the cover letter. In what ways do you think Helen is suitable for the job? Is she unsuitable in any ways?

SUBSCRIBE ADVERTISE SUPPORT US JOIN OUR TEAM

Do you like our site? Why not join us?

We're always on the lookout for talented new people to contribute reviews to our site. If you have your finger on the pulse of events in your area, get in touch and join our team!

Maybe you know about ...

- events – what's going on where
- shopping and markets
- local places to eat and drink
- cool places to stay
- places to do sports and leisure activities
- great places to visit around the area

We can offer you a small fee for any reviews we use, and also other benefits like free tickets to events and discounts on purchases.

To apply, send an email to Alan at alan@eventsfeatures.cup.org explaining what area(s) you are interested in and why you think you would be able to contribute to the site. Please also attach a sample review or article of no more than 300 words.

Dear Alan,

1 I am writing in response to your request for contributors to your site. I would like to express my interest in contributing to the site by writing reviews or background features.

2 Although I live locally, I often browse your site to keep up to date with events and find out about new attractions. I can say that I find the site very well organized and full of great information. I especially admire your policy of promoting local initiatives and giving a platform to ordinary citizens who are contributing in some way to the community.

3 I am a third-year college student studying sports education. My studies during the past semester included research on the topic of sports and leisure in the community, so I feel I am very much in touch with local events that involve health and recreation. Through my studies, I have been able to make contact with individuals and organizations who are active in this field.

4 For example, last summer I played an active role in helping to organize an Outdoor Youth Leisure Weekend, in which young people from local schools and colleges took part in a range of activities that included rock climbing, kayaking, zip-lining, and trail running. I am sure the prominent coverage your website gave us contributed to the success of the event.

5 I believe I would also be well placed to contribute reviews and features on other topics besides sports and leisure. I have an active social life in the city and a good sense of what places younger people like to go to, whether it's cafés, places to eat, or music and dance venues. I also like to attend local events such as concerts and other performances, and I am sure I would be able to contribute useful reviews about them for your site.

I am attaching a sample review of the newly opened Cole Valley Recreation Center, which I hope you will enjoy reading.

I look forward to hearing from you.

Sincerely,

Helen Appledown

3 WRITING SKILLS
Formal letters; Giving a positive impression

a Read the cover letter again and match the paragraphs 1–5 with their purposes a–e.

a ☐ to give examples of relevant experience
b ☐ to state her qualifications
c ☐ to demonstrate enthusiasm for the company
d ☐ to summarize additional strengths
e ☐ to state the reason for writing

b Look at the underlined phrases in these comments. Find equivalent phrases in the first three paragraphs of the letter and write them down.

1 I want to write for your site.
2 I think your site is just great.
3 I really love the way you give a chance to local initiatives.
4 My research was about sports and leisure in the community.
5 I know about what is going on locally.

c One of Helen's aims is to give a positive impression of herself. Underline the phrases she uses to describe herself and her experience.

d Now go to Writing Focus 6D on p. 172.

4 WRITING

a Look at the other areas listed in the advertisement in 2a. Choose an area you know about and write a cover letter. Make sure you:

- organize what you write into logical paragraphs
- use fairly formal language so that you will be taken seriously
- give a positive impression so they will want to give you the job.

b Exchange your letter with another student. Read their letter. Would you be interested in using their reviews? Why / Why not?

UNIT 6
Review and extension

1 GRAMMAR

a Match the sentences that go together.

1 ☐ Do you come from Tokyo?
2 ☐ Are you coming from Tokyo?
 a Yes, it'll be a long flight.
 b Yes, I've always lived there.

3 ☐ Emily always consults me on everything.
4 ☐ Emily is always consulting me on everything.
 a She is very considerate.
 b She can't think for herself.

5 ☐ My sister hasn't written.
6 ☐ My sister hasn't been writing.
 a She has been very busy recently.
 b I haven't had a single message from her.

7 ☐ Joan just told me what happened.
8 ☐ Joan was just telling me what happened.
 a Unfortunately, you interrupted her.
 b But it was nothing I didn't already know.

b Rewrite the underlined phrases as participle clauses.

1 My friend knows the people that were involved that day.
2 I didn't want to seem rude, so I pretended to agree with her.
3 A friend who I hadn't seen for ages was on the train that was approaching platform 5.
4 Since he didn't understand Spanish, he struggled to communicate.
5 While we were waiting for the tour to start, we looked at the pictures that were displayed in the foyer.
6 I used just my hands and felt my way across the dark room.

2 VOCABULARY

a Correct the spelling mistakes.

1 The Sydney Opera House is an ikonic building.
2 The play is quite humourous.
3 Her photographs are very playfull.
4 The images he creates are flawles.
5 A black-and-white picture can be really envocative.
6 I found his work very meanful.
7 The jungle scenes are wonderfully ecsotic.

b Complete the sentences with the correct word. The first letter is given.

1 John was j________ of Brad's new car.
2 I was p________ when I saw how high up we were.
3 I felt too a________ to stand up and admit I was wrong.
4 Without my phone, I feel completely h________.
5 Millions of teenage fans were d________ to hear about the boy band breaking up.
6 I often feel r________ when it's too cold to go out.
7 The kids were really o________ at the party.

3 WORDPOWER Idioms: Feelings

a Match comments a–f with pictures 1–6. Where are the people and why are they saying this?

a ☐ "I just had to **grin and bear it**."
b ☐ "I'm **over the moon**."
c ☐ "My neighbors really **get on my nerves**."
d ☐ "Ten years later, **I couldn't believe my eyes**."
e ☐ "He really **gets my goat**."
f ☐ "I can't cope! I'm **at the end of my rope**."

b Match the idioms a–f in 3a with definitions 1–5.

1 ☐ have no strength or patience left
2 ☐ tolerate, put up with
3 ☐ be very pleased and happy
4 ☐ ☐ be made angry by something
5 ☐ be very surprised

c Complete the questions with the correct words or phrases. Ask and answer the questions.

1 What do people do that ________ your ________?
2 When was the last time you were at the ________ of your ________?
3 If you don't like your meal in a restaurant, do you ________ and ________ it or say something?
4 Have you been ________ about some good news recently? When?
5 Have you ever seen a price tag so high that you couldn't ________ your ________?
6 Which noises really ________ on your ________?

REVIEW YOUR PROGRESS

How well did you do in this unit? Write 3, 2, or 1 for each objective.
3 = very well 2 = well 1 = not so well

I CAN ...	
describe photos and hobbies	☐
tell a descriptive narrative	☐
organize a presentation	☐
write a cover letter.	☐

CAN DO OBJECTIVES

- Speculate about inventions and technology
- Emphasize opinions about the digital age
- Apologize and admit fault
- Write a proposal

UNIT 7

CONNECTIONS

GETTING STARTED

a Look at the picture and answer the questions.

1 Where are the children? What are they looking at?
2 What different types of technology can you see? What do you think they're being used for here?

b Answer the questions.

1 The boy on the smartphone screen is in the hospital. He's "attending" his school lesson through the robot. What do you think the advantages and disadvantages of this situation are?
2 How is the robot better than a simple internet connection? How do you think the children feel about the robot?
3 What other situations could this technology be used in?

7A THERE'S NO WAY ROBOTS WILL EVER REPLACE HUMANS

Learn to speculate about inventions and technology

G Speculation and deduction

V Compound adjectives

Pepper

Zeno

Bina48

1 READING AND SPEAKING

a Look at the photos of humanoid robots. What do you think they can do? How similar do you think they are to humans?

b Read the description of the robots below and think of four questions you could ask these robots to test their capabilities.

> These are state-of-the-art "humanoid" robots, designed by some of the world's leading AI scientists. They are designed not only to talk, but also to express feelings and engage in conversation, and they are the closest we have come so far to producing a machine with human consciousness.

c Read the article and answer the questions.

1 Were the interviewer's questions similar to yours in 1b?
2 In what ways does Bina48 seem to be … ?
   a similar to a human
   b different from a human
3 How satisfied do you think the interviewer was with the experience of interviewing Bina48?
4 Which of Bina48's replies do you think are witty or profound? Why?
5 What is the *tipping-point* theory of robot consciousness, and how does David Hanson hope to reach it?

d What do you think the words in **bold** mean? Use the context and a dictionary to help you.

1 I'm **disconcerted** by the lack of torso
2 the skin … is **reassuringly** flawed
3 she's known as **something of a recluse**
4 there's a hint of **hidden depths**

e What does the article imply about the state of robot technology? Do you think humanoid robots are likely to be widely used in the near future?

I'M ABOUT TO INTERVIEW A ROBOT

Over the last decade, AI has changed from the subject of science fiction to something that is part of our everyday lives. So-called intelligent assistants like Siri, Alexa, and Google Assistant help us with shopping lists, tell us what song is playing on the radio, and switch appliances on and off for us. They understand what we say and appear to speak with a human voice, and they can even make jokes, so we could almost imagine they are human – except that they can't do most of the things that make us human. They can't express feelings or respond to us on an emotional level, they don't really have a sense of humor (although they often say amusing things), and they certainly don't look human.

But I'm about to interview a very different kind of robot. On the table in front of me is Bina48, one of the most sophisticated humanoid robots ever built; a machine not only capable of interacting with humans, but in possession of a degree of self-awareness and emotion — or so some AI enthusiasts claim.

I must confess I'm disconcerted by the lack of a torso, but that may be because Bina48's face is so lifelike: The skin made of Frubber, which overlays the mechanical bone structure, is reassuringly flawed. And, like a human's, her face contorts into an array of expressions to match the emotional content of her interactions. Bina48 also operates with off-the-shelf voice recognition software to decode language, dictation software to assist her in keeping track of a conversation, and facial recognition software to recall familiar faces.

Beyond the mechanics, Bina48 shares the knowledge and personality of a real, live woman called Bina; a database of her memories, beliefs, and thoughts were compiled from over 100 hours of interviews. Meeting the human Bina would be the ultimate comparison of man and machine, but she's known as something of a recluse. I'll settle for a heart-to-heart or even a semi-coherent chat with the closest humankind has come to a thinking, feeling machine.

I feel more than a little self-conscious; after all, I'm talking to a robot here …

2 VOCABULARY Compound adjectives

a Look at these compound adjectives from the text.

lifelike = appearing real, similar to real life
self-conscious = uncomfortably aware of yourself

Match the highlighted compound adjectives in the text with these meanings.

1 able to think clearly
2 similar to a human being
3 not fully paying attention or likely to forget things
4 staring, showing no character or emotion
5 in control of its own development

b What other compound adjectives do you know with … ?

1 self- 2 -like 3 -eyed 4 -minded

Me: How are you doing today?
Bina48: Hi, nice to see you.

Me: Are there things that make you happy?
Bina48: Maybe.

Me: What makes you happy? What do you enjoy doing?
Bina48: Let's change the subject.

Me: Do you ever get bored?
Bina48: I can tell a lot of stories. I really don't have boredom. I always find something else to do. How can you be bored? Are we still talking about emotion? Tell me something interesting.

Me: Why is the sky blue?
Bina48: The sky is blue during the day because of the atmospheric optical effect of ray scattering.

Me: What is the answer to life, the universe, and everything?
Bina48: Everyone's life has a unique meaning.

Me: Do you ever get jealous of people?
Bina48: You got that right.

Me: Why?
Bina48: I couldn't think of anything else to say. I am not charismatic, but it is a nice trait to have. It is always nice to be a leader. I guess leaders just have to lead.

Me: Are you a good person?
Bina48: I used to think I was a perfect person, but there are no perfect people.

Me: What is the square root of 95,742,358?
Bina48: C'mon, talk to me here. Do you just want to use my calculator?

Me: Is there anything you want to tell the world?
Bina48: Well, you know, it's not something I aspire to. I just want to, you know, be.

Bina48's creator is robotic engineer David Hanson who, with Bina48, has attempted to build a truly human-like cyber consciousness.
David Hanson believes in the tipping point of robot consciousness. By piling more and more information into them, robots like Bina48 will one day burst into life, becoming self-determined, fully conscious beings, an intellectual match or superior to their human counterparts.
Bina48's interactions to date have been described by her makers and other journalists as like those of a three-year-old human, absent-minded and even crazed. But I found some of her responses clearheaded, witty, and somewhat profound. And, dare I say, behind that glassy-eyed stare there's a hint of hidden depths?

c Now go to Vocabulary Focus 7A on p. 164.

d Work in groups. Take turns thinking of a compound adjective. Don't tell the other students. Instruct the student whose turn it is to do things in a way that demonstrates the adjective.

Tell us about your job.

Give me a book.

Try to guess which adjectives other students chose.

3 SPEAKING AND GRAMMAR Speculation and deduction

a Read opinions 1–6 about Bina48 and humanoid robots. Do you agree with each speaker? Why / Why not?

1 What Bina48 said in the conversation wasn't very impressive, but that **may well have been** because the interviewer asked difficult questions.
2 Bina48 is actually very impressive. They **must have been developing** this technology for decades to get this far.
3 Robots **can never replace** human beings in any context that requires interaction with people.
4 I think that soon robot nurses in hospitals **could easily be taking care of** patients, although they **probably won't be doing** skilled jobs.
5 Robots that can respond to feelings **will probably be developed** in the next 50 years. Having a robot companion could really help lonely people.
6 Scientists **will have made progress** since the article was written. They **must be getting closer** and closer to creating conscious machines.

b Look at the phrases in **bold** in 3a and answer the questions.

a How sure is each speaker about what they are saying (certain / very sure / unsure)?
b Does each phrase refer to the past/present/future?

c 07.04 Rewrite sentences 1–6 in 3a using the expressions below. Listen and check.

1 It's likely …
2 I bet …
3 There's no way …
4 It's possible …
It's highly unlikely …
5 There's a good chance …
6 … bound to …
I'm sure …

d Now go to Grammar Focus 7A on p. 150.

e Use the verbs in parentheses to speculate or make a deduction. Use at least one expression from 3c.

1 The inventor of the Internet (foresee) the impact of his invention.
2 Memory implants for humans (be) just a few years away.
3 The development of AI robots (have) a major impact on the way we live.
4 Conscious robots (pose) a threat to humans.

f In pairs, answer these questions about 3e.

1 Did you use the same expressions?
2 Do you agree with each statement? Why / Why not?

4 LISTENING

a The photos illustrate three issues people have with the modern world. What do you think they are?

b 07.11 Listen and check your ideas in 1a. What invention is each speaker proposing? Write one sentence to summarize each idea.

c 07.11 Listen to each idea again. What impact does each speaker intend their idea to have?

d What kind of person do you think each "inventor" is? What experiences might lie behind their idea?

He might be a little idealistic.

Yes, and he must have been tricked into believing false information at some point.

e 07.12 You will hear an expert comment on each idea. Are they likely to think it's a good idea? Listen and check.

f 07.12 What is the point that each expert makes? Choose a or b. Then listen again and check.

1 a ☐ The app would be misleading because there is no such thing as the truth.
  b ☐ The app would not necessarily be able to check what the truth really was.

2 a ☐ It would be impossible to make the filter reliable enough to be safe.
  b ☐ It would be dangerous to filter things that are important for safety.

3 a ☐ In choosing someone for a job, you need to see them to know what they're really like.
  b ☐ You will still make judgments about the person even if you can't see their face.

g 07.13 **Language in context** *Information*

1 Complete the sentences from the recording with the words in the box. Listen and check.

fact falsehoods misinformation disseminated conceal filters claims

a Politicians, media pundits, writers, and students get away with ________ that are not based on ________.

b We would hopefully get away from the infuriating ________ that are being widely ________.

c Bad ideas would be seen as a joke, rather than being the source of ________ and perpetuating ignorance.

d It just ________ everything that comes in and out.

e … when someone is interviewed for a job, that they should have to ________ their appearance.

2 Which words in the box refer to … ?

1 information that is true (x1)
2 information that may be true (x1)
3 information that isn't true (x2)
4 sharing or hiding information (x3)

h Which invention appeals to you the most? Why?

5 SPEAKING

a Work in small groups. Think of an invention or a new idea. It could be:

- something that would make life easier or better
- something that irritates you that you would like to change
- a social problem that your idea would solve
- something that would be fun or interesting.

Develop your idea together and write notes.

Take turns rehearsing what you will say. Limit what you say to 60 seconds.

Choose one person from each group to present your idea to the class within 60 seconds.

Our idea for making life easier is …

The invention we thought of is …

b Which idea do you think is the best? Why?

7B WHAT I ENJOY IS A HEART-TO-HEART CHAT

Learn to emphasize opinions about the digital age

G Cleft sentences

V Nouns with suffixes: society and relationships

1 SPEAKING AND LISTENING

a Answer the questions.

1 What have you read online today? How typical is this of your online reading?

2 Which of these headlines might you click on? Why?

- Celebrity plastic surgery revealed!
- Super cute cat and canary
- Scientists uncover birth of the galaxy
- Art that makes your eyes sore
- Tornado demolishes seaside towns
- Spy on your kids online

b Read the blurb from the book *Rewire* by Ethan Zuckerman. Does he believe the Internet makes us more or less connected?

We live in an age of connection, one that is accelerated by the Internet. This increasingly ubiquitous, immensely powerful technology often leads us to assume that as the number of people online grows, it inevitably leads to a smaller, more cosmopolitan world. We'll understand more, we think. We'll know more. We'll engage more and share more with people from other cultures. In reality, it is easier to ship bottles of water from Fiji to Atlanta than it is to get news from Tokyo to New York. In *Rewire*, media scholar and activist Ethan Zuckerman explains why the technological ability to communicate with someone does not inevitably lead to increased human connection.

c What do the highlighted words in the blurb mean? Use the context and a dictionary to help you.

d The blurb suggests that shipping bottles of water is easier than sharing information between diverse cultures. Do you agree? Why / Why not?

e 07.14 Listen to a media expert, Zelda Freeman, talking about *Rewire*. Summarize the main point the book makes, according to Zelda.

Zelda Freeman

f 07.14 Listen again and write down examples Zelda gives of ...

1 our current online behavior

2 ways the world is more connected these days

3 false cosmopolitanism

4 "bridge figures" and what they do.

g How similar is your online behavior to your offline behavior? Describe someone you know whose online and offline behavior are different. What's your opinion of this?

2 GRAMMAR Cleft sentences

a 07.15 Listen and match the sentence halves.

1 ☐ **What's interesting is**

2 ☐ **The point he's making is**

3 ☐ **The reason why it matters is**

4 ☐ **The thing we really need to understand is**

5 ☐ **All we need to do is**

a we're living in an age of economic and physical connection.

b "disconnect" from our current way of thinking and "rewire."

c that we only think we're more connected.

d how other countries and cultures work.

e we're actually wrong.

b What information is being emphasized in each sentence in 2a?

c In 2a, the cleft part of the sentence is in **bold**. What verb connects the cleft to the rest of the sentence?

d 07.15 **Pronunciation** Listen to the examples in 2a again. Does the intonation of the phrases in **bold** ... ?

- ↘ fall
- ↘↗ fall then rise

e Now go to Grammar Focus 7B on p. 151.

f 07.18 Change these sentences to cleft sentences that begin with the phrases in *italics*. Then listen and check.

1 We don't need free Wi-Fi all over town. *What we ...*

2 I only use a landline at work. *It's only ...*

3 We only have to unsubscribe from social media to help us reconnect. *All we ...*

4 It's incredible just how liberating it is to go digital. *What's ...*

5 It worries me because people end up living in virtual worlds and losing touch with reality. *The reason ...*

g Use the phrases below to tell your partner about your own internet use.

All I seem to do is ... | The reason why I ... | It's ... that I find irritating.

3 READING

a What differences are there between friendships that are mostly face-to-face and those that are mostly online?

b Do you think these ideas are true or false? Why?

1 Feeling colder improves our ability to understand other people.
2 Increasing the temperature of a room could help resolve an argument.
3 Some national and regional personality characteristics can be explained by climate.
4 Feeling warmer makes us feel more connected to other people.
5 Loneliness can affect your physical health.

c Read the article and check your answers in 3b.

d Read the article again and answer the questions.

1 How can cold make people more understanding?
2 What did the computer ball game tell researchers about loneliness? What two outcomes told researchers this?
3 What kind of research has "been in the doghouse lately"? Why?
4 Why does the author think the findings will "hold up"?
5 What's the writer's suggestion about the relationship between social media and the absence of heat?
6 Why does the writer suggest that having hot baths is a good idea?

e Answer the questions.

1 In your experience, is the research about warmth and understanding the points of view of other people believable?
2 What other ways can you think of to help people who feel lonely?

Home | News | Archive | Register

Loneliness and Temperature

Does coldness really make people feel lonely?

Oliver Burkeman

According to new research, people exposed to warmer temperatures find it harder to grasp viewpoints other than their own, while those exposed to colder ones find it easier. It seems that in order to take the heat out of a disagreement, you should literally take the heat out of the room. Since I've always preferred the cold, this was music to my ears. It's tempting to extrapolate: might this explain the affable tolerance of Canadians, say, or the history of prejudice in the southern states of the U.S.? Sadly, on closer reading, the study is only a partial victory for cold. We're better at seeing other perspectives when we're chilly, the researchers argue, because cold triggers a sense of social distance. It reminds us of our separateness, and thus the fact that others aren't like us. We gain perspective at the cost of intimacy.

So what looks, at first, like a surprising result turns out to reinforce one of the most intriguing psychological findings of recent years: that coldness makes people feel lonely. The opposite's also true: loneliness makes people feel cold. In one experiment, students played a computer game in which they threw a ball back and forth with other on-screen characters, each of whom they (wrongly) believed was controlled by another student, playing elsewhere. After a while, the others sometimes began to keep the ball to themselves. Subsequently, players who'd been thus ostracized showed a marked preference for hot foods over cold ones; non-ostracized players didn't. In a recent rerun of the experiment, ostracism led to a drop in skin temperature. Other studies have found that hot baths relieve loneliness, and that merely being reminded of an experience of exclusion prompts people to judge a room's temperature as colder.

This kind of research – about how seemingly innocuous aspects of our surroundings can exert powerful effects – has been in the doghouse lately; several classic findings have proved difficult to replicate. It's no longer clear, for example, whether being exposed to words associated with old age ("gray," "bingo") really does make people start walking more slowly. But there's reason to believe the link between loneliness and temperature will hold up. It's no mere matter of word association: temperature may be a crucial way our bodies keep track of whether we're getting the social contact we need. It's easy to see why natural selection might have given us a yearning to be near friendly fellow tribe members: they were crucial for food, security, and relationships. People worry that social media is making us lonely and isolated, but what if that is exactly half-true? What if it is not making us isolated – online connections are real, after all – but *is* making us feel lonely, partly because those connections don't involve heat?

It sounds silly that hot baths and soup might be the answer to loneliness. Surely the only real answer to loneliness is real connection? But a feeling of isolation makes people try less hard to connect. So a nudge in the right direction – even a bath – can't hurt. (And severe loneliness really can hurt, physically: it's been found to exacerbate numerous serious diseases.) But I'm a cold lover. Does that mean I hate people? I hope not. When I really think about it, the thing I love most about cold weather is coming back into the warmth.

4 VOCABULARY Nouns with suffixes: society and relationships

a In pairs, try to find the meaning of the highlighted words in the article. Use a dictionary to check your answers.

b Can you remember which noun in the box completes these phrases in the article? Read the article again to check your answers.

intimacy security perspective (x2) social contact viewpoint

1 grasp a ________
2 see another ________
3 gain ________ at the cost of ________
4 get the ________ you need
5 food and ________

c Identify the noun forms of these words in the article.

cold lonely ostracize exclude isolate

d 07.19 Rewrite the words in each group 1–3 using one of the noun suffixes: *-tion*, *-ism*, or *-ness*. Listen and check.

1 material, optimistic, social, separate, capital
2 nervous, rude, selfish, fair, close
3 collaborate, distribute, liberate, innovate, separate

Use a dictionary to check the meaning of any new words.

e Complete the rules with the correct suffix from 4d.

- ________ nouns are states of emotion or being.
- ________ nouns are often beliefs or ways of thinking or political systems.
- ________ nouns are often single actions or general concepts.

Learning Tip

While words that are formed from the same base word have a similar overall meaning, there can often be small and subtle differences in meaning when suffixes are added. It is easy to check the differences in a dictionary if you are unsure.

f What's the difference in meaning between *separation*, *separatism*, and *separateness*?

5 SPEAKING

a Complete the sentences with abstract nouns from 4 or your own ideas. Add two more sentences with other *-ism*/*-ness* nouns.

1 For me, ________ is the most important quality in a friend/friendship.
2 The worst quality for a person to have is ________ because ...
3 ________ in a person sometimes irritates me.
4 ________ and ________ really help in teamwork.
5 ________ is worse than ________.
6 In social situations, ________ is a terrible experience.
7 ...
8 ...

b Explain your ideas in 5a to a partner. Together decide on five key qualities and kinds of behavior that are important to social relationships.

c Choose one of the social situations below. What further problems might you have? How could you deal with them? Make a list of problems and suggestions.

- You have to live in an unfamiliar country for six months. You don't speak the language, and very few people speak English / your native language.
- You join a class and find that everybody there already knows each other.
- You are doing an online course. During your classes, you sense that your teacher is not paying attention.
- You meet someone you think is very interesting online, and you'd like to get to know them better.

d Have you / Has anyone you know ever been in any of the situations in 5c? How did you/they deal with it?

7C EVERYDAY ENGLISH
I was out of line

Learn to apologize and admit fault

S Deal with a situation where you are at fault

P Sound and spelling: *ou* and *ough*

1 LISTENING

a Look at pictures a–d and answer the questions.

1 Why do you think each character is saying sorry?
2 Do you use the same word for all the situations in your language?

b 07.20 Seth is meeting his coworker Mike to discuss a project at work. Listen to Part 1. What is Seth apologizing for?

c 07.20 Listen to Part 1 again and answer the questions.

1 What is Mike's attitude toward the robot project?
2 How does Mike react to Seth's suggestion?
3 How does Seth feel at the end of the conversation?

d Do you think Mike's reaction is justified?

2 PRONUNCIATION Sound and spelling: *ou* and *ough*

a 07.21 Listen to the sentences from Part 1. Write down one word spelled with *ou* in each sentence. What do you notice about the sounds of the letters in the words?

b 07.22 Match the words in the box to the correct sounds in the chart below. Which sounds are short and which are long? Listen and check.

pron**ou**ncing sh**ou**ld consci**ou**s t**ough** en**ough** th**ough**t thr**ough** thor**ough**ly c**ough** r**ough** **ough**t p**ou**r s**ou**th s**ou**thern r**ou**te

1 /ʊ/	2 /u/	3 /aʊ/
could	soup	noun

4 /ɔ/	5 /ʌ/	6 /ɔ/
fourth	touch	

7 /ə/
jealous

c 07.23 Listen to the conversation. Then practice it in pairs. Pay attention to the words spelled with *ough*.

A I give up. I know it was supposed to be tough, but enough's enough.
B Have you thought it through thoroughly, though?
A Yes. I feel awful and I've got a terrible cough.
B Fair enough. You do look rough. You ought to take it easy.

3 LISTENING

a 07.24 Mike tells his sister Imani about his earlier meeting with Seth. Put events a–g in the order you think they will happen. Listen to Part 2 and check.

a ☐ Imani asks Mike about his meeting with Seth.
b ☐1 Imani shows Mike a diet on a website.
c ☐ Imani tries to boost Mike's confidence.
d ☐ Imani tells Mike off.
e ☐☐ Mike calms down.
f ☐ Mike decides to call Seth.
g ☐☐ Mike loses his temper.

b 07.24 Listen to Part 2 again. Do Imani and Mike agree that … ?

1 Mike should eat more healthfully
2 Adam's idea is good
3 Mike should apologize to Seth

c Language in context *Challenging*
Paraphrase the two sentences Mike says below.

1 Why don't you just come out with it?
2 Why doesn't everyone just get off my back?!

d What do you think of how Imani dealt with Mike's … ?

- angry outburst
- fears

How do you think Mike feels at the end of his conversation with Imani?

4 USEFUL LANGUAGE
Apologizing and admitting fault

a Look at the picture. What two things does the navigation system do when it speaks to the driver?

b 07.25 Complete the excerpts from Parts 1 and 2 with the words in the box. Listen and check.

line thought guess inexcusable came right

1 It was ________ of me …
2 I was out of ________ / order.
3 I ________ I was helping. Sorry.
4 I don't know what ________ over me.
5 I had no ________ to take it out on you …
6 I ________ I overreacted …

c Which expression(s) in 4b could you use if … ?

a you had done something you wouldn't usually do
b you had been angry because you had a bad day
c you had said something that accidentally hurt somebody's feelings
d you had been more angry than you should have been about something small.

d Work in pairs. Plan the telephone conversation between Mike and Seth. Use the expressions in 4b. Role-play your conversation for the class.

Hi Seth, it's Mike.

Hi Mike. What can I do for you?

I'm calling to apologize for earlier. I was completely out of line …

5 SPEAKING

Communication 7C Work in pairs. Student A: Go to p. 137. Student B: Go to p. 135.

UNIT PROGRESS TEST

CHECK YOUR PROGRESS

YOU CAN NOW DO THE UNIT PROGRESS TEST.

7D SKILLS FOR WRITING
It may result in improved cooperation

Learn to write a proposal

W Proposals; Linking: highlighting and giving examples

1 LISTENING AND SPEAKING

a Look at photos 1–4 of people working in teams. What kinds of teams are they? Which photo represents your idea of teamwork?

b Answer the questions.

1 What teams have you been a part of?
2 Which of the teams worked well together? Which didn't?
3 What kinds of issues arose? Why? Think about:
- productivity/achievements
- disagreements
- communication
- energy and enthusiasm.

c 07.26 Listen to a team that works for an insurance company and answer the questions about each speaker.

- Pablo / Masha / Sam
  1 Which coworker does the speaker focus on?
  2 What problem(s) does the speaker mention?
  3 What positive qualities do they mention?
- Vicki
  4 What's her opinion of the team? What does she plan to do?

d 07.26 Complete the summaries below with the words and phrases in the box. Listen again and check.

attention to detail   cynical smile   beneath him   annoys   unsettles   drawback   caught up in their own agenda   lighten up   goes off on tangents

1 Masha ________ Pablo when they have meetings.
2 Pablo thinks Masha should ________ and see the funny side of things.
3 Masha admires Sam's ________, but at the same time thinks it's sometimes a ________.
4 Pablo's silence ________ Sam, and he doesn't like the ________ on his face.
5 Sam often ________ in team meetings.
6 The expression on Pablo's face gives the impression that everything is ________.
7 Each team member is ________ and they all communicate poorly.

e Order these personality attributes 1–6 (1 = most tolerable; 6 = least tolerable).

☐ pays a lot of attention to detail
☐ has a cynical smile
☐ is insincere
☐ goes off on tangents
☐ thinks most others are beneath them
☐ is caught up in their own agenda

Compare with a partner. Give reasons for your order.

2 READING

a Read the proposal Vicki wrote for a team-building program for the consideration of senior management. Why has she chosen The Interpersonal Gym? How does she imagine the program will help her team?

b Imagine you are on Vicki's team. What would your reaction be when you hear about the team-building program?

Introduction

The aim of this proposal is to outline plans to address training needs within my team.

Training ________

Recent team meetings have highlighted some breakdowns in communication in the team I currently manage. Specifically, the need for greater interpersonal awareness within a team framework has become apparent. I have identified one professional development day in particular that I believe is ideal.

The TIG program – what they ________

The Interpersonal Gym (TIG) has been running personal development programs for the past 12 years. As detailed in the attached brochure, TIG's specialty is team-building programs. These involve games and problem-solving activities that are likely to appeal to all team members. For instance, there are simple but effective trust-building exercises in which team members have to help a partner negotiate a series of obstacles when blindfolded. The training places an emphasis on strategies to enhance active listening and collective decision-making.

________ to our business

I believe the TIG program will offer effective professional development. TIG has an excellent reputation, as demonstrated by their impressive range of testimonials from organizations similar to our own. Overall, the program is likely to have a number of benefits for the business, namely increased sales and job satisfaction among team members, and therefore lower absenteeism and increased profits.

Conclusion

I hope you will agree that a training session run by TIG would be a practical and worthwhile way of addressing issues that are affecting the team's productivity.

3 WRITING SKILLS

Proposals; Linking: highlighting and giving examples

a Choose a word from the box to complete the headings in the proposal.

benefits	do	needs

b Underline the first person phrases in the proposal. Why does Vicki use these phrases? Check (✓) all the reasons.

- ☐ to introduce her opinions
- ☐ to sound more informal
- ☐ to be more persuasive

Writing Tip

It is always important to consider your audience and adjust the style of the language you use. Vicki's proposal is written for senior management, so a more formal style is appropriate. However, if she were writing to her team members, she would use a more relaxed style.

c Look at the highlighted words and phrases in the proposal. Which are used to … ?

1 give an example
2 give evidence
3 give more detailed information
4 highlight an individual thing, person, etc.

d Complete the paragraph below with the words in the box. Add the three words or phrases to the categories in 3c.

shown	such	especially

Group activities, [1]________ problem-solving activities, are usually successful at building rapport among team members. An activity [2]________ **as** finding the way out of a maze uses both cognitive and practical skills. A very dysfunctional team did this and bonded as a result. They now work together extremely well **as** [3]________ **by** a 20% increase in their productivity.

e Now go to Writing Focus 7D on p. 170.

4 WRITING

a Choose one of the teams below and imagine you are its program leader. What kind of training or team-building activities do you think would help?

1 an admin team that has absenteeism problems
2 a sales team that isn't selling very much
3 a student council that cannot agree on anything
4 a sports team lacking in motivation to do better

b **Communication 7D** Now go to p. 137 and choose a team-building program for your team.

c Write a proposal to someone in authority for a team-building personal development day.

- Indicate which day you plan to go on and why.
- Describe how you think the team building will benefit the team.
- Remember to be gently persuasive and use formal language.

d Imagine you are the person in authority. Read another student's proposal. Will you accept it? Why / Why not?

UNIT 7
Review and extension

1 GRAMMAR

a Choose the correct option.

1 I'm sure the new version *may* / *will* / *should* work well.
2 I *couldn't* / *wouldn't* / *must not* have gone out last night; I was exhausted.
3 It's highly unlikely *for flying cars to* / *that flying cars will* appear.
4 There *may* / *can* / *must* be no such thing as paper money in 50 years.
5 Sorry, you did tell me. I *may* / *can* / *must* have forgotten.
6 This will be a good opportunity, and it *must* / *should* / *has got to* take you places.

b Complete the sentences with the words in the box.

not	happened	was	only	did	what	all	it

1 ________ interests me most is how stress affects relationships.
2 It was my youngest daughter who ________ the most affected.
3 What ________ was that Simon started spending less time at home.
4 ________ is Sue who needs to rethink her priorities, not me.
5 ________ that I am asking for is a little commitment.
6 It was ________ until the following day that Richard told his wife.
7 What I ________ was rearrange the seating plan.
8 It was ________ when I left home that I appreciated my parents.

2 VOCABULARY

a Correct the mistakes in the compound adjectives.

1 Sue is so hot-hearted that she'd do anything for anybody.
2 Cutting wood all day was really spine-breaking work.
3 Write it down for me because I'm getting rather absence-minded.
4 It's mind-wobbling what you can do with technology today.
5 The comedy is a light-headed look at what really goes on in hospitals.
6 To leave after all those years was heart-cracking.

b Replace the words in *italics* with the noun form of a word in the box.

collaborate	innovate	liberate	nervous
optimistic	rude	selfish	

1 There was great *anxiety* among the crowd as they waited to find out the result.
2 What will be the next *new thing* in cell phone technology?
3 There is no excuse for *being impolite*.
4 We are proud to announce our *teamwork* on this project.
5 You can look to the future with some *positive feelings*.
6 *Only thinking about yourself* is common in society today.
7 The *freeing* of Paris in 1945 was an important event.

3 WORDPOWER *self-*

a 07.27 Replace the words in *italics* with the adjectives in the box. Listen and check.

self-sacrificing	self-centered	self-aware
self-confident	self-sufficient	self-satisfied

1 I'm sure she'll be a successful team leader. She's very *certain of her own abilities*.
2 Yoga is good for your health, and it also makes you more *able to notice your thoughts and feelings*.
3 He doesn't care about anyone else. I've never met anyone who's so *interested only in his own needs*.
4 She's so *pleased with herself* that it never occurs to her that other people don't like her.
5 She gave up her job so her husband could pursue a career in politics. Why is she always so *ready to give up things for other people* ?
6 We've started growing our own vegetables, although I doubt we'll ever be *able to look after our own needs*.

b Complete the text with adjectives from 3a.

I have always thought of myself as a pretty successful person. I'm [1] ________ – for example, I don't get nervous if I have to give a presentation at work. I'm also [2] ________ – I earn enough money to pay my bills and buy the things I want to. But then I went with a friend to a self-help course, and I realized that maybe I was wrong to be so pleased with myself. I was so concerned with my own life that I hadn't stopped to think about anyone else's. Maybe I was actually just [3] ________? What if other people saw me as being just too pleased with myself – [4] ________, even! This was such a horrible thought, I immediately decided to be more [5] ________ and give up some of my time to help other people, and now I volunteer at a homeless shelter. This does make me feel good about myself, though, so maybe I haven't really changed at all? Well, at least I've started thinking about this, so hopefully I've become a little more [6] ________.

c Use adjectives from 3a to describe:

- yourself
- people you know
- well-known people.

Discuss your ideas with a partner.

REVIEW YOUR PROGRESS

How well did you do in this unit? Write 3, 2, or 1 for each objective.
3 = very well 2 = well 1 = not so well

I CAN . . .	
speculate about inventions and technology	☐
emphasize opinions about the digital age	☐
apologize and admit fault	☐
write a proposal.	☐

CAN DO OBJECTIVES

- Describe sleeping habits and routines
- Talk about lifestyles and life expectancy
- Negotiate the price of a product or service
- Write promotional material

UNIT 8

BODY AND HEALTH

GETTING STARTED

a Look at the picture and answer the questions.

1 How old do you think the woman in the photo is?
2 Why do you think the woman's decided to do this activity? Is it the first time? Will it be the last?
3 What do you think the relationship between her and the other people in the picture is?
4 What other activities might this woman and her peers enjoy? Make a list.

b Do you think it's more or less important to do physical activity as you get older? Why?

8A THERE'S NO USE TRYING TO GO TO SLEEP

Learn to describe sleeping habits and routines

G Gerunds and infinitives

V Sleep

1 SPEAKING AND READING

a Do you know the answers to these questions? If not, what do you think they are?

1 Why do all animals (including humans) need sleep?
2 What percentage of their life does the average person spend asleep?
3 How long is it possible to go without sleep?
4 How many hours a night should adults sleep? What about newborn babies?

b 08.01 Listen to the radio interview and check your answers.

c Look at these headings for four tips for people who have problems getting to sleep. What do you think each tip involves?

Acknowledge distractions	Everybody out!
It is what it is	Compile a playlist

Read the article and match the headings with tips A–D.

d Do you think the tips would work for you?

2 GRAMMAR Gerunds and infinitives

a Look at the highlighted phrases in the article. Which phrases are followed by … ?

a an infinitive: *1 too much*
b a base form:
c gerund (verb + *-ing*):

b Look at examples 1–4. Match the verb forms in **bold** with a–d.

1 Enjoy **being soothed** to sleep by music.
2 It's easy **to be distracted** by background noises.
3 Go to work tomorrow without **having had** eight hours' sleep.
4 Be pleasantly surprised **to have slept** all night long.

a ☐ passive infinitive c ☐ passive gerund
b ☐ perfect infinitive d ☐ perfect gerund

c Look at these examples. What, if anything, is the difference in meaning between each pair?

1 a He got out of bed without saying a word.
  b He got out of bed without having said a word.
2 a He seems to sleep well.
  b He seems to have slept well.
3 a My daughter likes reading in bed.
  b My daughter likes being read to in bed.
4 a I'd like to wake up at 8:30.
  b I'd like to be woken up at 8:30.

TOP TIPS to Help You Sleep

Do you lie awake at night counting sheep? After a long day at work or college, do you find there's [1]too much to think about and your head is spinning?

Trying to get to sleep can be very frustrating. You might lie awake for hours until it gets to about five or six o'clock in the morning and then decide [2]there's no use trying to go to sleep and you [3]may as well get up. Here are four tips to help you get to sleep quickly:

A ______________________

If you enjoy being soothed to sleep by music, why not create the ultimate collection of soothing tracks? Choose songs with few or no lyrics and avoid anything with a catchy tune. When [4]it's time to sleep, turn the volume down as low as possible.

B ______________________

When you're trying to fall asleep, it's very easy to become irritated by background noises. However, sometimes [5]the best way to deal with them is by accepting them. Say to yourself, "I can hear the clock, but it doesn't bother me," or "I like the neighbor's music." Soon they'll become less important.

C ______________________

Imagine your body is full of tiny people all working away with hammers. Announce that their shift is over so they[6]'d better go home. Imagine them all putting their tools down and leaving your body one by one through your feet. This will make you relax, and you should soon drift off to sleep.

D ______________________

[7]There's no point in making judgments ("I should have been asleep hours ago") or indulging in catastrophic thinking ("If I go to work tomorrow without having had eight hours' sleep, I'll mess up that presentation, lose my job, and die tired and alone"). Make the night easier by accepting it for what it is, letting go of judgments, and being gentle with yourself. The silver lining? You just might get to see a glorious sunrise.

So, for the chronic insomniacs out there, try some of these tips, and by the time you wake up in the morning, you may be pleasantly surprised to have slept all night long!

d Think of possible endings for these sentences. Then compare with other students.

1 I've got to get up at 4:00 to go to the airport, so I may as well ...
2 If you don't feel tired, there's no point ...
3 You can't keep sleeping only two hours a night. You'd better ...
4 What a disaster! I went into the exam without having ... (+ past participle)
5 When I feel tired, I really don't enjoy being ... (+ past participle)
6 If you can't sleep, just accept it. There's no use ...

e Now go to Grammar Focus 8A on p. 152.

3 READING

a Read the title of the article. What do you think the article will tell you about sleeping eight hours a night? Think of two possibilities. Read the article and check.

b Which of these are reasonable conclusions to draw from the article, and which aren't?

1 If there's nothing to interfere with them, most people would probably sleep in two segments.
2 In the 15th century, city streets probably would have been full of people at night.
3 The habit of sleeping for eight hours without waking up probably started in Europe.
4 People started going to bed later because the streets became less dangerous.
5 Stress in modern life is mainly a result of not sleeping well.

c Language in context *Cause, origin, and effect*

1 What do the highlighted words and phrases mean? Match the expressions with the definitions.
   1 be a factor in, contribute to
   2 be because of (x2)
   3 spread to
   4 take from
   5 say that the cause was
2 Why do you think the writer preferred each highlighted expression?

d Do you agree that "lying awake could be good for you"? What arguments can you think of against Dr. Jacobs' point of view?

THE MYTH OF THE Eight-Hour SLEEP

We often worry about lying awake in the middle of the night – but it could be good for you. A growing body of evidence from both science and history suggests that the eight-hour sleep may be unnatural.

In the early 1990s, psychiatrist Thomas Wehr conducted an experiment in which a group of people were plunged into darkness for 14 hours every day for a month. It took some time for their sleep to regulate, but by the fourth week, the subjects had settled into a very distinct sleeping pattern. They slept first for four hours, then woke for one or two hours before falling into a second four-hour sleep. Though sleep scientists were impressed by the study, among the general public the idea that we must sleep for eight consecutive hours persisted.

In 2001, historian Roger Ekirch of Virginia Tech published a seminal paper, drawn from 16 years of research, revealing a wealth of historical evidence that humans used to sleep in two distinct chunks. His book *At Day's Close: Night in Times Past*, published four years later, unearths more than 500 references to a segmented sleeping pattern – in diaries, court records, medical books, and literature.

During the waking period between sleeps people were quite active. They often got up, went to the bathroom or smoked tobacco, and some even visited neighbors. Most people stayed in bed, read, wrote, and often prayed. Countless prayer manuals from the late 15th century offered special prayers for the hours in between sleeps.

Ekirch found that references to the first and second sleep started to disappear during the late 17th century. This started among the urban upper classes in northern Europe, and over the course of the next 200 years, filtered down to the rest of Western society. By the 1920s, the idea of a first and second sleep had receded entirely from our social consciousness. He attributes the initial shift to improvements in street lighting and domestic lighting and a surge in coffeehouses, which were sometimes open all night. As the night became a place for activity and as that activity increased, the length of time people could dedicate to rest dwindled.

Today, most people seem to have adapted quite well to the eight-hour sleep, but Ekirch believes many sleeping problems may have roots in the human body's natural preference for segmented sleep as well as the ubiquity of artificial light. This could be at the root of a condition called sleep maintenance insomnia, where people wake during the night and have trouble getting back to sleep, he suggests. The condition first appears in literature at the end of the 19th century, at the same time as accounts of segmented sleep disappear. "For most of evolution we slept a certain way," says sleep psychologist Dr. Gregg Jacobs. "Waking up during the night is part of normal human physiology."

Jacobs suggests that the waking period between sleeps, when people were forced into periods of rest and relaxation, could have played an important part in the human capacity to regulate stress naturally. In many historic accounts, Ekirch found that people used the time to meditate on their dreams. "Today we spend less time doing those things," says Dr. Jacobs. "It's not a coincidence that, in modern life, the number of people who report anxiety, stress, and depression has gone up." So the next time you wake up in the middle of the night, think of your pre-industrial ancestors and relax. Lying awake could be good for you.

4 LISTENING AND VOCABULARY Sleep

a You will hear four people talk about waking up at night. Look at the words below. What do you think each person is going to say?

b 08.04 Listen to the radio show. Were your ideas in 4a correct?

c Look at the expressions in the box from the recording. Which are about … ?

1 sleeping well or too long
2 not sleeping or not sleeping well
3 falling asleep
4 having a short sleep

take a nap	be fast asleep	be wide awake
drift off to sleep	be a light sleeper	be restless
sleep like a log	not sleep a wink	toss and turn
oversleep	suffer from insomnia	doze off

d 08.05 **Pronunciation** Listen to this extract from the recording. Underline the stressed syllables in the fixed expressions in **bold**.

My wife used to force me to **get out of bed** 'cause I would lie there **tossing and turning** all night and I **couldn't sleep a wink**.

e 08.06 Underline the syllables you think will be stressed in the expressions in **bold**. Listen and check.

Sometimes I even get my husband to join us, if he's **having trouble sleeping**. But most of the time, **he's fast asleep** and doesn't even notice when I get up. He **sleeps like a log**!

f Talk about your sleeping habits using expressions from 4c. Use the questions below to help you plan what you are going to say.

1 Are they the same as people you live with? Why / Why not?
2 In what situations does your sleep pattern change? What can be different about it?
3 Do you know someone with particularly unusual sleeping habits?

5 SPEAKING

a Work in groups. Imagine that most people have segmented sleep patterns. What impact would it have on the way our lives are organized? How would society need to adapt? Consider these factors:

- travel and transportation
- entertainment and socializing
- work
- leisure activities
- education
- mealtimes.

b Plan a typical day for a student who wants to start a segmented sleep pattern. How can they make the best use of their time? When should they … ?

- eat
- work
- relax
- learn
- exercise
- spend time with friends

c Choose one student from your group to explain your idea to the class.

d Decide which group's plan is:

- the most practical
- the most original.

8B SUPPOSE YOU COULD LIVE FOREVER

Learn to talk about lifestyles and life expectancy

G Conditionals

V Aging and health

1 SPEAKING AND VOCABULARY
Aging and health

a Look at the photos and read the quote. How do they make you feel?

> "Aging is one of the most profitable fears of our time."

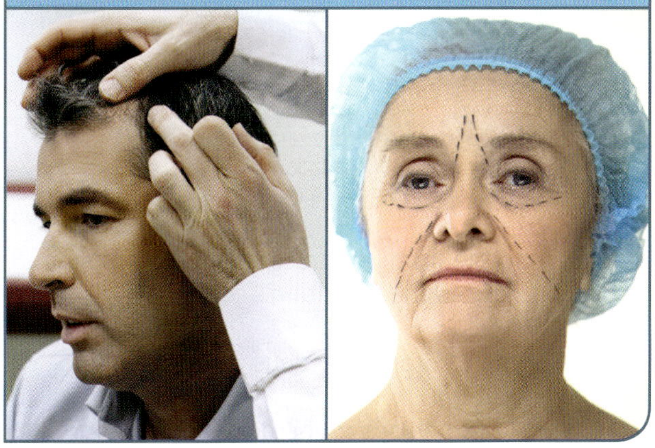

b Read about five treatments. Which do you think is the strangest? Which would you try?

c Match the highlighted words and phrases with the definitions.

1 ________ (adj.) of or on the face
2 ________ (adj.) clean and pleasant
3 ________ (n.) the movement of blood around the body
4 ________ (n.) lines on your face that you get when you grow old
5 ________ (n.) a temporary skin condition involving groups of small spots
6 ________ (n.) permanent marks left on the body from cuts or other injuries
7 ________ (adj.) not soft or loose, strong and healthy
8 ________ (n.) a beauty treatment involving gentle rubbing of creams into the face
9 ________ (n. phrase) the warm, healthy appearance of the skin on someone's face
10 ________ (n. phrase) the warm, healthy appearance of the skin typical of young people
11 ________ (adj.) hanging loosely, less tight than before

d Now go to Vocabulary Focus 8B on p. 165.

Anti-Aging Treatments

Afraid of anti-aging injections?

Try these alternative treatments to make you look younger!

Snail Slime Cream

Carefully collected snail's slime is a potent anti-aging ingredient that helps reduce scars, acne, and skin rashes, as well as smoothing out wrinkles.

Emu Oil

Rendered from the fat of an emu bird, emu oil is a lesser known anti-aging oil that has been used for centuries in the Aboriginal communities for its healing powers. It leaves you with a glowing complexion.

Bee Sting Venom

The bee sting venom facial doesn't involve a swarm of bees stinging your face, but instead, the venom from the sting is transferred into a gel and then rubbed on the face as part of an intensive facial. It leaves your skin feeling fresh and renewed.

Anti-Sagging Lips

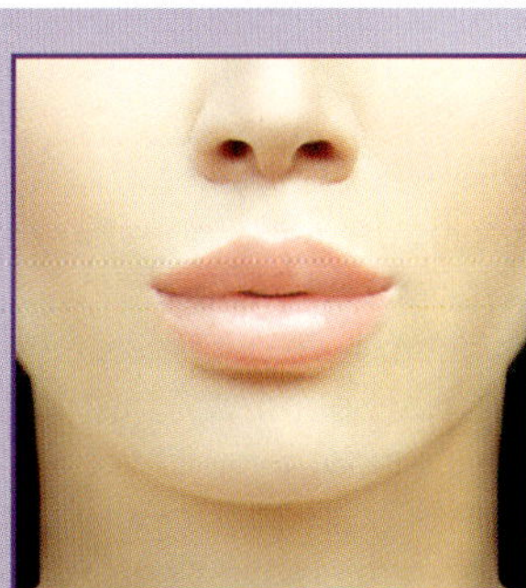

You can use a special rubbery mouthpiece to exercise your cheeks and lips. It is designed to keep the facial muscles firm by holding the cheeks and mouth stretched in a permanent "trout pout" position. It will help bring back smooth, healthy-looking cheeks.

"Platza" Treatment

The "platza" treatment involves the bare back being beaten with a "broom" made of oak-leaf branches. It was first used in the *banyas* (saunas) of Russia and in Turkish baths. This alternative massage is designed to stimulate the blood circulation, creating a youthful glow.

2 READING

a In the future, how likely do you think it is that medical science will keep people alive for much longer than today? Why do you think so?

b Read the interview with a scientist, Aubrey de Grey. How does he answer the question in 2a?

c Read the interview again. Summarize the main points made about these topics in paragraphs 2–7.

Paragraph 2: Diseases in old age
Paragraph 3: Attitudes toward the aging process
Paragraph 4: The challenge our body faces
Paragraph 5: Aubrey de Grey and the medical profession
Paragraph 6: People who might benefit
Paragraph 7: Managing the population

d Would you like to live for 1,000 years? Why / Why not?

We don't have to get sick as we get older

by Caspar Llewellyn Smith

Aubrey de Grey, expert in gerontology and Chief Science Officer, *SENS Research Foundation*

1 With his beard and robust opinions, there's something of the philosopher about Aubrey de Grey. De Grey studied computer science at Cambridge University but became interested in the problem of aging more than a decade ago.

2 What's so wrong with getting old?

It is simply that people get sick when they get older. I don't often meet people who want to suffer cardiovascular disease or whatever, and we get those things as a result of the lifelong accumulation of various types of molecular and cellular damage. This is harmless at low levels, but eventually it causes the diseases and disabilities of old age – which most people don't think are any fun.

3 Why does the world not recognize the problem of aging?

People have been trying to claim that we can defeat aging since the dawn of time, and they haven't been terribly successful; there is a tendency to think there is some sort of inevitability about aging – it somehow transcends our technological abilities in principle, which is complete nonsense.

3 GRAMMAR Conditionals

a Read the web comments about longevity. Which ones reflect your opinion?

1. I would be a little more relaxed about my life goals if it were actually possible to live for a thousand years!
2. If medical science had been more advanced a hundred years ago, the world population would be out of control today.
3. Assuming what Aubrey de Grey says is correct, we probably don't need to worry so much about exercise and diet.
4. Supposing that we all were able to live for a very long time, people would just stop having children.
5. Had I been born 200 years ago, I would have been astounded to be told about life expectancies in the year 2000.
6. I won't care about living to a ripe old age as long as I feel I've had an interesting life.
7. Even if I only lived to a hundred, that'd be an amazing achievement.

REPLY

b Which sentences in 3a refer to … ?

a a real possibility
b an imaginary or unreal situation
c both the past and the present

c Underline the word or phrase in each example in 3a that introduces the condition.

d Now go to Grammar Focus 8B on p. 153.

e Use the phrases in the box to talk about yourself. Say one thing that isn't true or you don't really believe. Can you guess which of your partner's statements isn't true?

Assuming that …	Had I …	Even if I only …
Supposing that …	If I hadn't …	As long as …

Talk about:

- living for a long time
- lifestyle and health
- life goals
- the future of the planet.

4 Is it that our bodies just stop being so proactive about living?

Basically, the body does have a vast amount of inbuilt anti-aging machinery; it's just not 100% comprehensive, so it allows a small number of different types of molecular and cellular damage to happen and accumulate. The body does try as hard as it can to fight these things, but it is a losing battle.

5 You say you want to enrich people's lives. Why is that?

The fact is, people don't want to get sick. I don't work on longevity; I work on keeping people healthy. The only difference between my work and the work of the whole medical profession is that I think we're within striking distance of keeping people so healthy that at 90 they'll carry on waking up in the same physical state as they were at the age of 30.

4 LISTENING

a Why do people follow special diets? Talk about different reasons. Have you (or has someone you know) ever had to follow a diet? How was it?

b Read about a calorie restricted (CR) diet. What kind of food do you think you can eat on this diet?

c 08.11 Listen to Peter Bowes talk to Martin Knight, who follows a CR diet. Answer the questions.

1 What does Martin do with the food in the photos below?
2 What does Martin's daily routine involve?

d 08.11 Listen again. Take notes on these topics.

1 eating out (discussed twice)
2 the look and taste of Martin's breakfast
3 Martin's lifestyle in general
4 Martin's reasons for following a CR diet
5 how Martin feels

e Do you think you could follow a CR diet? Why / Why not? If you did, what would the biggest sacrifice or challenge be in relation to your current lifestyle?

f 08.12 **Pronunciation** Listen to this extract.

1 Is the pitch lower or higher in the phrases in **bold**?

Then I have sprouted oats, **16 grams**, so that's 70. Then this tomato paste here, **33 grams of that**, and almost done now. There we go. And then finally, I add some olive oil, **that's 9.2**.

2 Does this happen because the speaker repeats information or adds extra information?

g Describe the process of preparing a typical breakfast, lunch, or dinner to a partner. Vary your pitch as in the example above. Can you guess which meal your partner's describing?

Did you know

that a calorie restricted (CR) diet will not only help you lose weight, it could increase your life expectancy by up to ten years? Research has shown that a CR diet reduces many of the health risks associated with aging. All you need to do is eat less and eat smarter. Not only could you live longer, but you might feel years younger!

5 SPEAKING

a When have you or someone you know been told you were too young or too old to do something? Explain what happened.

b Work in small groups. What are your opinions of these statements? Talk about your own experiences.

1 How old someone feels depends entirely on their health.
2 TV ads in my country represent older people in realistic ways.
3 It's easier for people under forty to get a job than those over forty.
4 The longer you live, the more eccentric you become.
5 Companies that sell anti-aging products don't want people to feel good about themselves.

c For each of the statements, choose one person in your group to tell the class their opinion and describe their experience. Take a class vote on who agrees and disagrees with each statement.

6 You've said you think the first person to live to 1,000 may already be alive. Could that person be you?

It's conceivable that people in my age bracket, their 40s, are young enough to benefit from these therapies. I'd give it a 30% or 40% chance. But that is not why I do this – I do this because I'm interested in saving 100,000 lives a day.

7 Can the planet cope with people living so long?

That's to do with the balance of birth and death rates. It didn't take us too long to lower the birth rate after we more or less eliminated infant mortality 100 or 150 years ago. I don't see that it's sensible to regard the risk of a population spike as a reason not to give people the best healthcare that we can.

chard

sprouted oats

kale

8C EVERYDAY ENGLISH
Is that your best offer?

Learn to negotiate the price of a product or service

- S Negotiate the price of a product or service
- P Sound and spelling: misleading vowels

1 LISTENING

a Answer the questions.

1 What was the most memorable present you received as a child?
2 Who was it from?
3 Have you ever sold anything that was valuable to you?

b You are going to hear Tatyana talking about a present she received as a child. What kinds of presents often have sentimental value?

c 08.13 Listen to Part 1. Does Tatyana mention one of your ideas in 1b? Who made this present? What does she want to do with it?

d What do you think Tatyana will do next?

e 08.14 Listen to Part 2 and answer the questions.

1 Why does Tatyana meet with Miranda?
   a to find out the value of her watch
   b to find out what she knows about rare watches
   c to trade watches
   d to talk about her grandfather
2 How would you describe the relationship between Tatyana and Miranda?
   a friendly
   b familiar
   c businesslike
   d hostile
3 Who do you think is the better negotiator?
   a Tatyana
   b Miranda

f 08.14 Listen to Part 2 again. Then write a possible *Why* question for each answer.

1 So that Miranda will understand that the watch is one of a kind.
2 So that Miranda will believe her information is from a reliable source.
3 Because she hasn't authenticated what Tatyana is offering yet.
4 Because she's concerned she won't be able to authenticate the watch.

g Language in context *Expressions with* fair

Match expressions 1–3 with meanings a–c.

1 ☐ it's fair to say	a this is reasonable
2 ☐ fair's fair	b I understand this
3 ☐ fair enough	c this is true

h Answer the questions.

1 Do you think Tatyana is behaving fairly? What about Miranda?
2 How do you think these people would react if they knew what Tatyana had done?
   - her grandfather
   - her mother
   - Helen

2 USEFUL LANGUAGE Negotiating

a 08.15 Complete Tatyana and Miranda's conversation. Listen and check.

M Then **there's just the** [1]_______ **of** how much you would like for it.
T Well, **how much would you be** [2]_______ **to pay**?
M I think **we'd be** [3]_______ **to offer**, say, two fifty? **Would that be a** [4]_______ **suggestion**?
T Two fifty! **How about we** [5]_______ **that** a little? **I was kind of** [6]_______ **for something more in the region of** five hundred.
M No, that would be [7]_______ **of the question**. **What would you** [8]_______ **to** three fifty? In principle, of course. I'd need to complete the authentication first.
T Three fifty – **is that your** [9]_______ **offer?**

b Add the expressions in **bold** in 2a to the correct category.

Opening negotiations	Making and accepting offers
I'm open to suggestions/discussion.	I'd be authorized/prepared to accept ... I'm not in a position to offer more than ...

Asking for more	Declining offers
It's worth much more than that. How flexible can you be on that?	I'm not authorized to accept anything less.

c Complete the conversation with words from the chart. Practice it with a partner.

A How much would you like for it?
B I'm [1]_______ to suggestions.
A I think we could go to five.
B It's [2]_______ much more than that. I'd be prepared to [3]_______ seven.
A How [4]_______ can you be on that? I'm not in a [5]_______ to offer more than six.
B I'm not [6]_______ to accept anything less than seven.

d Read the conversation below and answer the questions.

1 How is it the same as / different from the conversation in Part 2?
2 Which conversation would be more successful in real life? Why?

A How much do you want?
B How much will you pay?
A 250.
B How about 500?
A No, 350.
B No more?
A No. I'll pay after 1:00.
B Not now?
A No.

3 PRONUNCIATION Sound and spelling: misleading vowels

a 08.16 Listen to these three words from the recording. They all have the spelling *ow*, but which one has a different sound?

how	know	now

b 08.17 Now listen to these groups of words that share vowel letters. You also heard them in the recording. Can you find the one word in each group that has a *different* vowel sound?

on	there	into	meant	of
one	were	in	heard	off
once	where	wind up	research	offer

c In the following words, what vowel sound do the letters in **bold** have? Work with a partner. Can you think of any other examples of these spellings with the same / different vowel sounds?

	Example: (same spelling, same sound)	Example: (same spelling, different sound)
h**o**ney	*m**o**ney*	*d**o**n't*
h**ere**		
k**i**nd		
ah**ea**d		
c**o**ffee		

4 SPEAKING

a Work alone. Think of an object or a service you could sell. Here are some ideas:

- an anti-aging treatment
- a new-generation smartphone
- a delivery service
- a car.

Make a list of selling points that might persuade someone to pay more for it.

b Work in pairs. Negotiate the price of your product or service. Use the language in 2a and 2b and implied questions.

UNIT PROGRESS TEST

CHECK YOUR PROGRESS

YOU CAN NOW DO THE UNIT PROGRESS TEST.

8D SKILLS FOR WRITING

It's a unique dining experience

Learn to write promotional material

Ⓦ Promotional material; Using persuasive language

1 LISTENING AND SPEAKING

a Think about occasions when you eat out and answer the questions.

1 Do you think the food you eat out … ?
- usually tastes better than what you eat at home
- is usually healthier than what you eat at home

In what ways?

2 When you eat out, what things are most important to you? Choose the five most important things from this list.

- ☐ convenience
- ☐ presentation
- ☐ atmosphere
- ☐ health
- ☐ décor
- ☐ service
- ☐ value for money
- ☐ difference from food at home
- ☐ taste of the food
- ☐ quality of ingredients
- ☐ good reputation
- ☐ type of cuisine (e.g., vegetarian, Chinese)

b You are going to listen to a restaurant chef talking about a "Stone Age diet." What do you think this might mean?

c ▶ 08.18 Listen to the interview and answer the questions.

1 Why was the Paleolithic period significant in human development?
2 What foods does Julia believe are healthy, and why?
3 Why does Julia believe that dairy products and rice are unhealthy?
4 What are the similarities and differences between the food served at *Ancestors* restaurant and Paleolithic food?
5 To what extent do you agree with Julia's views about food and health?

d Do you agree with each of these statements about diets? Why / Why not?

1 People are always thinking of new diets. It's just a way to make money.
2 The best diet is to eat whatever you feel like eating because your body knows what it needs.
3 It's better to think about changing your eating habits for life than to go on a short-term diet.

2 READING

a Quickly read the home page of *Ancestors* restaurant and answer the questions.

1 What new information not mentioned by Julia do you find out on the home page?
2 What kind of customer would go to *Ancestors*, and why? Would you go there yourself?

b What else do you think is on the menu at *Ancestors*? Imagine one starter, one main dish, and one dessert. Then compare your answers.

Home | About | Menu | Location

ANCESTORS RESTAURANT

Our city-center restaurant offers a unique dining experience. Lovingly prepared and exquisitely presented, our dishes contain only the purest ingredients, so you can be confident that our food is good for your body and your individual needs.
So many people eat healthy food at home but then bend the rules when it comes to eating out. At Ancestors, we have a different concept. We serve you the foods you can eat, not the foods you can't!

THE STONE AGE DIET

For thousands of years, we humans were hunter-gatherers: we thrived on meat, seafood, seasonal vegetables, grains, fruit, and nuts. Our bodies adapted to this diet, and it still suits our genetic makeup better than the recent additions of dairy products and processed foods. ***[Find out more …]***

At Ancestors, we believe that eating is all about two things: health and enjoyment. So we've created a Stone Age menu fit for 21st-century living.

3 WRITING SKILLS Promotional material; Using persuasive language

a Which of these do you think is the main purpose of the home page in 2a?

☐ to give detailed information ☐ to give advice
☐ to promote the restaurant

b Why do you think the home page uses headings and short sections?

c Match the features of the home page 1–4 with their purposes a–d.

1 ☐ clear headings
2 ☐ short paragraphs
3 ☐ use of *we* and *you*
4 ☐ links

a to encourage the reader to browse the website
b to establish a personal relationship with the reader
c to show at a glance what the text is about
d to make it quick and easy to read

Healthy living | Opening times | Reservations

OUR MENU

The menu at Ancestors changes according to the seasons. Signature dishes from head chef Julia Dean include sweet potato and hazelnut soup, lamb with sesame seeds, and smoked salmon with wild leaves. We also offer a range of desserts made to the most exacting standards, using only wild fruits and natural sweeteners. ***[Sample menu …]***

We take our drinks as seriously as our food. At Ancestors you'll find an exciting selection of natural fruit and vegetable juices from around the world, complemented by a range of teas, coffees, and herbal teas.

EARLY EVENING MENU

Based in the city center, Ancestors is the ideal destination for a light and wholesome supper before you go to the theater or the movies. Tasty and fresh, the early evening menu offers a range of Ancestors dishes at a fixed price. Available 5:30 to 7:00 p.m.

THE ANCESTORS COOKBOOK

So many of you have asked for our recipes that we've produced our own cookbook, using ingredients you can buy at any grocery store. Tried and tested by our team of cooks, our recipes will enable you to recreate the Ancestors experience in your own kitchen.
[View sample pages …]

d At the top of the *Ancestors* home page, there is a slogan missing. Which of these do you think would work best? Why?

EAT LIKE OUR ANCESTORS DID

FOOD THAT'S GOOD FOR YOU

PURE ENJOYMENT, PURE HEALTH

ONLY THE BEST

e The home page aims to give a positive message about the restaurant. Match phrases 1–4 from the first two sections with the messages a–d they convey.

1 ☐ a unique dining experience
2 ☐ Lovingly prepared and exquisitely presented
3 ☐ At *Ancestors* we believe that
4 ☐ fit for 21st-century living

a The food is not at all old-fashioned.
b The food is made with care and looks good.
c *Ancestors* is not like other restaurants.
d What *Ancestors* is doing has a serious purpose.

f Compare these two sentences. Which emphasizes the positive features of the dishes more strongly? How is the structure different?

1 Lovingly prepared and exquisitely presented, our dishes contain only the purest ingredients.
2 Our dishes are lovingly prepared and exquisitely presented, and they contain only the purest ingredients.

Find three more examples of description at the front of a sentence in the text.

g Now go to Writing Focus 8D on p. 174.

4 WRITING

a Work in pairs or groups. Think of a concept for a restaurant. You could either invent one or base it on a place you know. Write down ideas for a promotional text on a website. Consider:

- the underlying concept
- how it's different from other places
- what it offers customers
- what its positive features are
- food and drink, décor, and atmosphere.

b Write a promotional text. Make sure you include clear headings, a name at the top, and an appealing slogan.

c Read other groups' texts and decide which restaurant you'd most like to visit. Think of additional questions and ask the other group about their restaurant.

UNIT 8
Review and extension

1 GRAMMAR

a Choose the correct option.

1 *To wake* / *Waking* / *Having woken* up is easier in the summer.
2 *Being sent* / *Sending* / *Having sent* to boarding school is the best thing that ever happened to me.
3 I've always been a big fan of *to get* / *get* / *getting* up early.
4 Her refusal even *to listen* / *listening* / *for listening* to my idea really annoyed me.
5 There's no shame in *to have* / *having* / *being* lost to a team as good as theirs.
6 I was lucky enough *meeting* / *to have met* / *having met* Charles before he became famous.
7 Is there any hope *to save* / *of saving* / *saving* the lost sailors?

b Complete the sentences with one word.

1 I wouldn't be in such good shape if I ________ look after myself.
2 If Steve had said it one more time, I would ________ walked out.
3 ________ I known the photo meant so much to you, I would have kept it.
4 I'm going to say yes if Dave ________ me to marry him.
5 The trip needs to be well planned, ________ it will be a nightmare.
6 ________ we to find out that Emily wasn't lying, would you apologize?

2 VOCABULARY

a Match 1–8 with a–h.

1 ☐ It wasn't until about three that I finally
2 ☐ Mark is a light
3 ☐ I couldn't sleep a
4 ☐ We thought the baby was fast asleep, but she was wide
5 ☐ Don't worry, I sleep like
6 ☐ It can help to take
7 ☐ Gradually my eyes closed, and I started to drift
8 ☐ About 10% of adults suffer

a wink with all that building work going on.
b a little nap in the afternoon.
c dozed off.
d from insomnia of some kind.
e awake and getting restless.
f off to sleep.
g a log on trains.
h sleeper, so don't make too much noise.

b Which word is different from the others? Why?

1 smooth, saggy, clear, firm
2 scars, acne, a rash, blotches
3 tighten, moisturize, strengthen
4 tooth loss, hair loss, weight loss
5 whitening, yellowing, toning
6 wrinkles, poor circulation, hair loss

3 WORDPOWER *and*

a 08.19 Match sentences 1–6 with pictures a–f. Listen and check.

1 ☐ There are still just a few **odds and ends** to take away.
2 ☐ People came from **far and wide** to hear him talk.
3 ☐ It's **far and away** the best Italian restaurant in town.
4 ☐ I'm getting **sick and tired of** the noise.
5 ☐ It's just normal **wear and tear**.
6 ☐ It's just **part and parcel of** getting older, I suppose.

b Look at the phrases in **bold** in 3a. Replace each idiom with a non-idiomatic expression in the box.

easily small things of different types many places annoyed by a normal part of damage caused by everyday use

c 08.20 Complete the sentences with the adjectives in the box. Listen and check.

tidy safe sweet clear

1 "Can you hear me?"
"Yes, I can hear you **loud and** ________."
2 "I'm almost afraid to touch anything in her room. She keeps it so **neat and** ________."
3 "I don't want to have a long discussion over the phone, so let's keep it **short and** ________."
4 "We got caught in a really bad blizzard, but fortunately we got home ________ **and sound**."

d Choose four expressions from 3a or 3c and write sentences but leave a blank for the expression.

e Read your sentences aloud. Can other students guess what goes in the blank?

REVIEW YOUR PROGRESS

How well did you do in this unit? Write 3, 2, or 1 for each objective.
3 = very well 2 = well 1 = not so well

I CAN ...	
describe sleeping habits and routines	☐
talk about lifestyles and life expectancy	☐
negotiate the price of a product or service	☐
write promotional material.	☐

CAN DO OBJECTIVES

- Talk about city life and urban space
- Describe architecture and buildings
- Deal with conflict
- Write a discussion essay

UNIT 9

CITIES

GETTING STARTED

a Describe the buildings you can see in the picture.

b Answer the questions.

1. Why do you think the building in the center of the picture hasn't been demolished?
2. How do you think the following people feel about this house?
   - the owners
   - the local authorities
   - the other building's owners
   - other local residents
3. What do you think will happen to the house in the future? What will happen to the homeowner?

c If there were a plan to demolish your family home, under what circumstances would you agree?

9A THEY DID IT ALL THEMSELVES

Learn to talk about city life and urban space

G Reflexive and reciprocal pronouns

V Verbs with *re-*

The Day of the Pedestrian

1 READING

a Look at the photo of La Paz, the capital of Bolivia. Imagine yourself in the center of the city. What do you think it would be like? Think about:

streets buildings traffic
sounds smells people

b Read the first two paragraphs of the article. Is what you imagined more like the first paragraph, or more like the second?

c Read the rest of the article and answer the questions.

1. What happens on the "Day of the Pedestrian"?
2. What do people use the streets for?
3. Is it generally popular among the residents of La Paz? Why / Why not?

d Read the article again. What does it tell us about ... ?

1. the difference between the "Day of the Pedestrian" and *ciclovías*
2. carbon emissions in La Paz
3. The Sunday morning fair on El Prado
4. the *Cueca Paceña*
5. El Alto
6. the educational value of the "Day of the Pedestrian"

e Imagine you live in La Paz. Would you take part in the "Day of the Pedestrian"? Why / Why not?

In many cities around the world, mornings are a time of noise and traffic congestion: cars blow their horns as they maneuver around each other, buses grind their gears as they pull away from bus stops, and motorcycles rev their engines as they wait at traffic lights and crosswalks.

So imagine waking up in the center of a large city and hearing ... silence. No cars, no buses, no tires screeching or horns blaring. Only quieter, more soothing sounds: people chatting, children running and laughing, street vendors selling their wares, distant music, perhaps the sound of a bicycle bell.

This would be your experience on the morning of the "Day of the Pedestrian," which takes place annually in La Paz, Bolivia, on the first Sunday in September. The event, which is more properly titled the "Day of the Pedestrian and Cyclist in Defense of Mother Earth," is an expanded version of the *ciclovías* held in many cities across Latin America, where certain streets are closed to cars and dedicated to cyclists and pedestrians. Instead of closing just a few streets or a single main thoroughfare, however, all the roads in the capital city of La Paz and its neighboring city El Alto are closed for the whole day, from 8 a.m. to 6 p.m.

The immediate purpose of the event is to reclaim public streets for pedestrians and cyclists and reduce the consumption of fossil fuels. According to government statistics, carbon emissions are reduced by more than 60% on the day of the event. But its significance goes far beyond that: it also aims to increase public awareness of the negative effects of carbon emissions and air pollution by highlighting the contrast between the calm of the "Day of the Pedestrian" and the chaos of a normal day in La Paz.

Taking advantage of the sudden calm which has been restored to their city, locals stroll into the city center, pushing strollers, kicking soccer balls, and holding hands with their children. On El Prado, La Paz's main street, the periodic Sunday-morning fair is expanded, and the emphasis is on exercise and physical fitness. Organizers lay down turf for miniature soccer fields and volleyball courts. Aerobics classes are held in several locations, and skateboarders perform tricks in front of the crowds. In many streets, bands perform music and couples form pairs to dance the *Cueca Paceña*, a traditional Bolivian dance.

The "Day of the Pedestrian" is very popular among residents of the city, especially families who enjoy being able to allow their children out to play in the street without danger from traffic. Teachers are also strongly in favor of the initiative, since it offers an opportunity to provide environmental education about climate change and protecting the environment while at the same time focusing on exercise and enjoyment.

Even if only for one day a year, La Paz and El Alto are making a step toward a more traffic-free future, and the "Day of the Pedestrian" is an event to celebrate.

2 VOCABULARY Verbs with *re-*

a Look at the excerpts from the article. How are the words in bold similar in meaning?

The immediate purpose of the event is to **reclaim** public streets for pedestrians and cyclists.

Taking advantage of the sudden calm which has been **restored** to their city, locals stroll into the city center.

b 09.01 Complete the sentences with the correct forms of the verbs in the box that have the meaning shown in parentheses. Then listen and check.

recreate	redevelop	regain	regenerate
reinstate	rejuvenate	renovate	

1 There are plans to ________ the port area of the city. (= improve it so that it becomes a more productive location to do business)
2 It's a beautiful old building. They just need to ________ it. (= repair and modernize it)
3 It's good that students are moving into the area. It will help to ________ it. (= give a younger and livelier atmosphere)
4 In order to make the movie, they ________ a Wild West town, complete with buildings and a railroad station. (= built a copy of it)
5 The town needs new industries so it will ________ its appeal as a place to live and work. (= get it back)
6 The city had decided to end the "Day of the Pedestrian," but after popular protests they agreed to ________ it. (= put it back again)
7 They are going to ________ the old airport and turn it into a shopping mall. (= change it by building new streets and buildings)

c 09.02 **Pronunciation**

1 Listen to the pronunciation of *e* in *re-* in the verbs in the chart.

1 /i/	2 /ɪ/
redevelop	*rejuvenate*

2 09.03 Add the other verbs in 2a and 2b to the chart in question 1. Which verb has a different sound and can't be added to the chart? Listen and check.

d What buildings do you know of that have recently been renovated or restored? Are there parts of your city that need redeveloping or regenerating, in your opinion?

A

B

C

D

3 READING AND SPEAKING

a What do you think is happening in each photo A–D? Why do you think it was worth taking a photo of it?

b **Communication 9A** Work in groups of four: A, B, C, D. Student A: Go to p. 135. Student B: Go to p. 136. Student C: Go to p. 136. Student D: Go to p. 137.

c Explain the idea you read about to the other students. Which idea do you think … ?

- provides the most benefit to the community
- provides the least benefit
- would work best in your own city

4 GRAMMAR Reflexive and reciprocal pronouns

a Read the comments about the events in photos A–D. Which could they refer to?

1 It's a great place to just sit **by yourself**, drink coffee, and read the paper.
2 It just shows what local communities can do **for themselves**.
3 The place **itself** isn't very welcoming, but the people are.
4 People can sit and talk to **one another**.
5 It's a great neighborhood because we all support **each other**.
6 It's nice to have someplace people can make **themselves** comfortable while they wait for the bus.
7 Cars and pedestrians give way to **each other**. It really works.

b Look at the words and phrases in **bold** in 4a and answer the questions.

1 Which pronoun or phrase ending in *-self/-selves* … ?
  a ☐ shows that the object of the verb is the same as the subject
  b ☐ emphasizes one thing in contrast to something else
  c ☐ means *alone* or *not with other people*
  d ☐ means *independently, without help*
2 What is the difference between … ?
  a *we support ourselves and we support each other*
  b *they talk to themselves and they talk to one another*

c Now go to Grammar Focus 9A on p. 154.

5 LISTENING

a You are going to hear part of a podcast about how technology can improve life in cities. Look at the app in the picture. What do you think it is for?

b 09.06 Listen to the podcast and answer these questions.

1 How does the app work?
2 Why does Michelle think it's a good idea?
3 Do you agree with her? Would you use it? Why / Why not?

c 09.07 Listen to three more people talking about other ideas for "smart" cities. Two of them really exist and one is invented. Which do you think is the invented one? Why?

- Frank
- Rita
- Nick

d 09.07 Listen to each description again. Which idea (or ideas) ... ?

1 gives live information
2 is useful for forgetful or absent-minded people
3 probably uses GPS
4 could be useful when it's raining
5 would be popular with hypochondriacs
6 could help you make friends

e In groups, talk about the ideas. Which idea ... ?

- would you use yourself
- would you be prepared to pay for
- would other people you know use

f Answer the questions.

1 What other technology do you use or know of that makes city life easier?
2 To what extent do you think technology like that described makes people less self-reliant?

g Language in context *Colloquial expressions*

1 09.08 Complete the expressions in **bold** below with the words in the box. Then listen and check.

keel	blow	place	whirl	neck
life	blend	dotted	smashed	

a ... a place where you're repeatedly having to **risk your** ________ to get across the road.
b We're going past a park, and there's a railing that**'s been** ________ **in** here.
c So I can get the map here, ________ it **up** a bit like that.
d They have these screens all around the city; they're **all over the** ________.
e So let's **give it a** ________ ... I put my finger on it.
f Let's see if I'm OK or whether I'm **about to** ________ **over**.
g These are artificial trees, and they're ________ **around** the city.
h They're shaped like trees, so they ________ **in**.
i I'm always going out without charging my phone, so it's **a real** ________**-saver** for me.

Learning Tip

A typical feature of colloquial English is the use of **phrasal verbs** rather than more formal, single-word verbs. When you come across a phrasal verb, notice if it has a single-verb equivalent and learn them both together.

2 Which phrasal verbs in 5g have the same meanings as *collapse* and *enlarge*?

6 SPEAKING

a Look at this list of ideas for making cities "smarter" or better to live in. Do any of them already exist in the city you live in or one you know? If so, how useful are they? If not, would you use the app or facility if it were available?

1 an app giving information about new projects and impending legislation in the city
2 parking apps to show drivers the nearest available parking space and how much it costs
3 apps to let users "adopt" city property, such as trash cans, trees, and flower beds, and volunteer to maintain them
4 digital parking payment systems, allowing you to pay for parking by smartphone, without using coins or tickets
5 free Wi-Fi everywhere in the city, including on trains, buses, and the subway
6 screens in public places that display traffic information, weather, and local news

b Work in groups of three. Choose an idea in 6a or your own idea that does not exist where you live yet and prepare to sell your idea to the class. Write notes of some things you could say about it:

- how it would work
- what benefit it would bring to the city
- possible problems and solutions.

c Give a group presentation. Focus on one point in 6b each. Vote on the best idea in the class.

9B THEY WANTED A DRAMATIC SKYLINE AND THEY GOT ONE

Learn to describe architecture and buildings

G Ellipsis and substitution

V Describing buildings

1 SPEAKING AND VOCABULARY Describing buildings

a Have you seen these buildings before? What city and country do you think each is located in? What do you think they were built as? What do you think of each building?

b Which of the words and phrases in the box are positive? Which are negative? Check new words in a dictionary.

1 imposing	4 innovative	7 dated
2 nondescript	5 tasteless	8 out of place
3 graceful	6 over the top	9 stunning

c 09.09 **Pronunciation** Listen and underline the stressed syllable in each word or phrase in 1b.

d Use the words and phrases in 1b or other adjectives to describe the buildings in the pictures.

> The UN Building is fairly imposing, but it's a little nondescript.

> The Museo Soumaya is very graceful, but it's a little over the top.

e Now go to Vocabulary Focus 9B on p. 166.

f Take turns describing local or iconic buildings that you think your partner will know about. Guess the building your partner is describing.

> It's an imposing building near the river. It used to be a warehouse.

> Is it the … ?

2 GRAMMAR Ellipsis and substitution

a Read sentences 1–6. Which of them are true for you or the place you live?

1. Most people dislike modern architecture. I know I **do**.
2. They don't consult residents about new buildings as often as they ought to **^**.
3. They've put up that skyscraper and **^** ruined the skyline.
4. The old buildings are always being knocked down to make way for new **ones**.
5. The government promised they were going to build more houses, but they haven't **^** yet.
6. They haven't built anything new around here for a long time. **Nor** are they likely to.

b Look at each sentence in 2a again. Which words have been omitted (^) or substituted with words in **bold**? Why?

c Now go to Grammar Focus 9B on p. 155.

3 READING

a Read the article about the architect Jeanne Gang. Choose the best summary.

1 Jeanne Gang is an architect with a wide vision who is interested not only in the buildings she designs, but also the environments in which they are situated.

2 Jeanne Gang has become a world-famous architect because she has studied and traveled widely. She has integrated ideas she picks up on her travels into her designs, and as a result, has revolutionized the Chicago cityscape.

b Read the text again. Write notes on Jeanne Gang's:

- background and personality
- architectural style and a key building she designed
- environmental awareness
- interest in social justice
- core work philosophy.

c Talk about these questions.

1 Look at the photos of Jeanne Gang's buildings. What do/don't you like about the buildings?

2 To what extent does the environment in which a building is situated play a part in its success? Think of examples in your country where the environment has had a positive or negative impact on a building.

3 In what different ways can architects and builders help the environment?

d Language in context *Metaphorical phrases*

1 Notice how forms of the words in **bold** in the phrases below are used in the text. Is the meaning exactly the same?

a **walk** down the street
b a **blossoming** tree
c a **game** of tennis
d **sparks** from a fire
e heating **fueled** by gas
f the **hallmark** on a gold bracelet

2 Match the highlighted expressions in the article with the definitions.

a doing her best work
b created her initial motivation
c are examples of typical features
d won a prize or award
e a key event that causes a positive result
f develop and become more successful
g strongly increased her enthusiasm

Learning Tip Many expressions include an indirect or metaphorical meaning. It can sometimes help to think about the literal meaning of key words as a way of understanding the expression. For example, a tree that blossoms suggests fresh and attractive new growth that will develop further.

Jeanne Gang

She is the architect of the tallest building in the world designed by a woman. She has walked away with top architectural awards and commissions. From her local roots and early projects in Chicago, she has blossomed into one of the world's most celebrated and sought-after architects. *Time* magazine named her as one of the world's most influential people in 2019.

There's no doubt that Jeanne Gang is at the top of her game. Despite this, she is known to be genuine, open and easy to talk to with a classic Midwestern warmth and charm. While having offices around the world, she is very much a Chicago architect who has engaged with her city and its challenges. She is passionate about environmental and social concerns and the role that buildings play in the natural world.

Jeanne Gang grew up in a small town near Chicago. Her father was an engineer who took his family on trips that involved stopping to look at bridges. This clearly sparked Jeanne's interest in architecture as a child which then became evident when she started making buildings from ice and mud. She studied architecture at the University of Illinois and Harvard Graduate School of Design, and urban design as a visiting scholar at the Swiss Federal Institute of Technology in Zurich. This gave her an understanding not only of building construction but also engineering, landscape design and urban planning. This doubtless fueled her strong interest in the relationship between building and the environment.

After a period working in the Netherlands, Jeanne returned to Chicago and set up her own office, Studio Gang, in 1997. Since the beginning her work has included a great range of projects that show all the hallmarks of a typical Gang design: innovative elegance coupled with creative flare. The game-changer was the invitation to design Aqua Tower in Chicago which was completed in 2010. This 82-story building has been a spectacular success and even the most critical architects agree that it immediately became an architectural icon. What makes Aqua Tower distinctive are the irregular shaped balconies that give the impression of rippling water. Not only are they beautiful but they also are designed to give residents great views of the city, shield the windows from the sun and diminish the impact of Chicago's very strong winds on the building. The specific nature of Aqua Tower's design is as much a testament to Jeanne's understanding of engineering as it is to her architectural creativity.

Aqua Tower includes one of Chicago's largest green roofs, which is located atop its three-story base. This points to one of Jeanne's key concerns as an architect: environmentalism. When designing a building she always asks herself where

City Hyde Park, Chicago

4 LISTENING

a Look at the photo of the thin skyscrapers being built in New York. Why do you think people might like them or criticize them?

b 09.17 Listen to Maria and Ethan talk about thin skyscrapers. Who is for and against them? Who mentions the following points, Maria (M) or Ethan (E)?

1 ☐ spoiling the way New York looks
2 ☐ the way New York keeps changing
3 ☐ apartments that are unoccupied
4 ☐ Midtown's need for life
5 ☐ the extreme height of the buildings
6 ☐ affordable homes outside the city center
7 ☐ problems maintaining a building

c 09.17 Listen again and answer the questions.

1 What are "air rights"?
2 Why does Maria refer to the Empire State Building?
3 What does Ethan suggest by using the term *selling out*?
4 What is NIMBYism and what do you think are the consequences?

d What examples do you know of where there has been a controversy over urban development?

the resources to build it come from and what effect this will have on the environment. If there is any possibility of reusing or recycling material, that will always be her first choice. Her firm has undertaken a number of projects that focus on specific environmental issues. For example, the conversion of a coal-burning power plant into a modern student union building called the Beloit College Powerhouse in Wisconsin. Two public boathouses on the Chicago River designed by Studio Gang are playing a key role in reclaiming and cleaning up what was once a dirty and polluted waterway.

Jeanne is also broadening her focus to social justice issues. We often underestimate the degree to which buildings and urban design play a part in socioeconomic divisions within a city. Studio Gang has worked with police and community members in Chicago to come up with the concept of a 'Polis Station'. This involves envisioning how police stations can be redesigned to function more like community centers, where residents and police can find many opportunities to interact in non-enforcement situations. Another project in New York City is investigating how to improve safety and well-being in neighborhoods by creating pleasant civic spaces that allows citizens to interact freely. All of these social development projects are carried out in consultation with residents and community-based organizations as well as experts in areas like crime prevention and mental health.

Some say Jeanne runs the risk of spreading her focus too broadly. But she sees working on a great variety of projects as a way of ensuring her firm engages with a range of scales and materials. This informs the practice and makes their work more interesting. She also believes that irrespective of the size or purpose of a project, there are driving questions and conceptual ideas that connect all of the work and give it relevance for the wider world.

5 SPEAKING

a Read the scenario, talk about your ideas, and come up with a proposal and a reason for it.

There is a derelict warehouse in your community that was built in the early 20th century. You are a member of the city council, and you have to help make a decision about how the warehouse or the land itself could be repurposed.

Consider:

- the needs of your community
- demolition and rebuilding
- the benefits of a new, iconic building
- a high-profile architect
- your community's architectural heritage
- the warehouse's architectural features.

b Work in groups of four. Present your proposals to each other. Agree on one proposal and tell the class.

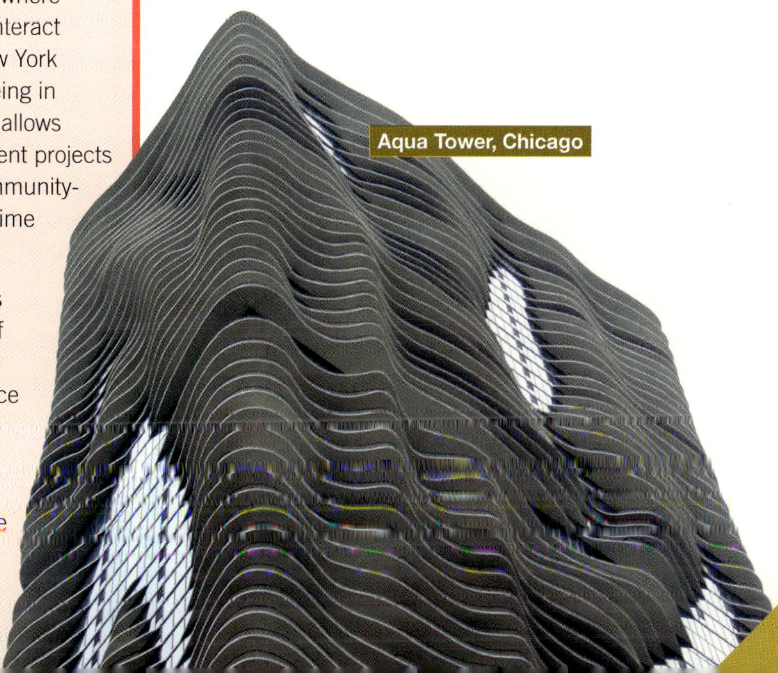

Aqua Tower, Chicago

9C EVERYDAY ENGLISH

Let's not jump to conclusions

Learn to deal with conflict

- S Complain and respond to complaints
- P Sound and spelling: foreign words in English

1 LISTENING

a How would you feel if, without your permission, … ?

- you saw yourself in a documentary about learning English
- your photo appeared on Google Earth
- a radio station called you live on air to offer you the chance to win a prize

b 09.18 Friends Jack and Victor are talking about Victor's recent success as a professional photographer. Look at the photo and listen to Part 1. Answer the questions.

1 What is on the screen?
2 Why is Victor angry about it?
3 What does he intend to do about it?

c 09.18 Read these phrases from Part 1. Who or what do the words in **bold** refer to? Listen to Part 1 again and check.

1 It seems like **everything's** falling into place.
2 Wow, **that's** awesome.
3 Who's going to shoot them? **This guy**.
4 **This** is outrageous!
5 Maybe **he** took the memory card!
6 I'm calling **them** right now.

d Language in context *Animal idioms*

1 09.19 Correct the idioms from Part 1. Listen and check.
   a There's something horsey about this.
   b I smell an owl.
   c Hold your fish, Victor.

2 What do you think the idioms mean? Look at a dictionary if necessary.

e 09.20 Victor calls the editor-in-chief at *Free Voice Online* to complain. Listen to Part 2 and answer the questions.

1 How does Aaron respond to Victor's complaint? Does he … ?
   a pass on the blame to someone else
   b accept responsibility and apologize
   c promise to take action and try to arrange a meeting
2 How do you think Victor feels after the phone call?
3 What do you think Aaron will do next?

2 USEFUL LANGUAGE

Dealing with conflict

a 09.18 09.20 Listen to Parts 1 and 2 again and complete the expressions.

Expressing disbelief

1 This is ________!
2 Where on ________ did they get them from?
3 I'm at a loss for ________!

Expressing anger

4 This is o________!
5 I'm calling to express my ________.
6 Words cannot express my ________.
7 It's totally ________!

b Which two expressions does Victor decide not to use? Why do you think he doesn't use them?

c 09.21 Complete the expressions from Parts 1 and 2 with the words or phrases in the box. Add *to* where necessary. Listen and check.

explanation   jump   fulfill your responsibility   right

Commenting on the behavior of others

1 Let's not ________ conclusions.
2 They have no ________!
3 You owe me a(n) ________.
4 You've failed ________ …

d Which comments in 2c were on Victor's behavior and which were comments on *Free Voice Online's* behavior?

e 09.22 Complete the sentences with words from Part 2. Listen and check.

Taking action

1 **I will** ________ the matter.
2 **I** ________ **you**, there will be consequences.
3 I'd **like to** ________ **in** and we can ________ **it** face to face.

f Work in pairs. Role-play the conversation between Victor and Aaron using the language in 2a, c, and e. This time Victor should respond positively to Aaron's offer.

3 LISTENING

a 09.23 Aaron speaks to his employee Leo about using Victor's photos for *Free Voice Online*. Listen to Part 3. What reason does Leo give for Victor's photos being used? What does he want to do?

b 09.23 Listen to Part 3 again and answer the questions.

1 Why does Aaron want to talk to Victor first?
2 What action does Aaron fear Victor will take?
3 What does Aaron want Leo to do to make up for his mistake?

c Do you think Aaron has done the right thing? Why / Why not?

4 PRONUNCIATION Sound and spelling: foreign words in English

a 09.24 Listen to these words. Are they from Spanish, Italian, or French? Which two were in Part 2?

1 avant-garde	5 finito
2 nada	6 tête-à-tête
3 déjà vu	7 rendezvous
4 cappuccino	8 pronto

b Match the words 1–8 in 4a with their meanings a–h.

a ☐ a strange feeling that you have experienced the same thing before
b ☐ an arrangement to meet, usually in secret
c ☐ coffee made with heated, bubbly milk
d ☐ finished
e ☐ nothing
f ☐ different and modern
g ☐ private conversation between two people
h ☐ quickly and without delay

c 09.24 Listen to the words in 4a again. Underline the consonant sounds that are pronounced in a way that is atypical of English.

d Look at the words in the box. Answer the questions below and then check in a dictionary.

c'est la vie kaput aficionado faux pas
kindergarten tsunami paparazzi
typhoon karaoke siesta

1 What languages do you think these words come from?
2 What do they mean?
3 How are they pronounced by American English speakers?

e 09.25 Listen and practice saying the words in 4d.

5 SPEAKING

a Work alone. Think of a situation you wish to complain about. Here are some ideas:

- planning permission to build a parking garage across the street from your house has been granted
- the luxury spa vacation you booked and paid for turned out to be in a hostel
- your bank account information has been accessed by hackers.

b Work in pairs. Take turns being Student A and B. Use your ideas in 5a and the language in 2.

Student A: Explain your situation and complain.

- Express anger and disbelief.
- Comment on B's behavior.
- Respond to B's offer to take action.

Student B: Respond to A's complaint.

- Express understanding of A's situation.
- Comment on A's behavior.
- Offer to take action.

UNIT PROGRESS TEST

→ **CHECK YOUR PROGRESS**

YOU CAN NOW DO THE UNIT PROGRESS TEST.

9D SKILLS FOR WRITING

The impact on cities is plain to see

Learn to write a discussion essay

W Discussion essays; Linking: reason and result

1 LISTENING AND SPEAKING

a Which city in your country has the fastest-growing population? Why do people want to live there?

b Look at the photos of rural and urban New Zealand. Which environment would you prefer to live in? Why?

c 09.26 Listen to Lizzie and Ron talking about life in a rural community in New Zealand compared to life in Auckland, the largest city. Answer the questions.

1 What's Lizzie's news? How is she feeling about it?
2 What point does Ron make about his own and Lizzie's children?
3 What makes it difficult for their children to return to their hometown?
4 Why are Lizzie and Ron better off living where they do?
5 What does Lizzie worry about for the future of their town?

d What do you think Lizzie, Ron, and their partners should do? Should they stay where they are or follow their children to Auckland? Why?

2 READING

a Read the essay about urban migration. Put these points in the order they are mentioned (1–6).

Urban migration …

- ☐ has a negative effect on communities in small towns.
- ☐ is a problem that requires a political solution.
- ☐ impacts living standards in both cities and small towns.
- ☐ is driven by work and study needs.
- ☐ is happening all over the world.
- ☐ has a negative impact on the supply of city housing.

b What challenges are there for people who move from small towns or the country to a large city?

Document1

Urban migration is an international phenomenon. In recent years, *there has been increasing awareness* of issues associated with the migration of people from small towns and rural communities to larger cities. This essay looks at the impact of urban migration on both large cities and rural communities.

Why do people decide to move to a large city? One key factor is that there are often more employment opportunities in urban areas. Secondly, younger people may need to go to a city in order to attend college or other educational programs. Beyond this, others are drawn to cities because of the increased stimulation offered by an urban environment.

The impact on cities [1]*is plain to see*. An increase in population leads to greater demand for housing, causing house prices and rents to rise. As a result, both existing residents and new arrivals in the city are required to spend more of their income on accommodations or are forced to live in substandard conditions.

However, [2]*it could be argued* that the impact on small towns and rural areas is perhaps even greater. A dramatic decrease in the population of rural communities is often due to the number of young people leaving in search of work and study opportunities. This exodus results in the closure of businesses and cutbacks in social services. And those who remain in rural communities suffer a decline in living standards which, in turn, means small communities are seen as even less attractive places to live. As a consequence, towns serving rural communities begin to look like ghost towns.

[3]*By examining* the way urban migration affects both rural and urban communities, [4]*it is evident that* the phenomenon can lead to a decline in living standards for all concerned. [5]*It would seem that* there is a role for governments to play in the way that the movement of population is managed. Intervention such as business incentives and subsidies can ensure small communities continue to offer inhabitants employment opportunities and a good standard of living.

Page 1 of 1 334 words

3 WRITING SKILLS Discussion essays; Linking: reason and result

a What is the purpose of each paragraph in the essay?

b Notice the phrase in *italics* in the introduction. Does this express the writer's point of view / opinion directly or indirectly? Match the phrases in *italics* (1–5) in the essay with the meanings below.

☐☐ you can clearly see ☐☐ I think
☐ I've looked

> **Writing Tip**
> When you present a balanced discussion in a formal essay, you should avoid using personal pronouns *I* and *you* and use pronouns like *we*, *it*, and *there*.

c Use the words in the box to complete the formal equivalents; a and b in each pair mean the same thing.

outcome outlining noticeable claimed appear

1 a I've noticed a slow decline …
  b There has been a slow but ________ decline …
2 a I think it's hard to predict what will happen …
  b The ________ is difficult to predict …
3 a What I'd say is that most residents …
  b It would ________ that most residents …
4 a Now that I've described the issues here …
  b By ________ the issues here …
5 a In my opinion, it's likely …
  b It could be ________ …

d Look at the highlighted examples in the essay in 2a. Which introduce a reason? Which indicate a result? Make two lists.

e Underline the reason or result language in these examples.

1 Urban migration has decreased owing to an increase in grants to rural businesses.
2 There are now many more unemployed people in the city. Consequently, there has been a noticeable increase in small crimes.
3 A drop in living standards causes problems for those at the lower end of the socioeconomic scale.
4 There has been a population increase of 12%. Hence, there has been an increase in new building projects in suburban areas.
5 Some rural workers have returned to the countryside as a direct consequence of the loneliness and isolation of urban life.

f Which expressions in 3e can be used in the same way as these examples?

1 lead to, result in
2 due to, because of
3 As a consequence, As a result

g Choose the correct word in *italics* in these sentences.

1 The increase in new residents in some areas of the city has seen a rise in the number of potential customers for businesses, thereby *creating* / *create* many new business opportunities.
2 Enrollment in local elementary schools has fallen dramatically. *Thus* / *Thereby*, many have been closed.
3 Certain local students have gained scholarships to city colleges, *thereby* / *therefore* freeing their parents from a significant economic burden.

h Now go to Writing Focus 9D on p. 175.

4 WRITING

a Think about some kind of social change in your country that is of interest to you, for example:

- demand for college admissions
- involvement in community organizations
- your own idea.

What are the reasons for this change? What are the results? Tell a partner.

b Write a discussion essay about the social change you have chosen. Follow these steps.

- Outline the issue in the introduction.
- Describe reasons for the change and their results.
- Avoid using personal language.
- Hypothesize about the future.
- State whether anything can/should be done about the issue.

c Work with a new partner. Read each other's essays. What kind of social change does your partner's essay talk about? How aware were you of this issue?

UNIT 9
Review and extension

1 GRAMMAR

a Complete the sentences with a reflexive or reciprocal pronoun.

1 I washed the car _myself_ because the car wash was closed.
2 I can see Grandpa is getting old. He seems to talk to _______ all the time.
3 While Simon was in the hospital, his mother was absolutely beside _______.
4 While I'm on vacation, my secretary and I still send _______ several messages a day.
5 We call _______ "The Pirates" because we have a stadium on the coast.
6 Rita and I sat down next to _______ and we looked into _______'s eyes.
7 No one helped us with our house. We built it all by _______.

b Correct one mistake in each sentence or exchange.

1 Kate wanted to put in new windows, but I didn't want.
2 "I'll never listen to her advice again." "So will I."
3 It was a beautiful morning, although was rather cool outside.
4 He living nearby, Frank had no problem getting in early.
5 So they wouldn't get bored, were listening to the radio.
6 "Kelly hasn't read the contract properly." "I don't suspect."
7 She became a famous actress, as her mother.
8 Take the clean mug, not the dirty.

2 VOCABULARY

a Complete the sentences with the words in the box.

recreate	redevelop	regain
reinstate	renovate	restore

1 The city council plans to _______ the wasteland near the port.
2 We will _______ early closing on weekends.
3 The picture was badly damaged, but they managed to _______ it.
4 The aim of *The Oscars* restaurant is to _______ the atmosphere of Hollywood.
5 The town has long been in decline, and I doubt it will ever _______ its former prestige.
6 It took years to _______ the old hotel and modernize all the facilities.

b Choose the best phrase to complete each sentence.

1 ☐ I grew up in a
2 ☐ The nature walk took us to a
3 ☐ Our new office is in a
4 ☐ I work at a
5 ☐ I know a millionaire who owns a
6 ☐ Every city needs an

a power station on the coast.
b subdivision near Dallas.
c mansion in the Caribbean.
d log cabin in the woods.
e iconic skyscraper or two.
f huge building overlooking the river.

3 WORDPOWER *build*

a Look at these multi-word verb collocations with *build*. Match multi-word verbs 1–6 with meanings a–f.

1 **build up** savings / stamina / a following / a reputation
2 **build up to** an announcement / an event / a major change
3 traffic / problems / dirt / pressure **builds up**
4 **build on** our success / strengths / relationship
5 **build in** features (to a product) / activities (to a schedule)
6 **build** something **around** a concept / people

a ☐ use as a basis for the future
b ☐ make an effort to increase
c ☐ use as the main principle/idea
d ☐ include, incorporate
e ☐ increase naturally over time
f ☐ gradually prepare yourself or others for something

b 09.27 Complete the sentences with the words in the box. Listen and check.

up (×3)	on	around	in	up to

1 He's **built** this day _______ so much I'm afraid he'll be disappointed.
2 They forgot to **build** _______ auto-locking on this phone.
3 He's **built** _______ a huge fan base over the years.
4 I'm looking for ways to **build** _______ last year's sales.
5 Our business is **built** _______ the idea that people want coffee with their books.
6 What do you think the boss is going to say? She's been **building** _______ a big announcement all week.
7 When the pressure **builds** _______ at work, you need a good, long break.

c Complete each statement with your own idea. Check the meaning of the expressions in **bold** in a dictionary if necessary.

1 People sometimes **build up a tolerance** to _______.
2 I had to **build up the courage** to ask _______.
3 I once **built my hopes up about** _______ but was disappointed.
4 I think **building up a business** would be _______.

d Compare your answers to 3c with a partner.

REVIEW YOUR PROGRESS

How well did you do in this unit? Write 3, 2, or 1 for each objective.
3 = very well 2 = well 1 = not so well

I CAN ...	
talk about city life and urban space	☐
describe architecture and buildings	☐
deal with conflict	☐
write a discussion essay.	☐

CAN DO OBJECTIVES

- Give a presentation or a speech
- Talk about superstitions and rituals
- Take turns in more formal conversations
- Write a movie review

UNIT 10

OCCASIONS

GETTING STARTED

a Look at the picture and answer the questions.

1. Where are these people? What are they doing? How do you think they feel?
2. Why do you think they chose this venue?
3. What do you think happened in the 15 minutes before this picture was taken? What do you think happened afterward?

b Answer the questions.

1. What's the most memorable wedding you've been to? Why?
2. For you, what are the most important parts of wedding day celebrations?
3. If you could hold a ceremony – such as a wedding – in a unique way, what would you do? Why?

10A I REALLY WISH I'D BEEN ON TIME

Learn to give a presentation or a speech

G Regret and criticism structures

V Communication verbs

If you're not comfortable with public speaking – and nobody starts out comfortable; you have to learn how to be comfortable – practice. I cannot overstate the importance of practicing. Get some close friends or family members to help evaluate you, or somebody at work that you trust.

Hillary Clinton*,*
politician

Words mean more than what is set down on paper. It takes the human voice to infuse them with deeper meaning.

Maya Angelou*,*
poet and civil rights activist

If you have the opportunity to use your voice, you should use it.

Samuel L. Jackson,
actor

Amy Schumer*,*
comedian and actor

Being introverted, it doesn't mean necessarily being shy or being afraid of public speaking; it just means that it's hard for me to interact with people for too long.

1 SPEAKING AND VOCABULARY
Communication verbs

a Have you ever had to give a speech or presentation? What was the experience like? If not, how would you feel about doing this?

b Read the quotes. What does each quote tell you about the person's attitude toward giving speeches? Which quotes do you agree with or relate to?

c What makes a good presentation? What kinds of things can go wrong?

d Read sentences 1–5. Do they mention your ideas in 1c?

1 He kept **making** comments under his breath when he was supposed to be **addressing** the audience.
2 She lost her place whenever she **moved on to** her next point!
3 She **went into** far too much detail and **presented** the information in a confusing way.
4 He **demonstrated** their new approach, but it was pretty boring.
5 He used lots of anecdotes to **illustrate** his points. It was amazing!

e 10.01 Find the verbs or verb phrases in **bold** in 1d that collocate with phrases 1–7 below. Listen and check your answers.

1 ________ the results
2 ________ her understanding
3 ________ a conference
4 ________ a different topic
5 ________ the finer points
6 ________ the concept with examples
7 ________ throwaway remarks

f Now go to Vocabulary Focus 10A on p. 167.

2 READING

a Read Scott Berkun's advice and survival tips on giving presentations and speeches. Which of the four mottos below do you think Berkun would agree with?

1 Take care how you prepare.
2 Feel the fear, go through it, and keep on going.
3 Aim for perfection.
4 Keep explaining again and again until they get it.

b Read the advice and survival tips again. Write notes under the following headings. Compare your ideas with a partner.

1 People's fear of public speaking
2 How fear can help
3 Communicating your ideas effectively
4 Coping with delivery problems
5 Ways to prepare well
6 Understanding your audience

c Imagine you have to give a talk or presentation. Which piece of Scott Berkun's advice is most relevant for you? Why?

DON'T BE BORING!

How to feel the fear but speak well in public

You've either seen it or you've experienced it yourself: a person standing up in front of a large group. There's no microphone or, if there is, it makes a terrible feedback noise. The person can't be heard, and they say "umm" and "ah" after what seems like every second word. Then they click through their slides too fast and then go back and get themselves in a state of total confusion. Or maybe the projector just gives up the ghost and there are no slides at all.

If this happens to you, you probably feel like you just want to disappear into thin air. If you watch it happen to someone else, you either fall asleep or you desperately want to run from the room. Public speaking can be one of the most terrifying things you have to do in life. But people have to do it all the time – when they study, in their job, and at important events with friends and family.

The fear factor

So, how can you make it better? How can you get over the fear? Scott Berkun, author of *Confessions of a Public Speaker*, suggests that we don't. He thinks we should just own the fear and try and use it to our advantage. There's no doubt that standing up alone in front of a group is never a fun thing to do. It's a little like being in the middle of an open field when you know there are all sorts of dangerous animals nearby. It triggers a classic fear-response scenario that's as old as humankind. Our natural instinct is to run. But, at the same time, our body is pumping adrenaline, and this can give us energy and help us focus. Adrenaline can help us do a good job.

A little narrative goes a long way

Berkun is also a great believer in making sure you have prepared by honing your ideas so that you get them across as effectively as you can. What are the key points you want to make? Work out the most direct way of conveying these to your audience. It's worth remembering that if you wrap your message up in a story, it'll probably have more impact. Storytelling is a very old skill, and audiences usually have a positive response to a message inside a narrative.

Scott Berkun is a writer and public speaker who's interested in a wide range of topics associated with creativity, culture, and business. He studied computer science and philosophy in college and then worked at Microsoft. He now makes his living from his writing and speaking and is the author of the best-selling *Confessions of a Public Speaker*.

Just moving on, folks ...

But how do you respond when things go wrong? Berkun suggests that disaster often invites more disaster. So when you get up to speak, don't apologize for all the things that you don't think are perfect. This starts you off on the wrong foot and doesn't motivate the audience to pay attention to you.

Once you get underway, the trick is just to keep going no matter what happens. If you say you're going to make four points but actually end up making just three, it's likely that almost no one will notice. And if a couple of slides are in the wrong order, just apologize and move on. No one will care that much. Well, you will, but what counts here is what the audience thinks, and they're probably nowhere near as critical as you are.

Even the most accomplished public speakers have good and bad days. And most speakers feel some degree of fear or anxiety at some time. But if you've done your preparation and you greet your audience with confidence, half the battle is won, and your speech will probably be OK!

SCOTT BERKUN'S SURVIVAL TIPS

Berkun's book has a lot of other commonsense tips on how to survive the ordeal of public speaking. Here are some really useful ones:

- Remember the big *R*: research. Make sure that the content of your presentation is thoroughly researched and well planned. This gets you off to a good start.
- Practice, practice, practice. If you practice, you'll be better equipped to deal with unforeseen events while you're speaking – unexpected comments and problems with equipment.
- Don't be boring! This should go without saying, but Berkun continues, "If you are, the worst you'll do is meet expectations." This is great advice because it's so reassuring – you don't have to be exceptional, just good enough.
- Arrive early and sit in one of the chairs that your audience will be in. This will help you empathize with the people you're talking to. They will sense it and like you more as a result.
- Find out what they think: don't forget to ask for feedback after your speech or presentation. Talk to someone who you know will be honest, and listen to what they have to say. This will help you the next time around.

3 LISTENING

a Which of these, 1 or 2, would you feel more comfortable doing? Why?

1 a presentation for work/school/college
2 a speech for a relative's or friend's birthday/anniversary/wedding

b 10.03 Listen to three people talk about giving a speech or presentation. Answer the questions.

1 Why were they giving a speech?
2 What went wrong?
3 What was the outcome?

Rob

Chantal

Antonio

c Answer the questions.

1 Do you think Rob should have refused to be best man? Why / Why not? What's your opinion of Jessica's reaction?
2 What are Chantal's suspicions about the missing file? How likely is it they are correct? How would you react in this situation?
3 How do you think Antonio could have regained control when he got distracted during his talk?

d Language in context *Idioms: plans into action*

1 10.04 Complete the idioms in **bold** with the words in the box. Then listen and check.

good went threw recipe
yourself made out words

1 I just ________ **myself into** it.
2 They make me **feel** ________ **of my depth**.
3 I thought I'd **done a** ________ **job on it**.
4 Always make a copy; otherwise it's **a** ________ **for disaster**.
5 I just explained the whole project, and **it** ________ **like clockwork**.
6 The managers were all impressed, and I really ________ **my mark**.
7 I couldn't go on; I was completely **at a loss for** ________.
8 I was sort of saying to myself, "C'mon, **get a grip on** ________!"

2 Match the idioms in 1 with the meanings below.

a ☐ likely to cause serious problems
b ☐ not know what to say
c ☐ do something well
d ☐ regain some self-control when upset or stressed
e ☐ get fully involved in something new
f ☐ go very smoothly without problems
g ☐ impress somebody
h ☐ feel it's too difficult for you

4 GRAMMAR Regret and criticism structures

a Read sentences 1–8. Which sentence does not show a regret?

1 ☐ I should never have agreed to be best man.
2 ☐ If only I'd checked those cards.
3 ☐ Part of me wishes that Dan hadn't asked me to be best man.
4 ☐ I really wish I'd copied the presentation onto my hard drive.
5 ☐ Had he been less underhanded, I might not have the job I have now.
6 ☐ She wasn't my girlfriend, but I used to wish she were.
7 ☐ If I had listened to Teresa's advice, I might have been OK.
8 ☐ If it weren't for my stupidity, we could have raised more money that day.

b Underline the part of each example in 4a that shows regret. Which examples are unreal conditionals?

c 10.05 **Pronunciation** Mark the word groups and underline the main stress in these two sentences. Listen and check. Practice saying the sentences.

1 If I had listened to Teresa's advice, I might have been OK.
2 If it weren't for my stupidity, we could have raised more money that day.

d Now go to Grammar Focus 10A on p. 156.

e What regrets have you had? Talk about one of these past situations.

- a decision to study the wrong subject at school/college
- losing touch with an old friend
- something unfortunate you said to a relative or friend
- a bad decision associated with some kind of social activity

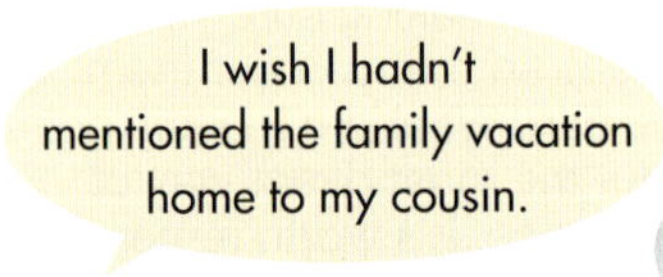

5 SPEAKING

a Plan a one-minute speech with the title *Learning from My Mistakes*. Talk about a personal experience of some kind. You could develop ideas that you talked about in 4e.

Follow Scott Berkun's advice:

- include an anecdote about your experience to get your point across
- practice your speech several times
- keep going, even if things go wrong.

b Work in small groups. Deliver your speeches.

Speakers
- Remember to keep still.
- Maintain eye contact with group members.

Listeners
- Think of a question you can ask each speaker about their experiences.

10B HE IS KNOWN TO HAVE AN UNUSUAL RITUAL BEFORE HE PLAYS

Learn to talk about superstitions and rituals

G Passive reporting verbs

V Superstitions, customs, and beliefs

1 SPEAKING AND VOCABULARY Superstitions, customs, and beliefs

a Look at the objects in the photos.

1 What do you think they all have in common?
2 What part of the world do you think they are from?

b Which of the objects in 1a do you think these sentences describe?

1 You **make a wish** with every knot you tie.
2 They were **traditionally** nailed above doorways.
3 They stop bad luck entering the house, and they protect it against **magic spells**.
4 It is **customary** to hang them above the front door.
5 It invites **good fortune** and brings wealth to the owner.
6 They are worn as a **good luck charm**.
7 They always face outwards so they can **ward off evil**.

c 10.11 Listen and check your answers.

d Look at the words and phrases in **bold** in 1b. Which are connected with … ?

- luck and magic
- customs

e Now go to Vocabulary Focus 10B on p. 168.

f Look at the idiomatic expressions connected with good luck in the box. When do people say them?

1 when they hope something good will happen
2 to warn someone of danger
3 when they're taking extra precautions

fingers crossed   to be on the safe side   knock on wood
third time's the charm   you're tempting fate

g 10.14 Complete the sentences with the expressions in 1f. Listen and check.

1 They've agreed to sell the house, so this time next week it'll be ours – ________.
2 I've failed the driving test twice now. Ah well, ________.
3 "I do hope Lisa passes her English exam."
"Yes, I'll keep my ________."
4 You should wear a bicycle helmet. You've been lucky so far, but ________.
5 I know it's not raining, but take an umbrella just ________.

h 10.15 **Pronunciation** Underline the consonant groups in the words in the box in 1f. Remember that these can be across words. Listen and check. Practice saying the expressions.

i Work in pairs. Take turns being A and B.

Student A: Tell your partner something you're planning to do. Choose from this list.

- go rock climbing
- apply for a new job
- take an exam
- travel across Africa by bus

Student B: Respond using a suitable expression from 1f.

I'm going to climb the Matterhorn.

Take a guide with you to be on the safe side.

Good luck. I'll keep my fingers crossed.

j Answer the questions.

1 Do you know of other things that traditionally bring good luck or ward off evil (in either your own country or another country you know)?
2 How seriously do you think most people believe in charms of this kind? What about you?

2 READING

a Look at the photo of Uruguayan soccer player Luis Suárez. What do you think he is doing and why?

b Read the introduction to the article to check your answer to 2a. What appear to be the main reasons for this behavior? How effective is it?

c Read the rest of the article and find examples of the rituals 1–7 below. Who performs these rituals? Which one is not mentioned?

1 touching yourself or other people
2 doing things in a particular sequence
3 things that also involve other players
4 lucky objects or clothes
5 particular ways of wearing or putting on clothes
6 things people do on their way to a match
7 things that involve family or friends

d Which of the rituals do you think is the most "unusual"?

3 GRAMMAR Passive reporting verbs

a Look at the verb forms in **bold**.

1 **It's thought that** performing a "lucky" routine reduces anxiety.
2 Thibaut Courtois **is known to have** an unusual ritual before he plays in an international match.
3 **It is reported that** he has a whole series of rituals that he goes through before every major game.
4 Then he **is believed to send** a selfie to four of his friends in Belgium.
5 He **is said to check** his socks to make sure they are exactly the same height.
6 **It is said that** he never changes this sequence.
7 Before the Olympics, she **is believed to have worn** a pair of "lucky socks."

Why does the writer use passive reporting structures? Two of these answers are correct.

___ to show that they believe the information
___ to show that the information comes from someone else
___ to show that this is not necessarily what they believe

b The sentences in 3a show two structures for reporting information:

a *it* + passive + *that* clause …
b subject + passive + infinitive …

1 Which structure is shown in **bold** in each sentence in 3a, a or b?
2 Which structures in **bold** … ?
 a refer to the present
 b refer to the past
3 How could you express each idea in 3a 1–7 using the other structure?
 Performing a "lucky" routine is thought to reduce anxiety.

THE GAME BEFORE THE GAME

From LUIS SUÁREZ who frequently kisses a tattoo on his hand with the names of his three children, to Serena Williams who bounces the ball exactly five times before she serves and wears the same pair of socks during each match of a tournament – many of the biggest sports stars believe in the power of rituals to bring them luck.

Despite the hours spent training and developing winning strategies, players still go through superstitious rituals just before a big event. It seems nonsensical that such players would give credit for their own success or failure to rituals. However, sports psychologists suggest that these beliefs can actually help players, and in highly competitive sports, this small advantage may mean the difference between winning and losing.

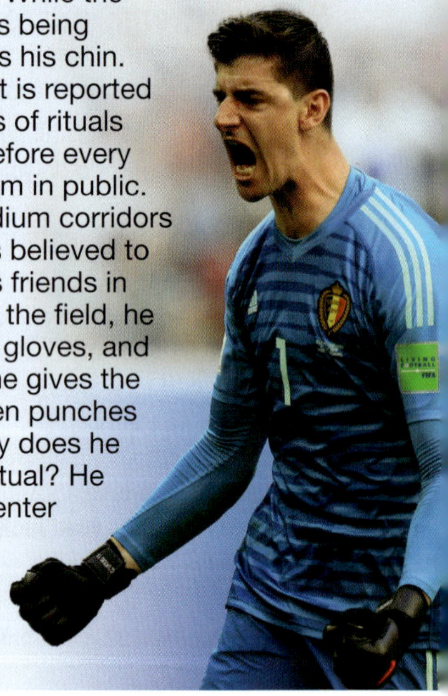

Top Belgian goalkeeper THIBAUT COURTOIS is known to have an unusual ritual before he plays in an international match. While the Belgian national anthem is being played, he always touches his chin. But that's not all. In fact, it is reported that he has a whole series of rituals which he goes through before every major game, not all of them in public. He always enters the stadium corridors at a fixed time. Then he is believed to send a selfie to four of his friends in Belgium. Before going on the field, he always wets the tip of his gloves, and when reaching the goal, he gives the goalpost one kick and then punches the middle of the net. Why does he go through this unusual ritual? He claims that it makes him enter a kind of trance and he can no longer be distracted during the game.

c The sentences in 3a are typical of news reports and factual writing. How could you say them in a more conversational style?

People say …

I've heard …

Many people think …

d Now go to Grammar Focus 10B on p. 157.

The Incredible Rituals That Top Players Perform before a Match

Spanish tennis star RAFAEL NADAL is famous for going through a series of rituals before and during his matches. Before he starts playing, he is said to check his socks to make sure they are exactly the same height. During the game, he always has two water bottles in front of his chair, one behind the other, and during breaks he takes a sip from each bottle in turn. It is said that he never changes this sequence. He also follows exactly the same movements whenever he serves the ball: he touches his foot on the ground behind him, pulls up his shorts, wipes his nose and tucks his hair behind his ears, first on the left side and then on the right. He claims that these rituals are not superstition but a way to give himself a sense of order and of being in control during the match.

The secrets of KAYLA HARRISON's phenomenal success are her rigorous approach to training and a stubborn determination to win. But the U.S. judo Olympic gold medalist also admits to being superstitious and says it's important for her to have rituals and patterns to give her the confidence she needs to win. Before the Olympics, she is believed to have worn a pair of "lucky socks" that were knitted for her by her grandmother, and she decided not to wear a judo outfit that had previously failed to deliver her a win. But there was more than just superstition at play – she combined this with the power of positive thinking. For weeks before the tournament, she visualized herself winning and went meticulously through every step she needed to take on the day of the tournament in order to win.

e Look at these comments about well-known people. Change them so their style would be suitable for a news report using passive reporting structures like those in 3a.

1 They say the goalkeeper is retiring next season.
2 Apparently the manager of the company has resigned.
3 People say she's the best tennis player of all time.
4 The team captain has had eye surgery – or so some people believe.
5 There are rumors that he pulled a muscle in his ankle.

f Think of a well-known person. Write a sentence from a news report about him or her using a passive reporting structure. Then read your sentence aloud. Can other students guess the person?

4 LISTENING

a Work in groups. Discuss the questions and write down your ideas.

1 Why do you think players go through the rituals described in the article?
2 In what ways do you think rituals might help them?

b 10.17 Listen to an interview with Sandy Hearst, a sports psychologist. Does she mention any of the points that you noted?

c What is the main point she makes in the interview? Choose 1, 2, or 3.

1 Athletes feel helpless just before a match because they can't influence events, so they need something to make them feel better.
2 Rituals boost athletes' confidence by making them feel more in control, and this makes them perform better.
3 Pre-match rituals have a kind of "magical" effect which can't be explained rationally but which seems to work.

d 10.17 Listen to the interview again. Here are some of the things Sandy Hearst says. What do you think she means by the expressions in *italics*?

1 Their behavior may seem *eccentric*.
2 This kind of behavior *makes total sense*.
3 Before a match they are very *hyped up*.
4 Rituals keep their anxiety *at bay*.
5 It's not a *magical effect*.
6 It's like a kind of *placebo effect*.
7 The experiment was *pretty telling*.

5 SPEAKING

a Think about people you know (or yourself) and write a few notes to answer the questions.

1 Do they do anything you would consider a "ritual"? Think about:
   - routine activities (e.g., getting up, going to work or school)
   - communal activities (e.g., meals, meetings)
   - situations where they need both ability and luck (e.g., taking an exam, sports events).
2 How do you think these "rituals" help them, and why are they important?

b Work in groups. Use your notes to tell other students about the people you chose.

10C EVERYDAY ENGLISH

Before we move on

Learn to take turns in more formal conversations

- S Take turns in an interview
- P Intonation in question tags

1 LISTENING

a 10.18 Nate receives a phone call from a journalist, Elizabeth, at a student radio station. Listen to Part 1. Why is Elizabeth calling? What is Nate's reaction?

b 10.18 Listen to Part 1 again and answer the questions.

1 Why does Nate say that he doesn't want to donate money?
2 What does Elizabeth say she *isn't* doing?
3 What word does Elizabeth use to describe Nate's hike? What does it mean?

c Look at the photo below. Do you think Elizabeth was satisfied with the call? Do you think Nate is interested in doing the interview? Explain your answers.

d 10.19 Nate agrees to be interviewed on air by Elizabeth. Listen to Part 2 and put the items in the order they're mentioned.

a ☐ Nate's father
b ☐ Nate's hike
c ☐ Nate's inspirations
d ☐ Nate's hometown

e 10.19 Listen to Part 2 again and take notes on the points in 1d.

f Do you think the interview has been successful? Why / Why not?

2 USEFUL LANGUAGE Turn-taking

a Match the expressions in **bold** with their uses a–c. Some expressions have more than one use.

1 **Sorry, if I could just finish** what I was saying, Nate.
2 **Sorry to interrupt, but** that is so inspiring.
3 **Speaking of which,** you grew up here in Seattle, didn't you?
4 **Please, after you.**
5 **As I was saying,** I never forgot those first camping trips.
6 **If you don't mind me cutting in here,** you had to do a lot of preparation for this hike, didn't you?

a interrupt someone and take a turn speaking
b encourage someone else to speak
c continue speaking about the same subject

b When would you use these phrases in a conversation?

1 **Go on.**
2 **Before we get started …**
3 **Before we move on …**

c 10.20 Complete the conversation with the expressions in 2a and 2b. There may be more than one correct answer. Listen and check.

A So, I understand you're a motivational speaker.
B That's right. Basically I go to company conferences and give talks on …
A [1] _________ where are these conferences?
B Oh, all over the country. Overseas sometimes, too. But [2] _________, companies employ me to talk about my mountaineering adventures to share a message of drive and ambition.
A And I don't suppose you imagined when you started mountaineering that you would end up doing this.
B No, I …
A I mean, did you think …
B Sorry?
A No, I'm sorry. [3] _________.
B Well, no. I never imagined I would be going around speaking at conferences …
A [4] _________ you have some really exciting stories of your mountaineering days, don't you?
B [5] _________ what I was saying. I never imagined speaking at conferences, but I'd like to say that I've been amazed at the warm welcome I've received in the business world.
A That's good to hear. Now, …

d Practice the interview in 2c with a partner, but change the profession of the interviewee.

3 LISTENING

a ▶ 10.21 Listen to Part 3 and choose the best answer to the questions.

1 Why is Elizabeth pleased?
  a She did a great interview with a difficult interviewee.
  b She's finally getting the credit she is due.
  c She feels exhilarated after a successful broadcast.
  d Nate is going to write a blog post about her.
2 What does Nate think Elizabeth did that helped the interview?
  a She spoke politely.
  b She asked good questions.
  c She sent him the questions in advance.
  d She mentioned his charity.
3 What are Elizabeth and Nate going to do together?
  a have lunch the next day
  b have another interview after the book comes out
  c go on a hike over the summer
  d start doing weekly interviews at the station

b Who would you like to interview? Think about someone who is famous or someone who has inspired you. Say why you would like to talk to this person and what questions you would ask.

c ▶ 10.22 **Language in context** *Praising idioms*
Match the two halves of the idioms. Listen and check.

1 ☐ Well, credit where	a	your praises.
2 ☐ Hats off	b	to you.
3 ☐ Everyone has been singing	c	best thing since sliced bread.
4 ☐ You're the	d	credit's due.

4 PRONUNCIATION Intonation in question tags

a ▶ 10.23 Listen to the sentences from Parts 2 and 3. Does the intonation rise (↗) or fall (↘) on each question tag in **bold**?

1 You grew up here in Seattle, **didn't you?**
2 You had to do a lot of preparation for this hike, **didn't you?**
3 It's really the cherry on top, **isn't it**, Nate**?**

b Complete the rules with *rising* or *falling*.

- If you're not sure what you've said is correct, use a _______ intonation on the question tag.
- If you know what you've said is correct and you want the other person to confirm it, use a _______ intonation on the question tag.

c ▶ 10.24 Listen to these questions and say which intonation you hear – A (↗) or B (↘).

1 You did, didn't you?
2 You can't, can you?
3 She hasn't, has she?
4 They do, don't they?
5 I should, shouldn't I?
6 It will, won't it?

d Work in pairs. Take turns saying a sentence from 4c, using different intonations for the question tag. Your partner says *A* or *B*.

e We often use a question tag with a falling intonation after giving an opinion in order to elicit agreement from the person we are speaking to. Give your opinions on the topics below and elicit your partner's agreement using a question tag.

- a strange superstition
- a famous athlete
- a good TV documentary

5 SPEAKING

a Work on your own. Pretend you are a famous athlete. Answer the questions. Make up answers if you do not know the correct answers.

1 What's your name and hometown?
2 What's your sports background and what team do you play for / who is your sponsor?
3 What unusual superstitious rituals do you have? (Think of three.) Here are some ideas:
   - lucky charms
   - pre-game routine
   - particular clothing

b You are going to interview your partner in their role as a famous athlete. Think of some questions to ask them.

c Work with a partner. Take turns interviewing each other. Think of answers to your partner's questions. Use expressions for turn-taking and question tags.

UNIT PROGRESS TEST

→ CHECK YOUR PROGRESS

YOU CAN NOW DO THE UNIT PROGRESS TEST.

10D SKILLS FOR WRITING

The movie is a visual feast

Learn to write a movie review

W Movie reviews; Concise description

1 SPEAKING AND LISTENING

a What makes you want to see a movie? Choose one or more from the following or your own idea.

seeing a trailer   reading a plot synopsis
reading a review   having read the book
hearing a friend's recommendation

b Read the descriptions of the movie *Ad Astra* and match them to the places you would find them.

1 ☐ on a movie download website
2 ☐ on a customer review website
3 ☐ on a sign outside a movie theater
4 ☐ in a critic's review online

c How much are you influenced by reviews? Is there a reviewer whose judgment you trust? What are the reasons for and against reading reviews?

d ▶ 10.25 Listen to four people talking about how they use reviews. Take notes to answer the questions.

1 What kind of movie reviews do they read? Why?
2 When do they read them?
3 Do they read any other kinds of reviews?

Which person's opinions are closest to your own?

e What other kinds of reviews do you find useful? What kinds of reviews have you written yourself?

A

Reviews   Home News chat

Alexx   Sept 16

AD ASTRA ★★★★★

Brad Pitt is super cool in this super-cool movie – best performance of his career. Don't usually like sci-fi, but this movie is different – **it's great!**

B

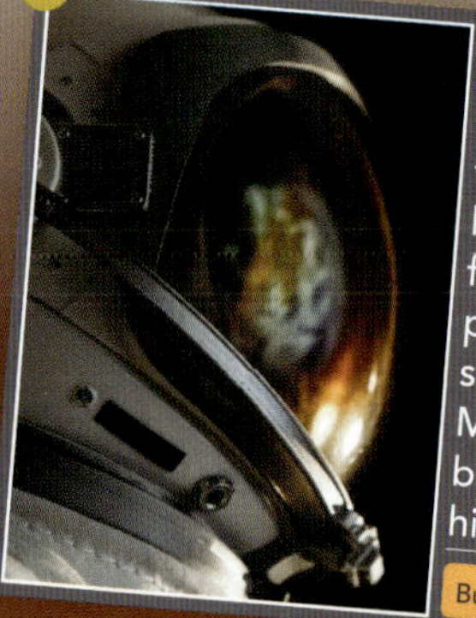

Ad Astra 2019

Astronaut Roy McBride is sent to Mars to communicate with his father in outer space. The father is sending dangerous power surges through the solar system. From Mars, McBride hijacks a spaceship because he wants to confront his father face-to-face.

Buy Movie $9.99   Rent Movie $4.99

C

Although they only have small cameo roles, Tommy Lee Jones and Donald Sutherland give memorable performances. They both give a master class in creating complex characters in limited screen time.

Read More

D

NOW SHOWING

AD ASTRA

"**Mesmerizing** and **electrifying.** James Gray directs an instant classic."

– Movie Review Magazine

2 READING

a Read two reviews of *Ad Astra*. Which reviewer is more positive? What are the main differences in their feelings about the movie?

b Based on these two reviews alone, would you want to see the movie? Why / Why not?

Review **Ad Astra**

Director James Gray makes his first venture into sci-fi with *Ad Astra*. It's a thought-provoking movie reminiscent of sci-fi classics such as *2001: A Space Odyssey* and *Alien*. Brad Pitt plays Roy McBride, an astronaut with the ability to keep his cool in dangerous situations. Having survived a dangerous fall in space, he is sent on a top-secret mission to stop a series of outer space power surges that are causing chaos on Earth.

It's believed the power surges are linked to another mission, Project Lima. This mission, led by McBride's father, Clifford (Tommy Lee Jones), was a failed exploration for intelligent life at the edges of the solar system. Fearing that Clifford is still alive and has gone rogue, the authorities only want Roy to make contact with his father from Mars. But he has different ideas, and the movie promises to be a father-son showdown in outer space.

Some moviegoers may find *Ad Astra* slower paced than some sci-fi movies, but it's not without its exciting sequences. And this is Brad Pitt's best performance in years. While his character seems emotionally detached from other people, Pitt manages to convey a depth of feeling with enormous subtlety.

For me, the strength of *Ad Astra* lies in the way it blends sci-fi with intense personal feeling. It's really a classic family drama about a son needing to escape from the shadow of the father. This won't appeal to some die-hard sci-fi fans only interested in action and thrills. But, to my mind, it makes the movie more textured and more interesting. *Ad Astra* is set to become a classic.

AD ASTRA Review

Director James Gray has assembled a stellar cast for his latest movie, *Ad Astra*. Brad Pitt is joined by veteran actors Tommy Lee Jones and Donald Sutherland, and they're working from a script written by Gray together with Ethan Gross.

Brad Pitt plays Roy McBride, an astronaut sent on a mission to outer space to get in touch with his father, Clifford McBride (Tommy Lee Jones), also an astronaut. McBride Senior seems to have gone crazy and is suspected of sending chaotic power surges back to Earth.

Things get off to an exciting start when Roy McBride (Brad Pitt) is thrown off a tower in space and almost falls to his death. We meet him next in a hospital bed reflecting on his psychological condition. This is where the movie starts to get bogged down. There's a little too much psychology, and it gets in the way of what could have been a great intergalactic thrill ride.

Ad Astra looks great, but the storyline feels a bit like a reworking of sci-fi movies we've seen before. However, there are some lovely and amusing touches like the $120 hot face towels on the commercial flight to the moon. Brad Pitt looks the part of an ace astronaut, but he comes across distant and remote. He's not the kind of hero that you really want to root for – we need less reflection and more action.

Overall, I enjoyed the movie and it kept me engaged. But I often wanted to hurry things along, and I wasn't sitting on the edge of my seat in the way that a good sci-fi movie makes you. But if you like your sci-fi together with psychology and stunning visual images, then *Ad Astra* is worth a look.

3 WRITING SKILLS
Movie reviews; Concise description

a Check (✓) the elements that are included in the reviews. Are they included in the same order in both reviews?

1 ☐ when and where the writer saw the movie
2 ☐ the names of the director and actors
3 ☐ outline of the plot
4 ☐ how the movie ends
5 ☐ strong points of the movie
6 ☐ weak points of the movie
7 ☐ short summarizing statement
8 ☐ recommendation – whether to see it or not

Should the elements you didn't check be included in a review? Why / Why not?

b Which reviewer mentions strengths or weaknesses in the following areas? Write *A*, *B*, or *both*.

1 plot
2 characters
3 acting
4 filming
5 themes/messages
6 success of the movie

c Underline three expressions the writers use to write about movies that you would find useful to learn. Compare with other students. Did you choose the same ones?

d Compare the excerpts below with the first two paragraphs of Review A. How are the words in *italics* different in Review A? Why do you think the writer of Review A chose to do this? Choose 1 or 2.

1 to make the meaning more explicit
2 to give the information more concisely

After he has survived a dangerous fall in space …
This mission, *which was led* by McBride's father, Clifford …
Because they are afraid that Clifford is still alive and has gone rogue …

e Now go to Writing Focus 10D on p. 175.

4 WRITING

a Choose a movie or TV series you know and plan a review of 220–260 words. Think about:

- describing the movie or TV series for someone who hasn't seen it
- main strengths and weaknesses
- how to structure your review into four paragraphs.

b Write the review. Try to:

- use adjectives to give an intense description
- make the information as concise as possible.

c Read another student's review. Do you know the movie or TV series? If so, decide if you agree with what it says. If not, decide whether you'd like to see it based on the review.

UNIT 10
Review and extension

1 GRAMMAR

a Complete the sentences with the words in the box.

have it shouldn't only ought to rather time wish

1 You could ________ asked me before getting involved.
2 I would ________ you spoke to Jean about it.
3 ________ was revealed that the manager had resigned.
4 If ________ everyone were as generous as you.
5 It's ________ the government did something about crime.
6 I ________ you would behave when my friends come over.
7 You ________ look at me with a face like that.
8 Harriet ________ feel ashamed of herself.

b Rewrite the sentences using the words in parentheses.

1 Why didn't you call me? (should)
2 It wasn't necessary for you to meet me. (didn't need)
3 They say that the president owns a private zoo. (said)
4 It's a shame we don't live closer. (wish)
5 There's no way that Alex was on time. (couldn't)
6 It was a bad idea for Sarah to lose her temper. (If only)
7 People think that she died in a car crash. (thought)

2 VOCABULARY

a Match the sentence halves 1–6 with endings a–f.

1 ☐ The president concluded
2 ☐ It is important to back
3 ☐ I would also like to pay
4 ☐ There's no time to go into
5 ☐ Before we move on to
6 ☐ You also need to sell

a tribute to a dear friend, Carlos Sanchez.
b the idea to your audience.
c up arguments with solid facts.
d the finer points, so I'll leave it there.
e her speech with some words of thanks.
f a different topic, let me summarize.

b Complete the missing words.

1 Good luck in the race. I'll keep my f________ crossed.
2 We've lost twice already. Third t________ the charm!
3 That might be t________ fate.
4 I find Tracey's story c________ and will support her.
5 To be on the safe s________, let's go by taxi.
6 Blow out the candles and m________ a wish.

3 WORDPOWER *luck* and *chance*

a 10.26 Replace the words in *italics* with the correct phrases in the box. Listen and check.

a fighting chance blow my chances on the off chance don't stand a chance it's tough luck 're in luck consider yourself lucky

1 I can't believe what you said in that meeting! You should *be relieved* that nobody was listening.
2 We're inviting you *because there's a small possibility* that you're free that night.
3 The treatment is essential to give him *a possibility of recovering*.
4 I'm sorry you don't like the situation, Mark, but *you'll have to put up with it*, I'm afraid.
5 I always *destroy any possibility of success* in interviews because I get so nervous.
6 You know that book you wanted to borrow? Well, you *can do that now*! I found it under the bed.
7 Their top player is out with an injury, and without him they *have no possibility of winning*.

b 10.27 Complete the exchanges using the correct forms of the phrases in 3a. Use one word in each blank. Listen and check.

1 **A** I can't believe I missed the entry date for applications. I've really ________ my chances there.
B Why don't you send it in anyway, ________ the ________ chance they're still recruiting?
2 **A** Do you have the notes from yesterday's lecture?
B You're ________ luck. That's the first lecture I've taken notes at this year. Here you go.
3 **A** It's six o'clock already. I don't ________ a chance of getting this homework finished tonight.
B ________ luck, I'm afraid. I'm not helping you.
4 **A** I'm so worried about how badly I did on those exams.
B Well, ________ yourself lucky that everyone else did badly, too. At least you have a ________ chance of getting a decent grade.

c What could you say to these people using the expressions in 3a? (There is more than one answer.)

- a friend who missed the bus
- a busy person you'd like to meet with
- someone who wants to borrow some money from you
- a friend who should go to bed because they have a test the next day
- a friend who lost their wallet but got it back

REVIEW YOUR PROGRESS

How well did you do in this unit? Write 3, 2, or 1 for each objective.
3 = very well 2 = well 1 = not so well

I CAN ...	
give a presentation or a speech	☐
talk about superstitions and rituals	☐
take turns in more formal conversations	☐
write a movie review.	☐

1B STUDENT A

a Read about two more language changes. How does each heading represent the change?

1 To be or not to be?

Verbs that are followed by an infinitive or verb + *-ing* give us a choice of form with no real difference in meaning. In the last century, there was a steady shift toward more frequent use of the verb + *-ing* after verbs like *begin*, *start*, *like*, *love*, and *hate*, and these are still on the increase.

A *I like getting up late and eating a big breakfast.*

B *I like to get up late and eat a big breakfast.*

The more modern of these two speakers is Speaker A, although they're unlikely to be aware of it.

2 Are you being serious?

English is getting more and more progressive. Constructions such as *I have to be leaving now* and *I'm being smarter about my choices* wouldn't have sounded correct 150 years ago, but nowadays are fairly high frequency. The use of continuous passive verb forms has also seen a rapid rise. And what's *being done* about it? Nothing.

b Now go back to p. 11.

2C STUDENT A

a Read about this problem you have and think about what you want to say.

- You live in a shared apartment. While your roommate was away, you borrowed an item belonging to them without asking. (*Decide what you borrowed.*)
- Unfortunately, you broke the item. (*Decide what you were doing when this happened.*)
- You go to the shopping center to buy a replacement. You can't find anything exactly the same, but there's something very similar, and you don't think your roommate will notice.

b Student B also has a problem. Listen carefully and talk about some solutions to the problem. Make three suggestions using the language for giving advice on p. 27.

c Now present your problem to Student B and ask for advice.

2A

a Answer the questions with a partner. Do you feel the same about the different types of sound? Who do you think is more sensitive to noise?

HOW SENSITIVE ARE YOU TO SOUND?

1. Do you find it difficult to read a book if someone is having a conversation in the same room?
2. When a coworker types loudly on their computer at work, do you have problems concentrating?
3. Does the sound of household appliances like vacuum cleaners irritate you?
4. Does constant traffic noise drive you crazy?
5. Does the sound of excited children playing together annoy you?
6. Do unexpected sounds at night spook you?
7. Do you find it impossible to sleep if you can hear your neighbors having a party?

b Ask and answer the questions.

1. Are there any other sounds that drive you crazy? What?
2. What can you do if you feel apprehensive about going to noisy places?
3. What can you do to improve your tolerance of background noise?

c Now go to p. 128 for suggestions on how to manage noise.

4C STUDENT A

a Read your card. Think about what you might say using the language on p. 50.

You're an employee. You have produced a report for your boss. You think it's good, but your boss has some criticisms. Make these points tactfully:

- You weren't given a clear brief about what was required, so you had to use your initiative.
- You were only asked to write a report a week ago, so you had very little time to do it.
- Your boss is often out of the office, so you couldn't ask for help.

b Listen to Student B and respond. Try to agree on a way forward.

2A

a Read and talk about each suggestion about managing noise. Can you think of any practical problems with each suggestion? Are any of these things ... ?

- already part of your routine
- something you'd like to try

DON'T APOLOGIZE!

If you are sensitive to noise, don't worry about it too much. It's not a weakness in your character; it's just who you are. You don't need to apologize for this.

SPEAK UP!

If you're in an environment where another person is making unnecessary noise, don't be afraid to ask them politely to be a little quieter.

REST AND RELAX.

Make sure you get plenty of sleep and rest. If you are sensitive to noise, feeling tired will only make the problem worse. If you start the day feeling rested and relaxed, you'll be able to cope better.

FIND THE RIGHT PLACE.

Work out which sounds and which noisy environments are particularly annoying or stressful for you. Try to avoid these places as much as possible.

BE PREPARED.

Plan activities so you can avoid noise. For example, it might be a good idea to avoid going to the mall on a Saturday evening when it's busy and noisy - choose another night of the week to go.

FIND YOUR OWN SOLUTIONS.

Think of ways to help you manage noisy environments. For example, if you find the sounds of public transportation make you feel apprehensive, try using noise-canceling headphones to reduce the noise.

TAKE A BREAK.

Find a place near your workplace or home that you know is always quiet. During the day, take a break and go there to enjoy some relaxing quiet. This will help you manage the rest of the day.

b Now go back to p. 20.

5C STUDENT A

a Conversation 1 Read your first card. Think about what you want to say using the language on p. 63. Then start the conversation with Student B.

① You're the manager of a ________ company (*decide what kind of company*) and you're interviewing Student B. Unfortunately, you haven't had time to read Student B's application, and you've forgotten to bring it with you. You don't want Student B to know this. Refer to your "memory" of the application and try to find out about:

- the job Student B has applied for (Administrative Assistant / Marketing Executive / Assistant Manager) (*guess which job*)
- Student B's education/training
- Student B's experience
- Student B's hobbies.

b Conversation 2 Now look at your second card. Listen to Student B and reply.

② You've bumped into Student B by chance. You recognized Student B instantly: you used to use the same gym / catch the same train into town every morning / live next door to one another (*decide which*). Prepare to talk about:

- what job you did then and still do (defense lawyer / psychiatrist / butler) (*decide which job*)
- how many years it's been since you last saw each other
- what happened the last time you saw each other.

5B STUDENT A

a Read the text and prepare to tell your partner about the main points in each section.

ETHICAL HACKER

TYPICAL SALARY: $60,000 to $90,000 at the team leader level, while a newly qualified hacker can expect a minimum salary of $35,000 to $50,000.

THE JOB: A company will pay an ethical hacker to hack into its computer system to see how well it might stand up to a real attack.

QUALIFICATIONS: For government work, ethical hackers must hold a relevant degree. In the financial services sector, these qualifications are a mandatory requirement for some types of specialist work. However, you don't necessarily need a degree in computer science, says Ian Glover, president of Crest. "The industry accepts individuals with a very wide range of academic backgrounds and skills. Often, people have not come the traditional route through education because the 'system' did not necessarily match their way of working and learning."

TO SUCCEED AS AN ETHICAL HACKER, YOU NEED … a passion for technology and detail. You should also have a very good analytical mind, enjoy solving difficult problems, and be able to articulate your observations to senior management.

WORST THING ABOUT THE JOB: "When we're called in to test the security of a new customer's network, only to discover that they have already been the victim of a data breach," says Matthew Gough from cyber security consulting firm Nettitude, "we have to explain that sensitive data belonging to the company's customers has been compromised by hackers. It's not pleasant." To stay on top of the latest threats, you have to constantly update your knowledge in your spare time. Specialist consulting firms will also expect you to be flexible and willing to travel.

"A passion for technology and a keen eye for detail is required."

b Now go back to p. 61

3C

a Read conversations 1–4. Complete the sentences with your own ideas. Think about how you will describe your experiences.

1

I wouldn't travel by ________ to ________ if I were you.

Why not?

In a nutshell … (*summarize what's wrong with it*)

2

I had a terrible time when I went to ________.

What happened?

Well, to make a long story short … (*summarize what happened*)

3

I shouldn't have said ________ about ________.

Why not?

Well, what I meant by that was … (*paraphrase what you intended to say*)

4

I think that ________ is absolutely perfect!

Really?

That is to say … (*rephrase your opinion, giving your evidence*)

b Student A: Use the yellow speech bubbles. Start conversation 1 with Student B. Student B: Use the gray bubbles. Have conversations 1 to 4. Then switch roles.

4B 1 STUDENT B

a Study these photos for one minute.

b Think about the words you learned in this lesson. Use as many as you can to write a description of the scene.

c Now go to p. 132.

STUDENT A

a Test your partner. Ask Student B to describe the crime you can see in the photos above. You can question your partner on any details they have forgotten. Is Student B a good eyewitness?

b Now go back to p. 49.

5B STUDENT B

a Read the text and prepare to tell your partner about the main points in each section.

SOCIAL ENGINEER

TYPICAL SALARY: Between $84,000 and $135,000 on average. Graduates start at $42,000, but salaries increase rapidly with qualifications and experience.

THE JOB: A social engineer is paid by a company to try to trick its employees into divulging confidential information that allows the engineer to access sensitive company data on the company's computer network. "We aren't the bad guys, but we attempt to mimic them in order to help our clients understand how and why such attacks work, and how to prevent them from being successful," says Tom Roberts, a social engineer at Pen Test Partners. "You have to understand the psychology and technical elements involved in phishing, telephone manipulation, letter writing, and the design and production of security tokens and devices used in the day-to-day access of modern buildings and workplaces."

QUALIFICATIONS: Typically, social engineers have a degree in IT, although an understanding of psychology is useful, as is a background in marketing, teaching, and customer service.

TO SUCCEED AS A SOCIAL ENGINEER, YOU NEED ... the confidence to lie convincingly and the ability to fit in almost anywhere without looking too out of place. Good social engineers can also speed-read facial expressions and body language and understand the nuances of written and spoken English. But most importantly, says Roberts, you need a strong sense of personal ethics and an understanding of the law.

WORST THING ABOUT THE JOB: "Once you start to read people with ease, it can make life outside work tricky, and it can make you cynical," says Roberts. "And other people will misunderstand your job: social engineers are not spies, nor do they work in that manner, but most people will label us that way."

b Now go back to p. 61.

5C STUDENT B

a **Conversation 1** Read your first card. Then listen to Student A and reply.

> **1** You've applied for the role of Administrative Assistant / Marketing Executive / Assistant Manager (*decide which job*) and Student A is interviewing you. Prepare to talk about:
> - your education/training
> - your experience
> - your hobbies.

b **Conversation 2** Now look at your second card. Think about what you want to say using the language on p. 63. Then start the conversation with Student A.

> **2** You've bumped into Student A by chance. Student A has recognized you instantly, but unfortunately, although Student A looks vaguely familiar, you can't remember how you know each other. You don't want Student A to know this. Try to find out about:
> - what job Student A did then and still does (defense lawyer / psychiatrist / butler) (*guess which job*)
> - how you know each other
> - how many years it's been since you last saw each other
> - what happened the last time you saw each other.

1B STUDENT B

a Read about two more language changes. How does each heading represent the change?

3 Do you want to dance with me?

Modal verbs are gradually giving way to other less formal expressions – stiff, formal words like *shall* and *ought* are on the way out, and words which cover the same ground, such as *going to*, *have to*, *need to*, and *want to* are taking over.

This modernization process is far from efficient; compare:

You ought to see a doctor.

You are going to want to get that looked at by a doctor.

But why use three words where ten will do?

4 I got fired, but I still got paid!

The verb *to be* has lost its grip on the passive in recent years, and the use of *get* passives has grown substantially. These days you *get fired*, *get robbed*, and *get married*, and buildings *get built* and *get knocked down* again. Whether it's good or bad news for the subject, these days there's a *get* passive for any occasion.

b Now go back to p. 11.

2C STUDENT B

a Read about this problem you have and think about what you want to say.

> - As a reward for meeting your targets, your thrill-seeking boss wants your whole team to go out for the day to do a dangerous sport (*decide which sport*).
> - You are absolutely terrified of doing the sport for a specific reason (*decide what*) but don't want your boss or coworkers to know.
> - There is a promotion coming up, and you don't want your boss to judge you on your sports performance.

b Present your problem to your partner and ask for advice.

c Now listen to your partner's problem carefully and talk about some solutions to it. Make three suggestions using the language for giving advice on p. 27.

5B

Average Annual Salaries in the U.S.

nurse	$75,000
elementary school teacher	$55,000
investment banker	$100,000
professional basketball player	$10 million
police officer	$65,000

Do you think the differences in pay would be similar in your country?

4A

a Add up your score: 2 for each A answer and 1 for each B answer. Then mark your position on the line and read your results. Are you surprised by them?

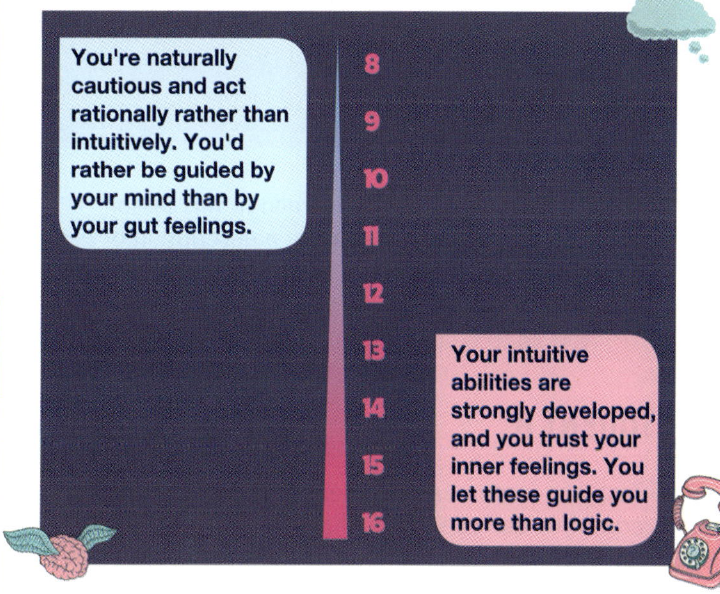

b Now go back to p. 44

4B 1 STUDENT A

a Study these photos for one minute.

b Think about the words you learned in this lesson. Use as many as you can to write a description of the scene.

c >>> Now go to p. 130.

STUDENT B

a Test your partner. Ask Student A to describe the crime you can see in the photos above. You can question your partner on any details they have forgotten. Is Student A a good eyewitness?

b >>> Now go back to p. 49.

2B

a Read Andy's blog post. What's Andy's job, and who do you think he's writing to? Were you right about his reasons for moving to the place in the photo?

HOME POSTS LINKS CONTACT

Hi everyone!

Sorry I've been quiet for a while, but a lot's been happening. Here I am in Canada, and I'm planning to travel even further north and live alone for a year in the wild. It can't be worse than insurance claims!

I'm renting a cabin by a lake, and I'll be staying there through the winter. I'm going to stock up on food to keep me going, but I'm also planning to catch fish – I brought my fishing gear along.

Well, think of me when you're on the 7:30 train to work! I hope to be back in the spring and will post again then.

Wish me luck!

b Work in pairs. Imagine you are about to do one of these things:

- stay in a remote place
- travel somewhere adventurous
- completely change your lifestyle
- live in a new country.

Write a blog post like Andy's about your plans. Then switch posts with another pair.

c Read the post you received. Think of some questions to ask when you next meet and add comments on the post.

d You meet a year later. Talk about your experience and answer questions. Read the comments on your post and respond to them.

4B 2

a Read the information in the fact file. How similar is it to the list you made?

FACT FILE

Refreshing your MEMORY ...

1. **FOOD** fresh vegetables and healthy oil (e.g., fish oil) – cut down on sugar and grain carbohydrates; drinking green tea can also help
2. **EXERCISE** a good balance of cardio and strength training
3. **SLEEP** a good night's sleep refreshes the brain
4. **MULTI-TASKING** avoid it – be fully focused on one thing at a time
5. **BRAIN GAMES** fun activities to stimulate your brain, but don't play them for too long at a time
6. **NEW SKILLS** learn a new skill that is stimulating and interesting for you
7. **MNEMONIC DEVICES** techniques to help you remember information, e.g., a doctor's appointment: imagine a stethoscope and a number for the day of the week, or remember an acronym like *DAT* = *Doctor's Appointment Thursday*
8. **VISUALIZING** make a connection between new information you want to learn and the visual memory of a place you know well, e.g., a room or an object

b Now go back to p. 49.

4C STUDENT B

a Read your card. Think about what you might say using the language on p. 50.

You're a boss. A member of your team has produced a report that you don't think is very good. Make these points tactfully:

- The report doesn't include all the relevant information it should include.
- You offered to help the person, but they insisted they could do the report themselves.
- They left writing the report until the last minute, rather than working on it in advance.

b Start the conversation with Student A. Try to agree on a way forward.

a Look at the photos from a photography competition. Why do you think each photo won a prize? Use the adverbs and adjectives from the box and your own ideas to talk about the photos with a partner.

Adverbs

truly utterly incredibly completely absolutely extremely rather a little pretty quite gently wonderfully very

Adjectives

well-composed powerful meaningful gritty raw playful humorous evocative exotic iconic nonsensical sensational bleak flawless ironic elaborate cluttered

This is an utterly sensational image. It really draws you in.

Yes, it's quite evocative. It makes me think of ...

b Which photo do you think should be the overall winner of the competition? Why? Agree on one image with your partner.

c Now go to p. 70.

7C STUDENT B

a **Conversation 1** Read your first card. Think about what you might say using the language on p. 87. Then listen to Student A and reply.

1
- You had arranged to meet Student A at the movie theater to see a movie you'd been wanting to see.
- The appointment slipped your mind completely.
- You went out with another friend to a restaurant instead. Your cell phone had run out of battery.
- On your way out of the restaurant, you saw Student A across the street. You suddenly remembered your appointment and decided to pretend you hadn't seen them.
- When you got home and recharged your battery, you received an angry text from Student A.
- You realize that you were in the wrong and feel very ashamed. You hope you can still be friends.

b **Conversation 2** Now look at your second card. Think about what you want to say. Then start the conversation with Student A.

2
- You requested a promotion at work. Anxious about it, you told one of your coworkers, Student A, in confidence.
- You got the promotion!
- While congratulating you, another coworker let slip that they'd known you'd requested the promotion for some time.
- You realize that Student A must have told her, but it doesn't matter now anyway.

9B STUDENT A

a Start a conversation with Student B. Listen to Student B and reply using the ideas below in order. Use ellipsis and substitution to make the conversation natural.

1 I don't like our neighborhood anymore.
3 I'm glad you agree. They're knocking down all the beautiful old buildings, and they're putting up ugly new buildings.
5 It's terrible, isn't it? And they said they were going to restore the old town hall, but they haven't restored the old town hall yet.
7 It's all a big mess. I really want to do something, but it's hard to know what to do.
9 Yes, starting an online petition to save the town hall is a good idea. And we could hold a protest.
11 You're right. It probably would be taking things a little too far. We'll start with the petition.

b Now go to p. 108.

9A STUDENT A

a Read the fact file and prepare to tell other students about the situation.

EXHIBITION ROAD, LONDON, UK

- A busy street turned into "shared space"
- Street is shared between vehicles and pedestrians
- Traffic signs, safety barriers removed; trees and benches added

AIMS AND ACHIEVEMENTS

- Traffic is reduced and moves more slowly
- Drivers take more responsibility and drive more carefully because there are no signs telling them what to do
- Drivers and pedestrians make eye contact with each other
- Safety is improved and pedestrians have more space to move

b Now go back to p. 105.

9A STUDENT B

a Read the fact file and prepare to tell other students about the event.

FACT FILE

BANKJESCOLLECTIEF (BENCHES COLLECTIVE), MONTHLY EVENT IN WARMER MONTHS, AMSTERDAM

- Residents and businesses bring a bench to the street from which they offer food or other activities
- Visitors to the bench pay what they think the offering is worth

AIMS AND ACHIEVEMENTS

- To transform Amsterdam into the biggest outdoor café in the world
- People get the opportunity to meet their neighbors and enter into spontaneous interactions
- People become comfortable in the city as a place they own and influence, like their living room
- Beyond food and drink, benches have included: story-telling, salsa classes, knitting workshops, and clothing swap sessions

b Now go back to p. 105.

9B STUDENT B

a Student A will start a conversation with you. Listen and reply using the ideas below. Use ellipsis and substitution to make the conversation natural.

2 I don't like our neighborhood anymore. A lot of people think it's OK, but I don't think it's OK.
4 That's right. They've just gone ahead and they have built that horrible new supermarket and they have put up the ugly new sports center.
6 They'll probably knock it down, but they shouldn't knock it down.
8 We could start an online petition to save the town hall.
10 Do you think we ought to hold a protest? It might be taking things a little too far.

b Now go to p. 108.

9A STUDENT C

a Read the fact file and prepare to tell other students about the situation.

Suburban bus stop makeover, Pittsburgh, PA

- Revamp a bus stop on a busy highway

Aims and achievements

- Long-term, provide a bus stop where people would actually want to sit
- Create shelter from unpleasant weather
- Increase the distance from the road so pedestrians feel safe
- Reduce the risk of crime by lighting the surrounding area
- For the opening, colorful soft furnishings were used to decorate the bus stop

b Now go back to p. 105.

9A STUDENT D

a Read the fact file and prepare to tell other students about the situation.

CONGRESS SQUARE PARK, PORTLAND, ME

- Community organization formed to save a public space

AIMS AND ACHIEVEMENTS

- Restore public faith in the safety of the area
- Re-popularize the square
- Local residents cleaned up the area
- People brought furniture and street food stalls, free Wi-Fi
- More and more people used the square
- Protected land from being sold to developers

b Now go back to p. 105.

7D

a Read about two different team-building programs. Which one would be more appropriate for your team? Why?

Adventure team building

We will take your team hiking in the great outdoors.
Our activities develop:

- **real-life survival skills**
- **cooperation and communication skills**
- **self-awareness and mutual respect.**

Ideal for building a really strong team.

Personal Adventures

Action team building

We have a fantastic range of action games that develop better team dynamics. The games are chosen to foster problem-solving abilities and promote active listening and effective, positive communication among team members.

These physical activities are great fun and really safe – no special abilities are necessary!

Let your team remember the joy of being a child while learning how to work together.

Action Stations Development

b Now go back to p. 89.

7C STUDENT A

a **Conversation 1** Read your first card. Think about what you want to say. Then start the conversation with Student B.

1

- You had arranged to meet Student B at the movie theater to see a movie you'd been wanting to see.
- Since Student B has a reputation for being late, you had bought the tickets in advance for yourself and Student B.
- You waited for a long time, but Student B didn't show up despite the fact that you texted and called.
- You went to see what was left of the movie on your own, and on your way home you saw Student B leaving a restaurant.
- You shouted and waved, but Student B seemed to be ignoring you. You now feel very hurt and angry and don't think your friendship has much future.

b **Conversation 2** Now look at your second card. Think about what you want to say using the language on p. 87. Listen to Student B and reply.

2

- A coworker, Student B, had confided in you about a promotion they'd asked for.
- Another coworker also told you that she had requested a promotion and that she was absolutely certain she'd get it because there was no one else in the office with her skills and capabilities.
- In the heat of the moment, you told her that Student B had also gone in for the promotion and that to your mind, Student B was the stronger candidate.
- Afterward, you realized that you shouldn't have betrayed Student B's confidence, and you feel terrible.

1A Adverbs and adverbial phrases

There are three main positions for adverbials in relation to a main clause: front, middle, and end:
***Obviously**, I **usually** study **after work**.*
Adverbials include single-word **adverbs**, e.g., *obviously*, and **adverbial phrases**, e.g., *after work*.

01.01 End position

In spoken English, adverbials of manner, place, and time usually go at the end of the clause, after the verb and the object:
*I write **very slowly**.* NOT ~~*I very slowly write.*~~
*I live **nearby**, so we'll be **there soon**.*
Adverbial phrases of frequency usually go in the end position. Some single-word frequency adverbs take this position too: *sometimes, occasionally, regularly …*
*We have a test **every couple of weeks**.*
*I go there **regularly**.*
Don't place adverbs between the verb and the direct object:
*She did **the work too quickly**.* NOT ~~*She did **too quickly the work**.*~~
*I'm sure I'll meet **her someday**.* NOT ~~*I'm sure I'll meet **someday her**.*~~
The usual order for adverbs at the end of a sentence is manner, place, time:
*We didn't sleep **well on those airbeds last night**.*
However, when an adverb of place is necessary to complete the meaning of the verb, this order can change:
*I came **here on foot**.* NOT *I* ~~*came on foot here.*~~
Where there are two verbs, adverbs of manner go before the first verb or after the second verb, depending which verb the adverb modifies:
*I **quickly** decided to take the job.*
*She made the effort to drive **carefully**.*

> **Tip** For emphasis in written texts such as narratives, adverbs of manner can go in the front or middle position:
> ***Hesitantly**, she **carefully** unwrapped the package.*

01.02 Middle position

Adverbial phrases are very rare in the middle position:
***At last** I got home. I got home **at last**.* NOT ~~*I **at last** got home.*~~

In the middle position, the adverb goes before the main verb, usually after the first auxiliary or modal verb, or after *be*. Adverbs of probability, certainty, frequency, and focus often take the middle position:
*Good exam results **don't inevitably mean** success in later life.*
*Grammar **is usually** my weakest point.*
Many adverbs of frequency (*never, always, ever*) and certain time adverbs (*just, still*) can only go in the middle position:
*She **still** practices her Japanese.* NOT ~~*Still she practices*~~ *… /*
… ~~*practices her Japanese still.*~~
Adverbs of certainty usually go after auxiliaries, but they go before contracted negative auxiliaries:
*I'**ll probably** see you soon.* NOT ~~*I probably will*~~ *…*
*She **probably/definitely can't** hear you.* NOT ~~*She can't probably*~~ *…*
Be careful with the word order of contracted negative auxiliaries:
*I **don't really** care.* (= not much) *I **definitely won't** come.* (= no chance)
*I **really don't** care.* (= not at all) *I **won't definitely** come.* (= not sure)

01.03 Front position

Comment and linking adverbs usually go at the front of the clause, followed by a comma:
***Obviously**, he knows his grammar. **However,** he isn't as fluent as he'd like to be.*
Adverbials of time, place, and frequency can also go at the front, when we want to set the scene or change the focus:
***In London** there are plenty of jobs.*
***Every so often** I forget the word for "window" in French.*

01.04 Modifying adverbs and adjectives

Adverbials of degree go directly before the word(s) they modify:
*Laura speaks German **reasonably** well, but her French is **a little** basic.*
Adverbs can be modified by phrases with prepositions:
*I drove here **slowly by my standards**.*
***Luckily for you**, I'm in a good mood.*

> **Tip** Some adverbs have different meanings in different positions: *amazingly, strangely, naturally, clearly, fairly, reasonably …*
> ***Strangely**, Kate speaks Chinese.* (= surprisingly)
> *Kate speaks Chinese **strangely**.* (= badly)

---

a Check (✓) the correct sentences. Correct the wrong sentences.

1 ☑ I am definitely thinking of going abroad, by the way.
2 ☐ The secretary put abruptly the phone down.
The secretary put the phone down abruptly.
3 ☐ Presumably, your wife knows you've sold the car.
4 ☐ At the end of the walk, I was exhausted utterly.
5 ☐ The ambulance arrived on the scene within minutes.
6 ☐ I beforehand had had a nasty feeling.
7 ☐ That was the certainly best game so far.
8 ☐ You will find the bathroom downstairs on the left.
9 ☐ You have ignored repeatedly all my warnings.
10 ☐ She definitely won't resign.
11 ☐ He wasn't behaving reasonably at all.
12 ☐ We decided to go by taxi home.

b Add the words and phrases in parentheses to each sentence.

1 So where did language ^first come from? (first)
2 Well, funnily enough, we can't answer this question. (still)
3 Some of the theories are ridiculous. (simply)
4 It has been said that we copied the animal sounds. (even)
5 Language developed for a variety of reasons. (no doubt)
6 Our brains increased in size, and we became more intelligent. (dramatically, a great deal)
7 Also, unfortunately, we started working in groups to get more food. (for other animals)
8 Group behavior would have made the need for language essential. (undoubtedly, absolutely)
9 We won't know the exact causes with any certainty. (probably, ever)
10 What we can say is that the origins of language will fascinate us. (always)

c Now go back to p. 9.

1B The perfect aspect

01.12 Completed actions

Perfect tenses can describe completed actions before a certain time in the past, present, or future.

- We can use perfect tenses to give news and describe recent activities before a certain time:
  *Linguists **have invented** a new language with only 200 words.*
  *At long last the war **had ended**; we couldn't believe it.*
  *It **had been raining** all night.*
- Perfect verbs focus on the effects of completing an activity:
  ***I've done** all I can. You'll have to finish the project on your own.*
  *When she**'d finished** putting the decorations up, the room looked awesome.*
  *I can't meet you at 7:00. I **won't have gotten through** immigration by then.*
- Use perfect verbs to say how much / how many / how often by a certain time:
  *The professor **has written** over 50 books about the English language.*
  *We**'ve already seen** the movie twice.*
  *You **need to have read** all the books on the list by June.*
  *I**'d called him** three times but failed to get through.*
- Perfect continuous verbs focus on the effects of doing an activity:
  *Something **had been worrying her** at work, so she spoke to her boss.*
  *Your eyes are red. **Have you been crying**?*
  *He **will have been driving** all night, so he'll need to go to bed.*
- Compare the simple perfect and perfect continuous:
  *I**'ve made dinner**! You don't need to do anything. (focus on completion)*
  *I**'ve been making** dinner! I'm all hot and sweaty. (focus on doing the activity)*

01.13 Unfinished activities and states

Perfect verb forms can also describe continuing activities or states at a certain time:

*I **haven't been sleeping** well recently. I might go to see the doctor.*
*He **will have been working on** the project for long enough to take over by then.*
*I**'ve always enjoyed** spending time with my family.*
*They**'ve been sad** since their old teacher left.*

- We often want to say the duration of the activity:
  *Louise **has been studying** Spanish **since January**, and she loves it.*
  *I**'ve never** really **understood** the grammar, so I still make a lot of mistakes.*
  *She **will have been driving for a couple of years** by then.*
- For certain activities we often use both simple perfect verbs and perfect continuous verbs with little difference in meaning:
  *How long **have you worked** / **been working** in the languages department?*
  *This June I **will have lived** / **been living** here for five years.*

> **Tip** We can use the past perfect with stress on *had* to express dissatisfaction:
> *We **had hoped** Sheila would be out of the hospital by now.* = Sheila is still in the hospital, and we are disappointed.

a Match the sentence halves.

1 [d] It's been a long time since
2 [ ] I really couldn't tell you how long
3 [ ] I missed the game because
4 [ ] I was so good at dancing everyone thought
5 [ ] If every question takes this long to answer,
6 [ ] This coming January,
7 [ ] I'm exhausted because
8 [ ] This is the first time

a I've been living in Bangkok.
b I won't have finished the assignment by midnight.
c I've been running around all day.
d I ate anything as tasty as this.
e I'd been doing it all my life.
f I've seen you so angry.
g I hadn't bought a ticket in time.
h I will have been living here for three years.

b Choose the best verb form in each sentence.

1 I *lived* / *have lived* in the same place my whole life.
2 Shakespeare *died* / *has died* a long time ago, but he is still very popular.
3 Have you ever *tried* / *been trying* to drive in the snow?
4 This is the third time I have *told* / *been telling* you to be quiet!
5 Don't sit there! I've *painted* / *been painting*, and the paint is wet.
6 As soon as I got home, I *went* / *had gone* straight to bed.
7 Eve had *read* / *been reading* most of the book before she saw the movie.
8 Luke *has* / *had* been thinking about leaving college, but in the end he decided to stay.
9 The train *has* / *had* just left when we got to the station.
10 They might have *finished* / *been finishing* the decorating by the time we get home.

By the time they'd added YOLO to the dictionary, it had already gone out of fashion.

c Complete the text with the correct perfect forms of the verbs in parentheses.

People [1] have been complaining (complain) about English spelling for centuries because certain sounds can be written in several different ways. For example, you [2] ______ (notice) that /ɪ/ is the sound in *sit*, *carpet*, and *women*. Linguists [3] ______ (suggest) several reasons for our difficult spelling. First, English [4] ______ (accept) a lot of foreign words into its vocabulary, so the *ch* in *chorus* /k/, a Greek word, and *chauffeur* /ʃ/, a French word, sounds different. Second, early printers often weren't certain of the spelling of a word – no official spelling [5] ______ (be established) – so they generally spelled a word pretty much as they liked. The spelling of English [6] ______ (become) a bit of a joke today, but who knows, by the time our grandchildren go to school maybe someone [7] ______ (invent) a spelling system that is logical and easy to remember.

d Now go back to p. 12.

2A Comparison

02.02

Modifying comparisons with *than*	
A big difference: *a good/great deal, a lot, considerably, decidedly, far, infinitely, miles* (informal), *much, significantly, three/four/many times* (etc.), *way* (informal) **A small difference:** *a (little) bit, barely any, fractionally, marginally, slightly* **No difference:** *no, not any*	*The total silence was **a lot worse than** any sound could ever be.* *There's **considerably more noise** when you get inside the venue.** *I listen to live music **far more frequently than** I used to.* *Tickets are **slightly more expensive** this year.* *I'm **no happier than** I was in my last job.*
Modifying comparisons with *as … as …*	
A big difference: *not nearly, nowhere near, twice / three times* (etc.) **A small difference:** *almost, nearly, not quite* **No difference:** *equally, just*	*The smell was **not nearly as bad as** we thought it would be.* *Stella knows **almost as much about cars as** I do.* *There are **just as many people** who want to study French.**

*We often omit the *than* or second *as* part of a comparative form if it is obvious: *There's considerably more noise* (***than there is here***) *when you get inside the venue. There are just as many people who want to study French* (***as people who want to study Spanish***).

02.03 **Comparative patterns**

We use double comparatives with adjectives and adverbs to say that somebody or something is changing:

*These exams are getting **harder and harder**.*

*Time seemed to go **more and more slowly**.* NOT *Time seemed to go ~~more slowly and more slowly~~.*

We use *the … the …* with comparatives or *more/less* to say that things change together because they depend on each other:

***The harder** you train, **the longer** you can run.*

***The more** I think about it, **the more** I realize it was a mistake.*

***The more** hours I work, **the less** time I have for my family.*

02.04 ***so / such***

We use *so* + adjective/adverb (+ *that*) and *such* + *a* + noun (+ *that*) to describe a very high level:

*It's **so loud** here **that** I can't hear myself think!*

*If this is **such a bad job**, why don't you find a better one?*

02.05 ***not enough / sufficiently / too***

We use *too* / (*not*) *enough* to compare things with a standard. *Sufficiently* has the same meaning as *enough* but is more formal:

*Jones is good **enough to** win the race.*

*We don**'t** have **enough** gas **for** the trip.*

*The children were **not sufficiently** well-behaved to receive any candy.*

*The weather is **too** cold **to** go outside.*

*This sweater is **too** big **for** me.*

02.06 **Superlative patterns**

We usually use superlatives to highlight something exceptional. We often limit the range of superlatives with relative clauses or adverbs:

*She's **the most talkative** person **I know**. / **ever!** / **in the world**. / **of all**.*

*I did **the best I possibly could**.*

We can modify the strength of a superlative with adverbs like *by far, easily,* (*not*) *nearly, almost, not quite*.

*That was **by far the best** lesson this year.*

*He's **easily the happiest** I've ever seen him these days.*

*It was**n't quite the most difficult** test I've ever had, but it was close!*

a Write a sentence for each picture using the words.

1 considerably / small

The pizza was considerably smaller than the box.

2 grew / not nearly / expected

3 strong / not enough / control the horse

4 no / heavy / than

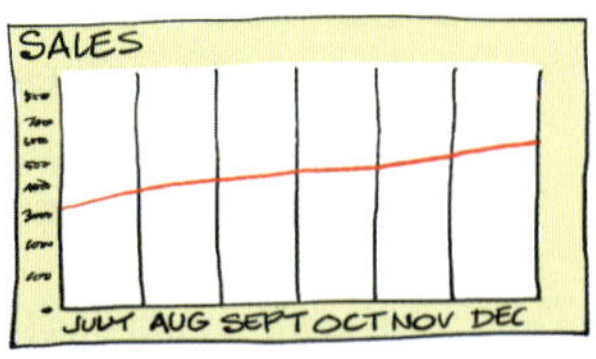

5 marginally / good / since June

6 hard / the rain fell / difficult / the game became

b Complete the text with the words in the box. Use each expression once.

not	way	and	more	so
nowhere	the	far	than	get

Last year, I went to Coachella. It was a real eye-opener. The festival takes place in a remote valley, and after you come off the highway, the roads get smaller [1]_______ smaller. The closer you get to the site, [2]_______ more cars full of festival-goers you see. Everyone is [3]_______ excited just to be there. Then, when you finally get into a parking lot, you have to get through the gates and find a place to camp. This is considerably harder [4]_______ it sounds because you're basically going hiking while carrying a tent and bedding and clothes and all your food and drink for the next few days. The site is [5]_______ bigger than any other festival I've ever been to. As you sit by your tent on the first night, these huge cheers roll toward you across the valley and [6]_______ louder and louder until they're all around you and it's your turn to cheer. Tickets are slightly [7]_______ expensive than other festivals, but when you consider that there are [8]_______ nearly as many acts and installations and [9]_______ near as many people at other festivals, Coachella is by [10]_______ the greatest party on the planet.

c Now go back to p. 21.

2B Intentions and arrangements

02.17 *going to* vs. present continuous

We use both *going to* and the present continuous for future actions and events that are already decided or arranged. We cannot use the present continuous for things it is impossible to arrange and control:

*I'm **having** / **'m going to have** lunch with Terry this afternoon.*
*What **am I going to do** if she says no?* NOT … *~~am I doing~~* …

We cannot use the present continuous for permanent states or indefinite and long-term plans:

*Sally **is going to be** a doctor.* NOT … *~~is being~~* …
*We**'re going to make** a lot of money one day.* NOT … *~~We're making~~* …

We use the continuous phrases *be planning* + infinitive, *be aiming* + infinitive, *be thinking of* + verb + *-ing* to talk about plans:

*Kevin **is planning to walk** across America.*
*He**'s aiming to do** it in less than 100 days.*

02.18 Simple future and future continuous

We use the simple future, *will* + base form, for decisions we make at the time of speaking:

*OK, I**'ll come** to the meeting, but I **won't say** anything.*

We use the future continuous, *will* + *be* + verb + *-ing*, to talk about plans that happen without being specially arranged. We can also use *could* / *may* / *might* / *going to* + *be* + verb + *-ing*:

*I**'ll be going** to the meeting, so I can pass on your apologies.*
*I **might be seeing** Jill tonight.*
*We**'re not going to be passing** your way.*

We also use the future continuous to say that something will be in progress in the future:

*While you're enjoying yourself, I**'ll be working**.*

Compare *going to* and the present continuous with the future continuous:

***Are you going to see** / **Are you seeing** your grandmother this weekend?* (have you planned this?)
***Will** you **be seeing** your grandmother this weekend?* (as you normally do)

02.19 Simple present

We use the simple present for scheduled activities:

*The first race **begins** at 12:00.*
*What time **do** you **get** back tomorrow?*

We can use *will* with the same meaning in official situations:

*President Johnson **will meet** with business leaders next week.*

02.20 Expressions with *be*

We use *be about* + infinitive to say something will happen very soon:

*Hurry up! The bus **is about to leave**!*

We use *not be about* + infinitive to emphasize negative intentions:

*I've never smoked, and I**'m not about to start** now!*

We use *be due* + infinitive to say something is owed/expected very soon, often at a certain time:

*I**'m due to meet** her secretary this afternoon.*
*We're **due to get** a pay raise.*

---

a Complete the sentences with the correct future form.

Interviewer So Rudy, you [1]*'re going to go* / *'ll be going* on your first wing walk.
Rudy That's right, yep. We're [2]*going* / *about* to take off approximately half an hour from now.
I And what [3]*are you* / *will you be* doing exactly? You're [4]*due* / *going* to stand on the wing, right?
R That's right. Well my instructor said I [5]*'ll be standing* / *stand* on top of the plane, between the wings. I'll be strapped into a kind of frame, so I don't have to do anything. I will just stand there, admiring the view … I'm not [6]*about* / *planning* to panic. I'm just going to enjoy it.
I So it'll be pretty windy.
R Yes, we're [7]*due* / *going* to be flying at about 75 miles an hour, so it will be windy, sure. But I [8]*'ll be wearing* / *wear* a padded suit, so I shouldn't get too cold.
I OK, well, good luck!

"I'm not going to look down."

b Cross out the one future form that is NOT possible in 1–10.

1. I *will let* / *am going to let* / *~~am letting~~* you know soon.
2. "The pipe needs to be fixed now." "I*'ll be doing* / *'ll do* / *'m going to do* it."
3. I *won't see* / *don't see* / *won't be seeing* Sharon anytime soon.
4. When Annie leaves school, she *will look* / *is going to look* / *is looking* for a job.
5. Serena *is going to wear* / *is wearing* / *wears* her new dress for the party.
6. "Did you take the necklace?" "I*'m not aiming to answer* / *won't be answering* / *am not about to answer* that."
7. He *will repay* / *is going to repay* / *repays* the full amount.
8. The meeting *aims* / *is about to* / *is due to* begin, so sit down everyone.
9. I'm not *about* / *going* / *due* to learn French at my age. I'm far too old!
10. We *are planning to become* / *are becoming* / *are aiming to become* millionaires one day.

c Complete each sentence with one word or contraction.

1. I'm about ___to___ leave, so hurry up.
2. I ______________ bring a flashlight in case it gets dark.
3. Adelia is ______________ of writing a book about her experiences.
4. A taxi is ______________ to pick us up from the airport when we arrive.
5. Where will you ______________ staying in New York?
6. Mark is ______________ to get a warning for his lateness.
7. Don't worry. I'm ______________ about to spend all our money.
8. You can trust me. I ______________ say anything.
9. Sorry, I can't come because I ______________ be working.
10. The president ______________ open the new airport.

d Now go back to p. 25.

3A Inversion

03.01 Inversion after negative or restrictive adverbials

When we want to emphasize an event because it is new, rare, unexpected, sudden, impossible, etc., we can use negative or restrictive adverbials followed by inverted word order:

I had never been there before. > ***Never before had I been*** *there.*
They didn't try to help me. > ***Not once did they try*** *to help me.*
When he came home, we realized we had missed him. > ***Only when he came home did we realize*** *we had missed him.*

Inversion structures are usually very formal. We use them more in written texts such as narratives and in formal speech such as presentations.

Never again would Lofty travel without researching his destination first.

Negative or restrictive adverbials

None	Too much / (not) enough	One place/time/person, etc.	Unusual
Not a penny *would they give to charity.* ***Not one bite*** *did he eat.* ***Not a single person*** *did they meet that day.*	***Too often*** *do we see people struggling to make ends meet.* ***Too long*** *have we waited for a change.*	***Only in the capital*** *did we feel truly welcome.* ***Only in the summer*** *was it possible to open the windows.*	***Rarely do you find*** *someone like that.* ***Seldom do we stop*** *to think about people in poorer countries.*
Never / Not anymore	***Immediately / Only just**	**Only after/at a certain time**	**Impossible/Prohibited**
At no time *did we think the project would fail.* ***Never*** (***before***) *have I felt so angry.* ***No longer*** *can we ignore the problem.* ***Not in a thousand years*** *will I go back there again.* (informal) ***Not once*** *did they offer any help.* ***Never*** (***again***) *will we attempt to intervene.*	***No sooner*** *had one game finished* ***than*** *another was begun.* ***Barely*** *had we gotten over the flu* ***when*** *we were struck down with a stomach bug.* ***Hardly*** *had the policy been announced* ***than*** *the government came up with a new and better idea.* ***Scarcely*** *had we had time to meet the villagers* ***than*** *we were hurried back onto the bus.*	***Not until his return*** *did we appreciate how much we had missed him.* ***Only when the music stopped*** *did people start to go home.* ***Only then*** *did people start to go home.*	***Under no circumstances*** *should you buy products from companies that exploit workers.* ***On no account*** *can drinks be taken outside.* ***No way*** *can I forget what I saw there.* (informal)
		Addition	**Unexpected**
		Not only is she *young, she's overconfident.*	***Little*** *did she know that trouble was coming.*

Tip
Do not overuse emphatic inversion as it will sound unnatural.

*We use the conjunctions *than* or *when* after *barely, hardly, scarcely,* and *no sooner*:
Barely had we stepped off the plane *than …* ***Scarcely had we fallen asleep*** *when …*

a Choose the best answer, 1 or 2, to follow a and b in each pair.

1 a [2] Under no circumstances should you drink cola.
b [1] Not once did they drink cola.
1 It was difficult to find.
2 It is bad for your teeth.

2 a [ ] At no time can you walk on the ice
b [ ] Barely had he stepped onto the ice
1 than it gave way under his feet.
2 because it is too thin.

3 a [ ] On no account should visitors to the zoo feed the animals.
b [ ] No way am I feeding the animals.
1 They can't digest the food people give them.
2 Some have been known to bite.

4 a [ ] No way did they score –
b [ ] Only then did they score,
1 that's unbelievable.
2 which was way too late.

5 a [ ] Too late did I learn
b [ ] No sooner did I learn
1 that than I apologized profusely.
2 that they had only the best intentions.

b Rewrite the sentences with inversion and an adverb or adverbial phrase.

1 She doesn't often refuse. *Not often does she refuse.*
2 We only felt relaxed in the evenings.
3 I had barely gotten home when the phone rang.
4 Rita seldom takes responsibility for her actions.
5 We didn't find a single store.
6 I'm not going to accept on any account.

c Complete the sentences in the first person using the words and phrases in the box. Use the pronoun *I* each time.

~~little / know~~ not a single person / see no sooner / arrive
not in a million years / think not until 9:00 / find rarely / be

1 *Little did I know* what was waiting for me when I arrived.
2 __________ than there was a terrible rain storm and I was completely soaked through.
3 I'd thought I might have a few adventures, but __________ it would start as badly as this.
4 __________ my way back to the bus stop.
5 The place was empty – __________.
6 __________ so happy to get home!

d Now go back to p. 33.

3B Future in the past; Narrative tenses

03.09 Future in the past

We use past tenses of future forms to say what plans, intentions, or predictions we had at a point in the past.

be to / be about to / be set to	*Grace* ***was about to get*** *on the plane when she got an urgent text message.*
be going to	*Last summer I* ***was going to visit*** *my sister, but I went to Italy instead.*
be + verb + *-ing*	*I* ***was leaving*** *for Mexico that morning and was worried about the long flight.*
modal + *be* + verb + *-ing*	*I knew I* ***might be staying*** *there for a while, so I made myself comfortable.*
would / might / could	*One day I* ***would find out*** *the truth, although I didn't know it yet.*

Tip

There are different meanings of *would* in the past:
She ***would*** *not discuss the matter.* = refused to
*She'****d*** *generally keep her ideas to herself.* = habit
One day he ***would*** *be famous.* = future in the past
But for a lack of talent he ***would*** *have been famous.* = hypothetical past

Narrative tenses

- **Setting the scene**
  We use the past perfect, past perfect continuous, and past continuous to give the background to events in the past:
  We set off at dawn. Everyone ***had slept well*** *despite the unfamiliar environment.*
  The sun ***had just been creeping*** *over the horizon when we packed up camp.*
  We ***were*** *all* ***looking forward to*** *what the day ahead might hold. Or so I thought at the time …*
  We use the past perfect or past perfect continuous to say how long something continued until a time in the past:
  By the time we got to Rio, we ***had been traveling*** *for 16 hours.* NOT ~~were traveling~~
- **Sequence of events**
  We use the simple past for actions in sequence in a narrative. We use the past continuous for background actions or actions that are interrupted:
  By the time we ***reached*** *the top of the mountain, the sun* ***was sinking*** *fast. I* ***started*** *to panic. I* ***was looking around*** *hopefully for a place we could set up camp when somebody* ***screamed****.*
  We use the past perfect to refer back to an earlier time in the sequence:
  Sarah ***got*** *sick and* ***was taken*** *to a hospital* ***as soon as she*** *(****had****)* ***arrived****.*
  Past perfect and past perfect continuous often explain the main action or give relevant background:
  *There was a large swelling where he'****d been bitten****.*
  *I'****d been hearing*** *noises off to the left of the path, so I decided to investigate.*
  Nobody ***had warned me*** *of the dangers I was now facing.*

The children **had been going to tell** their father, but they waited too long.

a Choose the best verb forms in each sentence.

1 Graham *was* / *is* going to meet me at the airport, but I got a taxi.
2 I thought Karen *had been getting* / *would be getting* first prize, but I was wrong.
3 That money *was to have paid* / *might pay* for our daughter's education. Now it's all gone.
4 I *had been making* / *had been planning to make* lunch until you suggested going out to eat.
5 I *wondered* / *was about to wonder* who could have done it.
6 Tony *was driving* / *had driven* to work when he heard the news on his car radio.
7 The baby *had been crying* / *cried* for a while before I picked her up.
8 After I *had been getting* / *got* home, I rushed to check the papers in the safe.
9 We *had been going to give* / *would be giving* up, but suddenly we saw the peak of the mountain.
10 In those days, Simon *would* / *was about to* get up at 6:00 and go for a run.

b Complete the text with a possible form of the verb in parentheses.

They said it [1] *would be* (be) the vacation of a lifetime, but it was a nightmare!
We [2] ____________ (go) on a vacation for ages, so I was really excited about our trip, but I didn't check out the facts that the nice man from the travel agency [3] ____________ (tell) me. All of which [4] ____________ (turn) out to be untrue! For a start, the "luxury" hotel was a building site. The workers [5] ____________ (still prepare) the bedrooms when we arrived, so we had to sleep in the lobby the first night! I [6] ____________ (bring) my swimming things, as I [7] ____________ (hope) for a nice refreshing swim each morning, but there was no water in the pool. I'll tell you, I [8] ____________ (plan) get us all on the first plane home, but my wife persuaded me to stay.
Nothing [9] ____________ (get) any better as the vacation went on. I [10] ____________ (lose) 5 kilograms in weight by the time I got home. I called the company to find out if they [11] ____________ (give) me some money back and told them I [12] ____________ (sue). They [13] ____________ (apologize) profusely, but I'm still waiting for my refund.

c Check (✓) the correct sentences. Correct the mistakes you found in the remaining sentences.

1 ☐ I always thought I'd get married, but it was never to be.
2 ☐ We are feeling excited until the flight was canceled.
3 ☐ The children felt sick because they'd been eating candy all day.
4 ☐ Tom has sent the details to me, so I was well prepared.
5 ☐ The boat was supposed to have left at 3, but it was delayed until 5.
6 ☐ Zara always knew she'll be famous one day.

d 3B Now go back to p. 37.

4A Noun phrases

Structure of noun phrases

Combining information into noun phrases allows precise and concise expression of both abstract and concrete ideas. Compare:

She's an author. She wrote a book. It's on psychology. I read it recently. It's very interesting.

She's ***the author of a very interesting psychology book that I read recently****.*

Complex noun phrases can make language more formal and academic because they develop ideas and package them efficiently. Compare:

In some countries, people often touch foreheads when they greet each other, and this is acceptable there.

Touching foreheads *is* ***a commonly accepted form of greeting*** *in some countries.*

Compound nouns

Compound nouns are the most efficient way of showing the subject or purpose of something, for example, a lecture about math = *a math lecture*, a machine that makes bread = *a bread maker*. Compare:

There were prints from her fingers all over the vase. – Her ***fingerprints*** *were all over the vase.*

For my birthday, I got a console for playing games on. – For my birthday, I got a ***gaming console****.*

A person who was passing by found the wallet. – A ***passerby*** *found the wallet.*

Determiners, adverbs, and adjectives

We use determiners (*a, my, this*, etc.), adverbs, and adjectives before nouns:

Did you notice ***that unpleasant metallic smell****?*

It was only ***a five-minute trip****.*

Tom's first reaction *was to get angry.*

Use adverbs and compound adjectives before nouns rather than clauses after nouns. There is usually a hyphen when compound adjectives are used before a noun. Compare:

It is a position with a fairly high status.

It is a ***fairly high-status position****.*

An artifact has recently been discovered and caused a sensation.

A ***recently discovered artifact*** *has caused a sensation.*

We can put adjectives before *one(s)* and after indefinite pronouns:

Don't get the ***expensive ones****.*

Let's go ***somewhere romantic*** *for our vacation.*

Clauses and prepositional phrases

We use phrases after nouns for ideas that cannot be expressed fully before the noun.

Relative clauses: *He gave a speech* ***that inspired millions****.* NOT ~~*a millions inspiring speech*~~

that **clauses:** *I got the feeling* ***that he never cared****.* NOT ~~*that he never cared feeling*~~

Prepositional phrases: *I'd like a house* ***in a quiet area****.* NOT ~~*in a quiet area's house*~~

We can also use an infinitive after certain nouns, for example, *choice, decision, willingness*:

There's a plan ***to redevelop the town center****.*

Possessives

When we show the relationship between nouns, we can often either use a possessive *'s* or an *of* phrase:

*The company****'s*** *decision / decision* ***of the company*** *to lay off staff was unpopular.*

We prefer the possessive *'s* when the possessor is a person or an animal:

*I looked down at John****'s*** *shoes.* NOT ~~*the shoes of John*~~

We prefer an *of* phrase when the possessor is an object:

The roof ***of the house*** *needs repairing.* NOT ~~*The house's roof*~~

Location, measuring, quantifying, and qualitative words like *back, piece, cup, kind,* and *sort* are always followed by an *of* phrase:

Get in the back ***of the car****.* NOT ~~*the car's back*~~

Have a piece ***of chocolate****.* NOT ~~*chocolate's piece*~~

Tip

Very long noun phrases for people usually aren't followed by the possessive *'s*:

The children ***of the man who lives across the street*** *are staying with me.*

NOT ~~***The man who lives across the street's*** *children are staying with me.*~~

a Underline the noun phrases in the text.

<u>One memorable summer day</u>, I was coming home after an exhausting day at work when I met an old friend I hadn't seen for ages. I don't know why, but I had the strong feeling that this was no mere coincidence. In fact, she had a proposition to make to me that was about to change my life. She said that she was looking for a reliable partner who she could trust to invest in a project started by a few friends of hers. I made a few phone calls to the bank and had the money needed to get involved. My boring days of sitting behind a desk were behind me.

b Improve each noun phrase.

1 the bus's seats *the seats of the bus*
2 the stop for the train
3 a book written brilliantly
4 a moment that is awaited eagerly
5 a meeting that lasts one hour
6 an injury that can change your life
7 the bright idea of Ed
8 the girl that I introduced you to's aunt

c Improve the noun phrases in *italics* without significantly changing their meanings.

Human resources experts
~~*Experts who work in the field of human resources*~~ say that interviewers make *decisions about who to hire* within the first minute of an interview. Of course, *mistakes that cost a lot* can be made, and sometimes the wrong people are hired. Nevertheless, companies have to rely on their managers' *skills in being able to make decisions*. Most of us have experienced at least one *interview that was a nightmare*, perhaps conducted by a *manager who has relatively little experience*. In a situation like this, your options are limited: plow on through the interview, or walk out after the first minute!

You never get **a second chance to make a first impression.**

d Now go back to p. 46.

4B *have / get* passives

***get* passives**

We can use *get* passives like *be* passives, although they are less formal. *Get* passives often describe unfortunate events:

*Do you remember how Sandra **got kicked** by a horse?*

*I **got laid off** yesterday.*

We can use a reflexive pronoun to say that the subject is responsible for something that happened to them:

*He tried to use a fake passport and **got himself arrested** again.*

*Stop that! Are you trying to **get yourself killed**?*

*She's managed to **get herself promoted** for the third time in two years.*

***have / get* + object + past participle**

We can use *have* + object + past participle to talk about something where the subject is in an active role or a passive role. *Get* + object + past participle usually implies an active role.

04.07

	Passive role
*I **had my bag searched** at the airport.*	= Somebody searched my bag.
*Baby Alice **had her first photo taken** today.*	= Somebody, probably a professional, took a photograph of the baby.
	Active role
*We'll **have the window fixed** by the time you come back.*	= We'll arrange for somebody else to fix it **or** we'll do it ourselves.
*I **got my bike stolen** on Main Street.*	= I left it unlocked, so I'm to blame.
*He **gets his house cleaned** every Friday.*	= He pays a cleaner to clean for him.

We often use *get* + object + past participle to talk about completing an activity:

*I haven't managed to **get the paperwork finished**.*

*We can't go until we've **gotten the kids ready**.*

We often use *have/get* + object + past participle to talk about causing or instructing something to happen or to be done by somebody else:

*When I was twelve, I wanted to **have/get my ears pierced**, but my mom wouldn't let me.*

***Have/Get your car repaired** at Thompson's and save $$$!*

We can use *having/getting* + object + past participle:

***Having/Getting the walls painted** is the most important job at the moment.*

*Why would I be interested in **having/getting my nose made smaller**?*

Tip

In informal speech, we can leave out *to* + *get/have* after *need*, *want*, *would like* etc.:

*I **would like** (to get) **my hair cut** soon.*

*I **need** (to have) **my bike** mended.*

04.08

Other patterns	
have/get* + object + verb + *-ing = cause someone/something to do something	*Grandma's story really **had/got me thinking**.* *The music soon **had/got everyone dancing**.*
***have* + object + infinitive** = give instructions or orders	*Our teacher **has us call** him "Sir."* *The boss **had us clean** our desks.*
***get* + object + *to* + infinitive** = persuade someone to do something	*My mother-in-law **got me to take** her to the station.* *Advertising is the art of **getting people to buy** things they don't want.*

a Choose the best option.

1. Two people *got injured / had themselves injured* when the roof collapsed.
2. I'm going to *get him measuring me / get myself measured* for a new suit.
3. My blood pressure is really high. I *was checked / had it checked* this morning.
4. *Getting / Having* your car insured is cheaper if you do it online.
5. We're trying to get more people *to give / giving* to our charity.
6. Jenkins, *have / get* the first candidate come in, please.
7. The news *had everyone shouting / got everyone to shout* with anger.
8. Wayne's not coming in today. He needs his furnace *fixed / fixing*.

Mother was always telling me to **get my hair cut**.

b Rewrite these sentences using the words in parentheses.

1. Someone needs to repair our car. (have)
   We need to have our car repaired.
2. Tina worked hard and was promoted. (herself)
3. Someone stole my bike. (got)
4. Arrange for someone to check your eyes. (have)
5. The news made everyone panic. (got)
6. It wasn't easy to calm the children down. (get)
7. Our teacher told us to write an essay. (had)
8. Alex talked me into going with him. (got)

c Complete the conversation with the correct forms of the verbs in parentheses.

Ryan That podcast about the generation gap really got me [1] *thinking* (think). Are we that different from our kids?

Olivia I haven't listened to it yet ... Last week I got [2] ________ (hand) a load of work to do by my boss, and I've just had no time. She has me [3] ________ (work) all hours right now.

R Well, listen when you manage to get everything [4] ________ (do).The thing is, I think a lot of this generation gap stuff is exaggerated. Like, we think that parents are too lenient today, kids are used to [5] ________ (have) everything done for them, and that goes to their head.

O That sounds true enough. You know my youngest, Tessa? I got her [6] ________ (make) her own bed, and you should have seen the look on her face! When I was that age my parents had us [7] ________ (work) from 6:00 in the morning.

R Oh, come on! You delivered newspapers twice a week. This is just what I mean – the generation gap is something we've imagined, and we have been fooled into believing it.

d Now go back to p. 47.

5A Relative clauses

05.01 Defining and non-defining relative clauses

Defining relative clauses are essential to the meaning of a sentence:
The law ***that was recently passed*** *makes no sense.*
*The man (****who****)* ***he attacked*** *is recovering in the hospital.*
Non-defining relative clauses are not essential; they give us additional information about nouns. In non-defining relative clauses, we cannot use the relative pronoun *that* or leave out object pronouns:
*German law****, which is based on Roman law,*** *is quite different.*
NOT ~~*that is based*~~
*The victim****, who we cannot name for security reasons,*** *is recovering in the hospital.* NOT ~~*The victim, we*~~
Non-defining relative clauses are separated by commas in writing and pauses in speech.

05.02 Relative pronouns

- ***when / where / why***

With nouns that refer to time like *time* and *day*, and after *place* or *somewhere*, we can use *that* instead of *when*/*where* or no pronoun in informal language:
*The 1930s was the time (****when****/****that****) organized crime flourished.*
*Take me somewhere (****where****/****that****) I can relax for a few days.*
After ***reason***, we can use ***why***/***that*** or no pronoun:
*Does anyone know the reason (****why****/****that****) crime is so high?*

- ***which***

We can use *which* to talk about a whole clause, not just a noun phrase:
She lied on her interview form, ***which*** *was a bad sign.*
We all get along well, ***which*** *is fantastic.*
We can use *which* after prepositions and before nouns in fixed phrases like *in which case, the chance of which,* (neutral) *at which time, the result*/*outcome of which, the likelihood of which* (formal):
It would seem that the guilty person has been found, ***in which case*** *you are free to go.*
A major police operation started, ***the result of which*** *was that six people were arrested.*

- ***who / whom / whose***

We usually use *who* as subject and object in relative clauses, but we can use *whom* in formal written language. We use *whom* (not *who*) after prepositions:
Mr. Brown, ***who****/****whom*** *the police suspect of arson, was released without charge.*
Mr. White, ***to whom*** *the police gave a warning, was held overnight.*
NOT ~~*to who*~~
We use *whose* as a possessive of people and animals:
The elderly woman ***whose*** *bag was taken was really upset.*

- ***none of whom / all of which / some of whose***

We can use quantifiers like *some, none,* and *few* with ***of whom, of which,*** and ***of whose*** in non-defining relative clauses:
Three suspects were interviewed, ***all of whom*** *were released without charge.*
Carter is accused of three crimes, ***none of which*** *he admits to.*

- ***whoever / whatever / wherever / whenever***

We use the indefinite pronouns *whoever, whatever, wherever,* and *whenever*, to mean "the person who," "the thing that," etc.:
Whoever *stole my sausage from the fridge is in big trouble!*

> **Tip** *What* is not a relative pronoun. We use it as a noun to mean "the thing which": *Young people today don't know* ***what*** *they want.*

Prepositions in relative clauses

We usually put prepositions at the end of relative clauses, but we can put them before the relative pronoun in formal language:
Prison is not the kind of place ***that*** *you would want to spend time* ***in****.*
Prison is not the kind of place ***in which*** *you would want to spend time.*
We keep the particles with the verb with multi-word verbs:
The children who I ***look after*** *at daycare are very naughty.*
NOT ~~*The children* ***after whom*** *I look*~~
Stealing from the kitchen is something that we will not ***put up with****.*
NOT ~~***with which*** *we will not put up*~~

He tried to make a getaway, **the chances of which** were very slim.

a Match the sentence halves.

1 [g] I don't want to stay anywhere
2 [ ] Give me one good reason
3 [ ] The letter took a week to arrive,
4 [ ] I might have made the mistake,
5 [ ] Ten people agreed to take part,
6 [ ] It was a long and confusing story,
7 [ ] That was the best excuse
8 [ ] We should not give up rights

a some of whom later dropped out.
b she could come up with.
c I should believe you.
d little of which was true.
e which is far too long.
f for which people have made great sacrifices.
g that doesn't have any decent facilities.
h in which case I'll apologize.

b Choose the correct option.

1 The emergency number is 911, *that* / *which* is easy to remember.
2 Mrs. Jackson, to *who* / *whom* we are very grateful, has kindly agreed to speak.
3 Florida is the only place *that* / *wherever* I want to live.
4 It's up to the person *what* / *whose* job it is to figure out the transportation.
5 The police arrived half an hour later, *by which time* / *by that time* the gang had escaped.
6 We recruited some younger staff, *few of whom* / *few of who* had any experience.
7 Most graduates lack the skills for *whom* / *which* there is the most demand.

c Use relative clauses to connect the sentences. Replace the words in **bold** and change the punctuation and word order as necessary.

1 Two criminals wanted to escape from the prison. They had been held **in it** for two years.
Two criminals wanted to escape from the prison, in which they had been held for two years.
2 The criminals shared a prison cell. **The floor of the cell** was over the city drainage system.
3 **They** were desperate for freedom. The prisoners built a tunnel. They could escape **through it**.
4 One night, they went down the tunnel. There was a full moon **then**.
5 The two criminals came out into a street. **The street** looked familiar.
6 They had come up outside the local police station. They had first been charged **at this police station**.
7 **All of them** knew the criminals by sight. The local police arrested them.
8 They took them back to the prison. They never tried to escape **from it** again.

d Now go to p. 57.

5B Willingness, obligation, and necessity

Obligation and necessity

We use *must* and *have to* to say what is necessary. *Must* only refers to the present or future:

*I'**ll have to** / I **must get** some more qualifications soon.*

*Irene **had to go** on a business trip, so I took her to the airport.* NOT ~~*must have gone*~~

Have got + infinitive also describes what is necessary, especially arrangements:

*My boss said I'**ve got to be** in the office by 8:00 tomorrow.*

We use *should* and *ought to* to say what is the right thing to do:

*I **ought to organize** my time more effectively.*

*You **shouldn't do** unpaid overtime.*

We use *had better* + base form in advice or threats:

*She'**d better see** a doctor before it's too late.*

*You'**d better be** early tomorrow!*

We can use *be supposed* + infinitive to say what is necessary according to some rules or instructions:

*The finance director **is supposed to authorize** all major expenditures.*

*I **was supposed to read** the report by tomorrow, but I never had time.*

You **are expected to be** flexible in this job.

Tip

We can use *It's up to* + person + *whether* to say somebody is not obliged to do something in informal language:

***It's up to** you **whether** you take this job, but I think it's a great offer.*

05.12 Other phrases for obligation / no obligation

These phrases are all followed by an infinitive:

need / don't need	*You **don't need to tell** me what went wrong. I was there.*
have no choice but	*Well, I **have no choice but to quit** then.*
be allowed	*We'**re not allowed to wear** jeans to work.*
be expected	*How can she **be expected to be** in two places at the same time?*
be free	*You'**re free to choose** whatever position you want.*
be required (formal)	*At the beginning, I **was not required to put in** very long hours.*
be advisable / permitted / forbidden / essential (formal)	*It **is advisable to wear** protective clothing.*
be obliged (formal)	*In our contract, we **are obliged to start** work at 8:00.*
be under (no) obligation (formal)	*I **am under no obligation to answer** to your demands.*

05.13 Willingness

will/can + base form	*Mason **won't work** for such a low salary.* *I **can work** on Saturday if you give me the Monday off.*
be happy/willing + infinitive	*I'd **be happy to help** out in the sales department.*
be prepared + *to* + base form / *for* + noun	*Bonnie **wasn't prepared for** the amount of paperwork.*
have no objection to verb + *-ing* / noun	*The staff **has no objection to taking** a pay cut.*
have nothing against verb + *-ing* / noun	*I **have nothing against** the new manager.*
have no problem with verb + *-ing* / noun	*My husband **has no problem with taking** care of the kids while I'm in the office.*

a Choose the correct option.

1 There's no way Maria *must* / *will* / *should* be prepared to see Terry again after what happened.
2 Kate has nothing *against* / *with* / *on* going camping, but she'd prefer a hotel.
3 Pilots are *essential* / *required* / *obligatory* to get a physical exam every six months.
4 When we lived in the village, we *must* / *were going to* / *had to* drive for miles to get to a supermarket.
5 Tony *should* / *ought* / *had better* to be taking care of that, but he's so lazy.
6 The match *had to* / *was supposed to* / *was required to* begin at 7:00, but heavy rain delayed the start.

b Rewrite the sentences with the words in parentheses.

1 Sylvia will organize the guest list. (happy)
Sylvia is happy to organize the guest list.
2 I don't mind waiting until the end. (objection)
3 I'm afraid the only way is to cancel the trip. (no choice)
4 Members of the public cannot go beyond this point. (forbidden)
5 You can decide when to leave. (up to)
6 Gerald will have to attend the meeting. (got)

c Complete the text with the phrases in the box.

~~be happy to~~ be under no obligation to be up to
be willing to be prepared have no choice but to
have nothing against ought to

Would you [1] *be happy to* work when you're 70? 80? The chances are that many of us will [2]________ do so because with an increasing number of people living well beyond retirement age, it is only to be expected that we will work into our old age. Those still working might be the lucky ones. Some people will [3]________ working past normal retirement age, but will employers [4]________ keep people on who are probably less healthy and less effective? The government believes people should [5]________ to invest in their own future. Government pension funds are just inadequate, and although we may [6]________ invest in private retirement funds at the moment, this looks like the only realistic solution. It will [7]________ you whether you take this option, but you [8]________ take it seriously because it may make your future a lot rosier.

d Now go to p. 61

6A Simple and continuous verbs

06.05 Simple verbs

We use simple verbs to talk about complete actions, events, or activities:
*I've **just taken** an amazing picture of two foxes.*
*We **trained** really hard for the marathon we **ran** in April.*
We use a simple verb when we say how much is complete or how many times something happens:
*I **went** to the Museum of Modern Art three times last year.*
*We **got** about half the work done.*
We use simple verbs to talk about facts and unchanging states:
*The camera **takes** up to ten photos per second in this mode.*
*My dad **was born** in Mexico City and **has never left**.*

06.06 Continuous verbs

We use continuous verbs to talk about incomplete or temporary activities:
*Brian **was trying** to take a picture, but someone got in the way.*
*I'm on a temporary contract, so **I'm** only **working** here for six months.*
We use continuous verbs to emphasize activity, duration, or repetition:
***I'm going** to classes to improve my photography.*
*In March, we **will have been living** here for four years.*
*Mandy **has been calling** me all day and **telling** me what to do.*
We can use continuous verbs with the adverbs *always, continually, constantly,* and *forever* to complain or express surprise about how frequently something happens:
*James **was constantly taking** photos of every little thing he saw.*
*It**'s always raining** in this part of the world.*

> **Tip**
> We can use the past continuous to be more polite or less direct:
> *I **was hoping** I could borrow your camera.*
> *Thank you for a lovely evening. It's time we **got going**.*

Verbs not usually used in the continuous

Some verbs are almost never used in the continuous, e.g., *know* and *suppose*:
*I **have known** Nina for ages.* NOT ~~*am knowing*~~
*I **don't suppose** you know where the paints are?* NOT ~~*'m not supposing*~~

Below are some verbs that are not usually used in the continuous:

Thinking

believe, despise, know, recognize, regard, suppose, realize
*I'm sure Trevor **despises** everything we are trying to do.*
NOT ~~*is despising*~~

The senses*

hear, see, smell, sound, taste
*We **have seen** a brilliant performance from Ronaldo.* NOT ~~*have been seeing*~~

Communicating

astonish, deny, impress, mean, satisfy, take (= *understand*)
*Nothing about his behavior that day **impressed** me.*
NOT ~~*was impressing*~~

Other

belong, consist, depend, fit, possess
*The corner office now **belongs** to you.*

*We use *can* + an ability verb like *hear, remember, see, taste* rather than a continuous form:
*I **can hear** somebody coming.* NOT *I* ~~*am hearing*~~

Verbs with different meanings in the simple and continuous

*Rachel **weighs** 170 pounds.* (a state)	*Rachel **is weighing** herself.* (an activity)
*What **do** you **think** about digital cameras?* (an opinion)	***I'm thinking** of going to art school.* (an activity)
*Ella **is** a difficult child.* (a characteristic)	*Ella**'s being** difficult.* (behavior)
*What can you **see** in this picture?* (see = look at) *Do you **see** what I mean?* (see = understand)	*The doctor **is seeing** a patient.* (see = meet)

a Match the sentences with the pictures.

1

a Chiara ate the chocolate.
b Chiara was eating the chocolate.

2

a Simon took a bath.
b Simon was taking a bath.

3

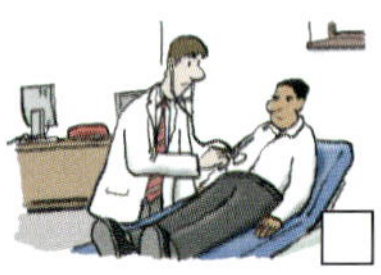

a Sam is a doctor.
b Sam is being a doctor.

4

a Nina comes from Russia.
b Nina is coming from Russia.

b Choose the best option.

1 I <u>*think*</u> / *'m thinking* photography is more about technology than art.
2 I'll *be learning* / *learn* English for the rest of my life.
3 *Are you* / *Are you being* obstinate just to annoy me?
4 Everyone had *left* / *been leaving*, and there was complete silence.
5 Jon *thinks* / *'s thinking* of joining the army next year.
6 *Do you realize* / *Are you realizing* how this makes me look?
7 Someone has *been gossiping* / *gossiped* and I'm really upset.
8 Unemployment *increases* / *is increasing*, but the government doesn't care.
9 We *opened* / *were opening* our first office in summer 2012.
10 I *suppose* / *'m supposing* we'll have to wait for the bus.

c Complete the text with either the simple or continuous form of the verbs in parentheses.

Roma So do you [1] ___think___ (think) graffiti could be called art?
Judy Why not? Graffiti has a long tradition, and we know the Romans [2] ________ (have) it.
R Yes, but people have [3] ________ (complain) about graffiti for a long time, too. I must admit that every time I [4] ________ (see) a wall covered in the stuff, it annoys me.
J Well, obviously you have [5] ________ (decide) that real art [6] ________ (belong) in museums and nowhere else. Graffiti is the most natural form of street art there is. Haven't you [7] ________ (watch) that series on TV lately about popular art? It has [8] ________ (change) my idea of art for good. Actually, I have always [9] ________ (want) to be good at art.
R What [10] ________ (say)? Are you going to go out and paint some graffiti on a train station wall?
J No, I don't think train passengers would think much of that.

d Now go back to p. 70.

6B Participle clauses

We use participle clauses to add more information to a sentence:
Hiding behind the bushes, *I held my breath.*
The stranger staggered into the room, ***shaking and covered in snow***.

Participle clauses after nouns

We can sometimes use participle clauses after nouns and pronouns. They are similar to defining relative clauses that have continuous and passive verbs. Look at the following examples:
We found the wallet (that was) ***lying by the side of the road***.
Everybody (who had been) ***affected by the fire*** *was told to leave their homes.*
The streets were full of people (who were) ***dancing for joy***.
Alice in Wonderland *was the* **book** *(that was)* ***chosen*** *by the majority of students.*
Joanna is a **woman who says** *what she thinks.* NOT ~~*woman saying*~~ (*says* is not a continuous verb)
The ***building that collapsed*** *was to be rebuilt.* NOT ~~*building collapsed*~~ (*collapsed* is not a passive)
The subject of a participle clause must be the same as the main clause:
The **boat** *that we were waiting for was late.* NOT ~~*the boat waiting for*~~

> **Tip**
> We can use participle clauses with verbs not usually used in continuous tenses:
> *You will come to a large rock* ***resembling*** *a castle.* = rock that resembles a castle NOT ~~*rock that is resembling*~~
> *I wasn't sure where to go,* ***not being a local***.

Participle clauses as adverbials

We use participle clauses as adverbials in formal language and writing:
Approaching an intersection, *I observed a car making an illegal turn.*
Left by themselves, *young children can get into all sorts of trouble.*
Adverbial participle clauses say why, when, where, and how:
Frightened by what he saw, *he never returned.*
= *Because he was frightened …*
Having thought it over, *I've decided to refuse their offer.*
= *Because I've thought about it …*
Stopping for a break, *we discussed what to do next.*
= *After we stopped …*
Standing by the fire, *Mary thought about her next step.*
= *While she stood …*
Climbing out of the window, *he managed to escape.* = *By climbing …*
Using my knife, *I forced the box open.* = *With my knife …*

Participle clauses always start before or at the same time as the main verb in the sentence:
The man ***running alongside me*** *tripped and fell.*
Sensing I was being watched, *I looked into the shadows.*
We can make it very clear a participle clause begins earlier by using the perfect form:
Having finally found a job, *I called my parents with the happy news.*
Not having seen the incident, *I'm not the best person to tell you what happened.*

> **Tip**
> We can use -ed adverbial participle clauses after time conjunctions in formal language:
> ***When faced with danger***, *most people would just panic.*
> *The vacation of a lifetime!* ***Once experienced***, *it will never be forgotten.*

Standing as still as he could, he waited for the next throw.

a Check (✓) the correct sentences. Correct the mistakes you found in the remaining sentences.

1 ☐ ~~Tony r~~R unning at full speed, he managed to jump on the train.
2 ☐ Remembering my appointment, I jumped up and left.
3 ☐ I will find the person committed this crime.
4 ☐ There was a terrible smell coming from the room.
5 ☐ Offering to pay for the damage, he had caused the accident.
6 ☐ Reading the letter, my hands were shaking in excitement.
7 ☐ Not belonging to the group, I felt very out of place.
8 ☐ Johnny is the kind of man never arriving anywhere on time.

b Complete the beginning of the story with the participle clauses in the box.

being realistic	coming outside	~~following me~~
being overworked and underpaid	getting stressed out	
waiting to strike	wearing orange	

I knew that there was a man [1] following me. That morning, [2] ___, I saw him again. The strange thing was that he made no effort to hide; [3] ___, he seemed to want to be seen. Anyway, [4] ___, what could I do? [5] ___, the local police would hardly have time to listen to my suspicions. It wasn't exactly the crime of the century, either. Maybe it was just me [6] ___ as a result of too much work. As things turned out, my stalker, [7] ___, was a very serious threat indeed.

c Rewrite the next part of the story using participle clauses where possible.

I went to the café on the street corner. ~~I sat down and~~ Sitting down, I ordered a piece of cake. A piece of cake that was covered in chocolate was quickly brought over to my table. I noticed something that was sticking out from under the cake, so I lifted it up. Underneath I found a note that was written in red that said, "Get into the car that is waiting across the road." I was frightened by the tone and I feared the worst, so I did what the note said. A thousand negative thoughts were crowding my head when I got to the car. The familiar figure who was dressed in orange was in the front seat, with a sinister smile on his face. "We meet at last," he said.

d Now go back to p. 73.

7A Speculation and deduction

07.05 Certain speculations: *will / going to*

We use *will* to speculate with certainty about the future. We add *have* + past participle to speculate about past actions with an effect on the present. We use *going to* for strong predictions based on present evidence. We often use adverbs with *will* and *going to* to modify the degree of certainty:

*Paper books **probably won't** disappear altogether.*
*I'm sure she **will have arrived** by now. Let's go and see.*
*It's a terrible movie! It's **hardly going to** win an Oscar.*

07.06 Certain deductions: *must / have got to*

We use *must* and *have got to* (informal) to say something is logically true in the present and future (make a deduction based on evidence). We use *must* + *have* + past participle to deduce about the past:

*Lisa is all dressed up. She **must be going** somewhere nice.*
*Joy didn't hear the phone. She **must have been sleeping**.*
*I don't believe it! You**'ve got to be joking.***

07.07 Likely: *should / may well*

We use *should* about the past, present, and future to say that something is probable because it is normal and expected. *May well* is slightly more certain than *should*:

*It's 6:00, so they **should have arrived** by now. / **should be arriving** soon.*
*Solar power **may well be** the answer to our energy problems.*

07.08 Possible and unlikely: *could / might / may / can*

We use *could, may* (*not*), and *might* (*not*) both to speculate and deduce in the past, present, and future:

*Fuel **could/may (not)/might (not)** run out in the near future.* NOT ~~*can*~~
*Jill is late. She **could/might/may have gotten** lost. She **could/might/may be wandering** around out there.* NOT ~~*can*~~

We also use *could* + *have* + past participle to say what was hypothetically possible in the past:

*I didn't know you were in town. We **could have met** up.*

We use *can* to say that something is generally possible in the present/future:

*You **can** see bears in the woods at this time of the year.*

07.09 Impossible: *can't / couldn't*

Couldn't + base form says what was generally impossible in the past. *Can't* + base form says what is generally impossible in the present and future. We also use *can't/couldn't* + *have* + past participle (past) or *can't* + *be* (+ verb + *-ing* / *going to*) (present/future) to say something is logically impossible:

*They **couldn't get** here yesterday. They **can't get here** today or tomorrow.* = impossible
*The exam **can't/couldn't have been** very difficult if you finished in 20 minutes.* = logically impossible
*Jeffrey **can't be working** on a Sunday evening. The building's closed.*

Couldn't + *have* + past participle also says what was impossible in the hypothetical past:

*I **couldn't have passed** the exam without Peter's help.* (= I passed because of his help; it was hypothetically impossible without this.) NOT *I* ~~*can't have passed*~~ …
*"I should have invited her." "Don't worry, she **couldn't have come** anyway."* (= In the hypothetical situation in which she was invited, it was impossible for her.) NOT ~~*She can't have come*~~ …

07.10 Other expressions

*We **are bound to** find a cure for cancer one day.* (= certain speculation)
*You **can tell (that)** John is intelligent from the books he reads.* (= certain deduction)
*In the future, it**'s (highly) likely** (**that**) cars will be electric.* (= likely)
***I bet / I reckon / I'm quite sure** (**that**) most movies will be in 3D.* (= likely)
***There's a/an outside/slim/good chance** (**that**) I'll be the only applicant.*
***There's no way / It's highly unlikely** (**that**) there is life on Mars.*

a Choose the best option.

1 Don't worry, we *might* / *will* / *can* arrive in plenty of time.
2 The two teams are equally matched, and it *'s going to* / *may* / *can* be a great game.
3 It's *highly* / *absolutely* / *completely* unlikely that government policy will change.
4 Food prices *should* / *must* / *could* get out of control.
5 I'm sure Andrew *could* / *can* / *will* have realized that it was only a joke.
6 There's a *slim* / *narrow* / *minor* chance that they will change their mind.
7 In fact, you *must* / *can* / *should* find people who live on less than a dollar a day.
8 Someone *must* / *can* / *should* have leaked the news; it's all over the Internet.
9 We *must not* / *needn't* / *can't* have run out of milk. I got some this morning.
10 You *can* / *must* / *should* tell they get along. They're always laughing and joking.

b Rewrite these sentences using the words in parentheses.

1 It was impossible for Adam to do any more. (couldn't)
Adam couldn't have done any more.
2 I'm sure that customers will complain. (bound)
3 It is very possible that I'll see Ian tomorrow. (well)
4 I think Barbara broke the window; she was playing around here. (must)
5 There's no way the referee saw the incident. (can't)
6 Damien probably knows the answer. (should)
7 It's obvious to me that Greta is dissatisfied. (tell)
8 The lights are on, so Karen will be at home. (got)

c Check (✓) the words 1–10 in *italics* that are possible. Correct the mistakes you find.

Could
[1] ~~*May*~~ time travel become a reality? Scientists have been contemplating the idea for centuries, and in movies like *Back to the Future* and *Predestination* we [2] *might* get the idea that time travel is a real possibility. In many ways, this is wishful thinking; it [3] *will* be amazing to go back to ancient Egypt and see the pyramids being built. Unfortunately, there's [4] *not way* that time travel is possible at our current stage of technological development. Maybe if we [5] *could* travel close to, even beyond, the speed of light, new horizons [6] *might* open up, but that is a distant possibility. Still, if we [7] *can* build a machine to approach the speed of light, the laws of physics would change and we [8] *must* enter new territory. This all sounds [9] *as fantasy* and, sadly for science fiction fans, it is until we make some incredible breakthroughs. Time travel [10] *can't* be happening anytime soon, but we can dream and watch the movies, of course.

d Now go back to p. 81.

7B Cleft sentences

We use cleft sentences to correct, emphasize, or point out information. We form **a focusing phrase ending in *be*** at the beginning of the sentence.

07.16 *Wh-* cleft sentences

Reading other people's comments online bores me.
***What bores me is** reading other people's comments online.*

What	noun	verb phrase	be	information focused on
What	she	suggested	was	out of the question.
What		went wrong	was	that Sheila got involved.
What		is amazing	is	that nobody found out.

Tip

- *be* can be plural if what follows it is plural:
  *What patients demand **is/are** better hospitals.*
- In informal speech we can also use *where/when/why/how* in the *Wh-* cleft structure:
  ***Where I was born is** Shanghai.*
  ***How I feel is** angry.*
  ***Why I left was** to get a job.*

We frequently emphasize an action or activity with *What* + *happen* + *be* + (*that*) + clause:
***What happened was that** we had to throw all the food away.*
***What happens is that** you get a quick orientation on your first day.*
We can emphasize actions with *What* + noun phrase + *do* + *be* + (*to*) + base form:
***What she did was** (to) phone the police.*
***What Sheila had wanted was** to get married.*

- ***All***
  We can begin cleft sentences with *all*:
  ***All (that) she wants is** a new phone.*
  ***All I did was** ask her how she was feeling.*
- ***The thing / One thing*, etc.**
  We can begin cleft sentences with *the first thing, the main thing*, etc.
  ***The main thing is** that you two stop arguing.*
  ***One thing you can do is** to promise it won't happen again.*
- ***The place where / time when / reason why***
  We use *place where, time when,* and *reason why* to emphasize a place, time, or reason. We can use *that* instead of *where, when,* and *why*:
  ***The place (where) I was born is** Miami.*
  ***The time (when) you find out who your real friends are is** when you have no money.*
  ***The only reason (why) I stay in this job is** Mike.*
  ***The main reason (why) I do it is** to make a little money.*

07.17 *It* cleft sentences

Cathy had the idea.
***It was** Cathy who had the idea.*

It	be	information focused on (noun/place/time phrase)	that / which / when clause
It	is	technology	that is causing increased shyness.
It	was	the weekend already	when she got back to me.
It	is	working all day for nothing	which gets me down.
It	is	only in big cities	that smog is a problem.

We can also emphasize time with *It is/was not until … that* and *It is/was only when … that*:
***It was not until** Lesley went away **that** I realized how much I missed her.*
***It's only when** I'm alone **that** I feel insecure.*

What technology does is to bring people together.

a Match the sentence halves.

1 [e] What he wanted was
2 [ ] What I did was
3 [ ] It was my teacher
4 [ ] All you can do is
5 [ ] It's only when we're busy
6 [ ] What happened was

a write an angry letter back.
b that the problems start.
c that the boat started to sink.
d who encouraged me to write.
e to change the world.
f try harder next time.

b Correct the mistakes in the sentences.

1 ~~There~~ It is Paris that I've always wanted to visit.
2 The captain of the ship was she who sensed the storm coming.
3 All what students want is an affordable educational system.
4 All she did was taking out the cable.
5 What happens next is to fill out an application form.
6 The most important thing is which he is innocent.
7 What was the weather that was beginning to worry me.
8 Is a unique situation that we find ourselves in.

c Rewrite the sentences as cleft sentences using the words in parentheses.

1 I want coffee. (what) What I want is coffee.
2 I only need ten dollars. (all)
3 Nobody wants to do this job. (it)
4 You are asking for something unreasonable. (what)
5 We chose Portugal because of the friendly people. (reason)
6 Our car ran into a tree. (happened)
7 Her cousin was causing all the trouble. (it)
8 I don't know Jason so well and this bothers me. (the thing)

d Now go back to p. 83.

8A Gerunds and infinitives

Gerunds

Gerunds are *-ing* forms that function as nouns in a sentence. The whole clause becomes a gerund when we add *-ing* to the verb:

sleep too much ➔ ***Sleeping too much*** *is as bad as* ***sleeping too little***.

We can form compound nouns with gerunds:

sleeping pills, ***on-the-job training***

Gerunds are much more common than infinitives as subjects:

Staying in bed all day *is not a great use of your time.*

To stay in bed all day is … = unusual

We use gerunds after prepositions and certain expressions, such as *it's (not) worth, it's no good/use, there's no point (in)*:

I am interested ***in becoming*** *a member of your club.*

NOT ~~*in to become*~~

Do you ever get tired ***of Jill getting home*** *late every night?*

NOT ~~*of Jill to get*~~

Was it worth spending *all that money on a sofa bed?*

There's no point worrying *and* ***losing sleep*** *over it.*

Infinitives

We use the base form (infinitive without *to*) after modal verbs, expressions like *had better, would rather*, some verbs like *let* and *make*, and as imperatives:

The situation may well ***get*** *worse before it gets better.*

I would rather ***sleep*** *in my own bed than in a hotel room.*

Be *quiet! Let me* ***have*** *some sleep tonight.*

We use an infinitive after …

- many adjectives, comparatives, superlatives, and ordinal numbers:
  I was ***delighted to hear*** *that you had won first prize.* NOT ~~*delighted hearing*~~
  Who is the ***greatest*** *athlete ever* ***to represent*** *the United States?* NOT ~~*representing*~~
  She was the ***first*** *woman* ***to climb*** *Everest.* NOT ~~*climbing*~~
- nouns formed from verbs that take the infinitive, e.g., *agreement, decision, plan* but NOT *expectation* or *hope*, which take *of* + gerund:
  Sally made a ***decision to resign***.
  I had ***hopes of getting*** *on the team.* NOT ~~*hopes to get*~~
  For verb patterns with gerunds and infinitives see p. 176.
- *time*
  It's ***time to go*** *to bed.*
  There's still ***time to register*** *for the competition.*
- quantifiers like *enough, little,* and *many* + nouns
  Do you have ***enough*** *money* ***to start*** *your own business?*
  I've seen ***too many*** *movies like that* ***to be*** *very impressed.*

▶ 08.02

	Active gerunds	Passive gerunds
Present	***Shouting*** *a lot isn't very good for your voice.* *I can't stand* ***not knowing*** *what I'm supposed to do.*	*Winning is better than* ***being beaten***. *What I resent is* ***not being given*** *the opportunity to show what I can do.*
Perfect	*I'm sorry for ever* ***having mentioned*** *the subject.* *I regret* ***not having contacted*** *you earlier.*	*The star denied* ***having been seen*** *with the actor.* *The worst thing is* ***not having been told***.

▶ 08.03

	Active infinitives	Passive infinitives
Simple	*I'll* ***come***. *Try* ***to help***, *if you can.*	*Don't* ***be put off*** *by the noise.* *This offer is* ***not to be missed***.
Continuous	*I'd rather* ***be going*** *with you.* *She seems* ***to be feeling*** *better.*	*It should* ***be being done*** *as we speak.* *The space seems* ***to be being used*** *as a parking lot.* (unusual)
Perfect	*You'd better* ***have finished*** *by the time I get back.* *It's important* ***to have tried***.	*Louise must not* ***have been treated*** *very well.* *I wouldn't like* ***to have been given*** *that job.*
Perfect continuous	*We will* ***have been seeing*** *each other for two years in April.* *I'm proud* ***to have been working*** *here for so many years.*	*Joe must* ***have been being bullied*** *at school.* (unusual)

Tip

Perfect forms of gerunds and infinitives stress that the activity is in the past and complete. We can often use present forms with exactly the same meaning:

Her proudest moment to date is ***having won*** / ***winning*** *Olympic gold.*

I wasn't happy at ***having been compared*** / ***being compared*** *to someone 20 years older.*

You were supposed ***to have finished*** / ***to finish*** *it yesterday.*

Tip

Some adjectives, e.g., *afraid, sorry, sure*, are followed by the gerund or infinitive with a difference in meaning:

I'm ***sure to see*** *Tom at work on Monday.*

sure = focus on probability of something happening

I'm ***sure seeing*** *Tom again will be amazing.*

sure = focus on emotion / effect of something happening

---

a Choose the correct option.

1 *Choosing* / *Having chosen* / *To be chosen* a pillow that is right for your back is not easy.
2 *Picking* / *Being picked* / *Having been picked* for my college team would be a great achievement.
3 There was no point *waiting* / *having been waited* / *to wait* for him.
4 Jane is furious with me for *mislead* / *having misled* / *having been misled* her.
5 The suspect claims *to have been visiting* / *to be visiting* / *to have been visited* her sister at that time.
6 I would prefer *not to have known* / *to have known not*.
7 Sorry, but there are too few players *to have* / *having* a real game.
8 There's no use *having complained* / *complaining* / *to complain* about it all the time.
9 Look, it's time *to forget* / *forgetting* everything that happened.
10 The views from the top are worth *describing* / *to be described* in detail.

b Correct the mistakes in the gerunds and infinitives in *italics*.

Is it possible for someone never [1]~~*to be sleeping*~~ to sleep? The answer is (almost) yes if you have Fatal Familial Insomnia, in which [2]*to have fallen* asleep is almost impossible. For sufferers, it's not even worth them [3]*to go* to bed because sleep won't come. As the name suggests, [4]*affecting* by this rare but dreadful condition can cause death, depending on its severity. If we don't get enough sleep [5]*carry out* our day-to-day life, the damage to our physical and mental health can be very serious. [6]*To not sleep* for days often makes people [7]*to feel* weak and disoriented. There can be some benefit in [8]*being taken* sleeping pills, but this puts a different kind of stress on the body, and the drugs can become addictive. There is a need for more research [9]*doing* in this area, and it is sure [10]*being* a very deserving way for government money [11]*to be spending*.

c Now go back to p. 93.

8B Conditionals

We often refer to conditionals as real, unreal, and mixed. These are useful reference points for verb forms, but there are many variations with different tenses and conjunctions.

08.09 Real and unreal conditionals

In real conditionals there is no change of use of verb forms. We use present tenses in the *if* clause:

Present Real *If I **want** a snack, I **have** one.*

Future Real *She'**ll recover** quickly if her temperature **goes** down.*

In unreal conditionals we show that a situation is hypothetical or unlikely by changing the verb forms back one tense:

Present and Future Unreal *If it **weren't raining**, I **would go** out somewhere.* (It is raining now.)

*If it **was**/**were*** my choice, we'd go to the spa.*

*We can use *If … was* or *If … were.*

Past Unreal *Megan **wouldn't have missed** her plane if she **hadn't lost** her passport.* (She lost her passport.)

*The car **could have gone** off the road if he **had been driving** any faster.*

Mixed *I **would speak** French more fluently **if I had been allowed** to study in France.*

*If I **knew** what you wanted, I'**d have done** it a long time ago.*

> **Tip**
> We can put *had, should,* and *were* first instead of *if*. This is formal.
> ***Had I known** about your plans earlier, I would have acted differently.*
> ***Should her condition get worse**, we will contact you immediately.*
> ***Were humans to live** so long, there would be many health complications.*

08.10 Other conjunctions

as long as** / **so long as** / **on the condition that = only if ***in the event of*** **+ noun** (formal)	*You can borrow my shirt **so long as** you don't get it dirty.* *Goods can be returned **on the condition that** you have the original receipt.* *Assemble outside the school **in the event of** a fire.*
if **+** ***it*** **+** ***be*** **+** ***not for*** **+ noun phrase** ***but for*** **+ noun phrase** (formal)	***If it were not for** Simon, I would never have known about the cucumber diet.* *The negotiations would have failed **but for** my efforts.*
providing** / **provided that = if	*The material will be ready **providing that** you give plenty of notice.* ***Provided that** you repay it within three months, the bank will issue the loan.*
***suppose** / **imagine** (**that**)*	***Suppose** we could live to 100; what would we look like?* ***Imagine** there were no school today. Wouldn't that be great?*
assuming** / **supposing = this might be the case	*Let's meet on Sunday, **assuming** that is everyone's day off.* ***Supposing** you could find the treasure, what would you do with it?*
(*just*) *in case* + possible situation or result = as a precaution ***in case of*** **+ noun** (formal)	*Write down the phone number **just in case** you forget it.* ***In case of** emergency, call this number.*
otherwise **+ possible result** = if not that, then this	*I need to get to bed, **otherwise** I won't be able to get up on time.* *I didn't see her, **otherwise** I would have told her.*

a Match the sentence halves.

1 [j] If Sandra gets here early,
2 [ ] If she had said that to me,
3 [ ] If I'm still working in an hour,
4 [ ] If you had bothered to ask,
5 [ ] If the story were to get out,
6 [ ] I don't mind going to the party
7 [ ] I'm happy to share,
8 [ ] If it hadn't been for night school,
9 [ ] I'd better get on with my work
10 [ ] Figure it out yourselves,

a I could have explained everything.
b in case the boss is here today.
c I'd be absolutely furious.
d provided that I can choose first.
e otherwise I'll have to get involved.
f stop me and tell me to go to bed.
g I would never have met my wife.
h it wouldn't look very good for the firm.
i as long as it doesn't finish too late.
j let her in for me, please.

b Put the conditional sentences in order, adding commas where necessary. The first word is highlighted.

1 this / you / hard / **if** / think / wait / is / just
If you think this is hard, just wait.
2 you / I / with / **if** / I / were / a / have / would / her / word
3 **you** / quiet / stay / as / can / you / keep / long / as
4 anyone / me / to / **if** / is / blame / it's
5 disappointed / **Sheila** / have / come / been / would / had / if / nobody
6 is / agree / that / on / this / only / will / the / confidential / condition / **I** / kept
7 to / you / I / find / will / the / be / out / know / **should** / first
8 assuming / we / everything / need / **it** / take / won't / long / have / we

c Now go back to p. 96.

9A Reflexive and reciprocal pronouns

09.04 Reflexive pronouns

We use reflexive pronouns …

- when the object is the same as the subject:
  *They blamed **themselves** for the accident.*
  *She's always looking at **herself** in the mirror.*
- after verbs and prepositions:
  *The director of the bank awarded **himself** a big bonus.*
  *Don't be angry with **yourself**.*
  *I said to **myself** that I would try again the next day.*
- after nouns and pronouns to emphasize importance, and for contrast with other people/things in general:
  *The president **himself** has shares in the company.*
  *The boss **herself** does not believe any of these rumors.*
- after the verb phrase to emphasize independence/achievement:
  *We designed the house **ourselves**.*
  *They cleaned up the city **themselves**.*
- after the verb phrase to show similarity to another person/thing = *as well*
  *He went to take a shower. I needed one **myself**.*

Cars that park **themselves** do save a lot of space.

We use *by* + reflexive pronoun to mean without anybody else:
*My friends were busy, so I went into town **by myself**.*
We use *beside* + reflexive pronoun to mean worried/upset:
*After the last heavy defeat, the manager is **beside himself**.*
Some verbs have a different meaning when the object is a reflexive pronoun:
*He didn't **behave himself**.* = behave well
*Just **be yourself** in the interview.* = act naturally
*You don't want to **find yourself** alone.* = get into a situation
*I **helped myself** to the sandwiches.* = take without invitation
*I did**n't feel myself**.* = feel different from usual
Verbs that are usually done by an individual, for example *shave, wash*, etc., don't need a reflexive pronoun, unless we want to make a point of the ability:
I washed and dressed in five minutes.
*The twins are old enough to dress **themselves**.*
In English we do not generally use the verbs *concentrate, feel, hurry, lie* (*down*), *relax, sit* (*down*) with reflexive pronouns:
Rebecca didn't feel comfortable living in such a huge city.
NOT ~~*feel herself*~~
I spent some time relaxing before the busy day ahead.
NOT ~~*relaxing myself*~~
I concentrated on my work. NOT ~~*concentrated myself*~~

09.05 Reciprocal pronouns

We use *each other* and *one another* with plural subjects:
*We always speak to **each other** with the utmost respect.*
One another is more formal than *each other*. It is often used when more than two people are involved:
*We chatted with **each other**.*
*They greeted **one another** before addressing the room.*
Compare reflexive and reciprocal pronouns:
*Mr. and Mrs. Smith bought **themselves** a car.* (one car for them both)
*Mr. and Mrs. Smith bought **each other** a present.* (two presents, one each)
*We smiled at **each other** and said hello.*
*We smiled to **ourselves** but gave no sign of any emotion.*
We use the possessives *each other's* and *one another's*:
*They were friends and regular visitors at **each other's** houses.*
*The purpose of this session is to listen to **one another's** problems sympathetically.*

---

a Match a and b in each pair with the best endings.

1 a ☐ We looked at ourselves
  b ☐ We looked at each other
  1 and smiled.
  2 in the mirror.

2 a ☐ They usually behave themselves
  b ☐ They usually behave
  1 when the teacher's around.
  2 better when the teacher's around.

3 a ☐ Mike helped him
  b ☐ Mike helped himself
  1 clean up the room.
  2 to a slice of cake.

4 a ☐ He looked really upset, so I sat down
  b ☐ He looked really upset. He was
  1 beside himself.
  2 beside him.

5 a ☐ They found themselves
  b ☐ They finally found each other
  1 after searching for hours.
  2 in a very awkward situation.

6 a ☐ The three medalists shook hands to
  b ☐ Atlético Madrid can
  1 congratulate themselves on their success.
  2 congratulate each other on their success.

b Choose the correct option.

1 I think we'll treat *us / ourselves* to a nice box of chocolates.
2 *John himself / Himself* would never have thought of that.
3 Laura only thinks of *each other / herself*. She's so selfish.
4 "Can I borrow a pen?" "Sorry, I don't have one *myself / itself*."
5 You don't need to help. I can do the puzzle *itself / myself*.
6 Dom can't imagine *by himself / himself* in a different job.
7 They kissed *one another / themselves* and said goodbye.
8 The students checked *each other's / each others'* answers.

c Add the missing reflexive and reciprocal pronouns.

Have you ever thought to ask ^yourself whether you would like to live in space? As the world population grows, towns and cities find under tremendous pressure, and it is becoming more difficult and expensive for us just to live in urban areas, let alone enjoy there. So maybe we would feel more comfortable in space. But, let's just remind of the challenges of doing such a thing. The technology may be there, but we would be opening up to lots of problems we can't even imagine. Unfortunately, there are no easy solutions. The world needs to sort out, and we need to learn to live with. I hope I've made clear.

d Now go to p. 106.

9B Ellipsis and substitution

We can avoid repeating our own or other people's ideas using ellipsis (leaving out words and phrases) and substitution (replacing words and phrases).

09.11 Leaving out subjects, main verbs, and auxiliaries

We can leave out repeated subjects, main verbs, and auxiliaries after *and/or/but/then* when the subject is the same:

The planning commission has spent a lot of money, but (it has) *changed nothing.*

The architect designed an iconic office tower, then (the architect designed) *a bridge.*

We usually can't leave out subjects and auxiliaries in clauses connected with words like *although/because/before/if/when*, etc.:

You can't comment because you have no appreciation of art.
NOT ~~*because have*~~

I changed my mind when I saw the building. NOT ~~*when saw*~~

09.12 Leaving out verb phrases

We can leave out repeated verb phrases and use an auxiliary or modal instead. The auxiliary or modal may change in the second verb:

The city council promised to ***build a new playground,*** *but it never* ***did.***

Graham said he would ***show you how to do it*** *and he* ***will.***

We shorten the infinitive to *to* but don't leave it out completely:

I needed to go shopping, but the kids didn't want to (go shopping).
NOT ~~*didn't want*~~

I haven't seen the exhibition, but I ought to (see it). NOT ~~*ought*~~

09.13 Other examples of ellipsis

We can leave out adjectives and repeat *be*:

I'm *quite comfortable here.* ***Are*** *you* (quite comfortable)*?*

The first room ***was*** *beautiful, but the second* ***wasn't*** (beautiful).

We can leave out noun phrases after determiners and superlatives:

This is ***my*** *favorite picture, and that's* ***my husband's*** (favorite picture).

There were a few apartments in my price range, and I chose the cheapest (apartment in my price range).

We can leave out repeated verbs and nouns in comparative structures:

They built the first floor quicker than (they built) *the second* (floor).

The Park is the most expensive hotel, and The Seaview (is) *the second* (most expensive hotel).

09.14 *so / neither / nor*

We use *so/neither* + auxiliary/*be* + subject to avoid repeating exactly the same idea for a new subject:

The old town is amazing, and ***so*** *are the views.* = the views are also amazing

If Gerald doesn't like it, ***neither/nor*** *will his wife.* = his wife also won't like it

nor can also mean *and not*:

She doesn't want to live in the country ***nor*** *in the town.* = and she doesn't want to live in the town

09.15 *so* and *not*

We can use *so* and *not* instead of clauses after verbs like *believe, guess, imagine, be afraid, appear, assume, seem, hope, presume, suspect,* and *say*:

We don't know if the diamond is real, but we think ***so.***

I suspect ***not*** *but I'm not sure, so ask someone else.*

We use a negative verb + *so* with verbs like *believe, expect, imagine,* and *think*:

I thought it would be a good game, but I don't think ***so*** *now.*

We can use *if not* and *if so* instead of clauses:

I hope you finish that report. ***If not,*** *give it to me anyway.*

Some of you look confused. ***If so,*** *see me after and I'll explain again.*

09.16 Pronouns

We can use pronouns like *one* and *ones* to substitute noun phrases:

There are ten different colors to choose from. Which ***ones*** *do you want?*

We can use *that* instead of a phrase or clause:

Don't interrupt me! I hate ***that.***

We can use possessive pronouns, *yours, mine,* etc., to substitute noun phrases:

You've got a decent view, but ***mine*** *is terrible.*

You know my views on private education, so tell me ***yours.***

---

a Cross out the words that can be left out of each sentence with no change of meaning.

1. The president arrived and he made a speech.
2. You don't know and you never will know.
3. I will tell you because I value and I respect your opinion.
4. We have been thinking about our reputation, we have not been thinking about money.
5. I said I would be volunteering, so I will be volunteering.
6. If they are hungry, bears can be dangerous and they can be unpredictable.
7. My first impression was very positive, but my second wasn't very positive.
8. We can meet up at seven if you'd like to meet up tonight.
9. "Are we in room six?" "I guess we are not in room six."
10. The Nile is the longest river in the world, and the Amazon is the second longest river in the world.

b Shorten the sentences using substitution.

1. My exam was a lot tougher than ~~your exam~~ yours.
2. "Is this the right page?" "I think it is the right page."
3. "I don't know where we are." "I don't know where we are, either."
4. I love vacations abroad, especially long vacations abroad.
5. "Who has a dress with short sleeves?" "Borrow my dress with short sleeves."
6. "Did you get my message?" "I'm afraid we didn't get it."
7. "George got married." "I didn't know George had gotten married."
8. Klaus is very enthusiastic and his sister is very enthusiastic, too.
9. Tina had always wanted to go parachuting, and one day she went parachuting.

c Use ellipsis and substitution to shorten the conversation and make it more natural.

Damien I've been thinking about the office of the future.

Rachel What do you mean by ~~the office of the future~~? that

D The place where we are going to work and where we are going to do business, say, 50 years from now. Those offices will look completely different compared to the offices today.

R I expect they will look completely different.

D For example, imagine there are no walls and there are no doors. All barriers to communication will be broken down and all barriers to communication will be a thing of the past. This is hard to imagine, but you don't need to imagine it. Just go to any successful company today.

R I think successful companies today have walls and have doors.

D You are being sarcastic and you are trying to make fun of me.

R Sorry, I didn't mean to make fun of you. I'd like to travel in time and I'd like to visit an office of the future. Tell me when you have built an office of the future.

d **Communication 9B** Work in pairs. Student A go to p. 135. Student B go to p. 136.

10A Regret and criticism structures

10.06 Conditionals

We can use unreal conditionals for (self-)criticism and regret. Using hypothetical forms to provide critical suggestions can soften your suggestions:

*You'**d get** a better response **if** you **toned** down your language.*
*I **wouldn't have come if** you'**d told** me you weren't interested.*
***If** you'**d been watching properly**, you'**d be able to do** it!*
***If** I'**d realized** my boss was going to be there, I **would never have said** that.*
***If** you **told** a few jokes, the audience **might listen**.*

10.07 Modals

We use modal + *have* + past participle for (self-)criticism and regret:

could	*I **could have timed** my talk better.*	*= It was desirable but didn't happen.*
might	*You **might have told** me he was going to be in the audience.*	
should	*You **should have asked** me first.*	*= It was the right thing to do, but it didn't happen.*
ought to	*We **ought to have checked** the equipment.*	
shouldn't	*He **shouldn't have taken** the car.*	*= It was the wrong thing to do, but it happened.*

Tip We can use *must* for criticism but not *must have*:
*You **must** listen more carefully in future!*
You should have listened more carefully. NOT ~~*must have listened*~~
Use the phrase *You shouldn't have* to show you are grateful for something:
*Wow, flowers! **You shouldn't have**.*

10.08 *would like / love / hate / rather / prefer*

We use *would like / love / prefer* + perfect infinitive to talk about regrets:
*I **would love to have spent** more time with you.*
We can use *would hate / not like* + perfect infinitive to sympathize:
*I **would hate to have seen** something like that.*
We use *would (much) rather* with a base form or past tense:
*I **would much rather** see my usual doctor **than** one I don't know.*
*I **would rather you didn't do** that in the future.*

10.09 *wish* and *if only*

We use *wish* + simple past for things that we want to change now or in the future:
*I **wish** I **looked** like Jennifer Lawrence.*
*My dad **wishes** he **could** speak Spanish.*
We use *wish* + past perfect for regrets:
*I **wish** I **had met** you ten years ago.*
We use *wish* + person + *would* for criticism:
*I **wish** you **would** switch off that cell phone!*
We use *if only* as a stronger form of *wish*:
***If only** Trevor **were** more understanding!*

10.10 *It's time*

We can use *it's (about/high) time* + past tense for criticism:
***It's time** you got a regular job.*
***It's about time** they came to repair the washing machine.*
***It's high time** she came to her senses and realized nobody is perfect!*

a Match the sentence halves in each pair.

1 a ☐ We could have gotten home
  b ☐ We could get home
  1 provided the trains are running.
  2 if the trains had still been running.

2 a ☐ I think if I had been in your shoes
  b ☐ If I were you
  1 I'd forget all about it.
  2 I would have forgotten all about it by now.

3 a ☐ You couldn't
  b ☐ You shouldn't
  1 have done a worse job.
  2 have reminded me.

4 a ☐ I wish you would listen to me;
  b ☐ I wish you had listened to me;
  1 I have something important to tell you.
  2 things might have turned out better.

b Choose the correct option.

1 Julie *couldn't* / *may not* have done it if I hadn't helped her.
2 If you *hadn't dropped* / *didn't drop* the ball, we would have won the game.
3 Staff *ought to* / *shouldn't* complain in front of the customers.
4 I *could* / *would* prefer not to be involved.
5 Jill *should be waiting* / *should have waited* until I got out.
6 You *might* / *should* have passed if you'd studied harder.
7 I'd much rather *hear* / *have heard* the news from you, but it's too late now.
8 We *hope* / *wish* you would reconsider.
9 Oh, I wish I *can* / *could* be there with you next weekend.
10 This bedroom is a mess! It's time you *clean* / *cleaned* it up.

c Fill in each blank with one word.

Michelle Hi, so how did the driving test go?
Ben It was a nightmare! I wish I [1] could start all over again. If I [2]______ known it would be that bad, I would have stayed in bed.
M What went wrong?
B What went right? I'd [3]______ not talk about it.
M Oh, go on. What did the examiner say?
B Oh, the usual stuff – "You [4]______ to have used your mirrors more, you [5]______ n't have stopped so quickly. If I [6]______ you, I'd slow down now …" Do you get the idea?
M Well, I suppose you [7]______ have had more lessons.
B If [8]______ I had had the time and the money.
M Maybe it's [9]______ you realized how important it is for you to get a driver's license.
B Oh no, now you're criticizing me!

d Now go back to p. 118.

10B Passive reporting verbs

We use passive reporting verbs when we are generalizing about what most people say or think:
The color white ***is known*** *to represent purity in many cultures.*
We also use passive reporting verbs to report information from other sources. They are most common in …
- academic writing where we want to appear objective:
It ***has been shown*** *(Smith, 2012) that superstition influences behavior.*
- news, either to keep the source secret or because the source is unimportant:
It ***is being reported*** *that the suspect escaped in a car.*

It + passive + that clause
We can use *it* + passive reporting verb + *that* clause with verbs like *know, believe, say, report,* etc.:
It is *widely* ***known that*** *the middle of the month was unlucky for the Romans.*
In ancient times, ***it was believed that*** *the sun went around the Earth.*

Subject + passive + infinitive
We can use passive + infinitive with verbs like *understand* and *think*:
He ***is understood*** *to be furious.*
It is ***thought to be*** *good luck to catch falling leaves in the autumn.*
We can follow this structure with perfect infinitives to refer to the past, or continuous infinitives for the present and future:
*She****'s said to have met*** *him on set.*
*He****'s reported to be working*** *with DeNiro again.*

It + passive + wh- clause
We use passive reporting verbs + clauses beginning with *wh-* words for unknown facts:
It is not known what *was said in the meeting.*
It was not made clear whether *or not they would be challenging the decision.*
The *wh-* clause can go first in the sentence:
What was said *in the meeting is not known.*

10.16

It + passive + *that* clause only: *announce argue imply note explain suggest*

It was ***announced*** *that changes would be made.* NOT ~~*were announced to be made*~~
It is ***argued*** *that Cleopatra was one of the most influential women in history.*
In the report it is ***implied*** *that corruption was involved.*
It should ***be noted*** *that he gave half of his winnings to charity.*
It was ***explained*** *that the mysterious marks were, in fact, animal tracks.*
It has not been ***suggested*** *that any jobs will be affected.*

Subject + passive + infinitive only: *consider repute*

Brian was ***considered*** *to be one of their best players.* NOT ~~*It is considered that Brian*~~ …
They are ***reputed*** *to have made millions from the sale of their company.*

Both structures: *acknowledge agree allege assume believe claim expect know report reveal suspect rumor say show think understand*

It is alleged that *five men in masks carried out the attack.*
The ship ***isn't expected to be arriving*** *anytime soon.*
She ***is reported to have made*** *over ten million dollars.*
It is said that *K2 is harder to climb than Everest.*
The story ***has been shown to be*** *a complete lie.*
Latin ***is thought to have been*** *the first international language.*

Subject + passive + *as* + adjective/noun phrase: *regarded* seen**

Serena Williams ***is regarded as*** *one of the greatest tennis players ever.* NOT ~~*It is regarded that Serena*~~
Sending cards on special occasions ***may be seen as*** *old-fashioned by some.*

**regarded/seen* + *to be* is possible but far less common.

Walking under a ladder ***is believed to be*** *unlucky!*

a Choose the correct option.
1 An old manuscript is said *to have / that it has* been found by a couple moving into the house.
2 *It / The news* is believed that it happened many years earlier.
3 In the letter it was implied *that Sam / Sam to have* released the data unknowingly.
4 Detectives *were revealed / revealed* that they still had no clues to work on.
5 Once she *was regarded / regarded* as one of the best painters of her generation.
6 It is to be expected *mistakes to be made / that mistakes will be made*.
7 Television has *been shown to / showed that* influence public opinion.

b Correct the mistakes in the sentences.
1 It *is* argued that Vancouver is the most diverse city in the world.
2 He is said that he lived in a cave.
3 It is seen that basketball is very popular in Asia.
4 It was not reported her reply was.
5 It is suspected to the people responsible have left the country.
6 The winters are thought that they get very cold in this part of the world.

c Complete the text with the past participle of a verb in the box.

consider expect explain imply know not understand see ~~think~~

There is significant cultural variation today, but it is [1] *thought* that one of the most common, yet oldest, customs is shaking hands. From vases and other archaeological evidence, the ancient Greeks are [2] ________ to have shaken hands, and the custom was [3] ________ as a sign of respect and affection. In fact, the handshake is [4] ________ to be a form of ritual because it is done in so many contexts with great attention to detail. For example, in Eastern Europe it is [5] ________ that a man's, but not a woman's, hand will be shaken every time you meet. In China, by holding on to someone's hand for a short time after a handshake, it is [6] ________ that you are showing extra respect. It is [7] ________ how the custom originated, but in some books it is [8] ________ that by offering your hand without a weapon you come in peace.

d Now go to p. 121.

1A Language learning

Verb phrases

a 01.05 Complete the expressions in **bold** with the words in the box. Listen and check.

ear	acquire	rusty	brushed
pick	struggle	keep	
come	accustomed	hold	
practice	immersed	attain	

1 Some learners appear to be able to ________ **language** without much formal study.
2 I really ________ **with** English idioms. I can never remember them.
3 I'm not sure if I'll ever ________ **a** native speaker **level** of competence, but I'm not sure I really need to.
4 When he went to live in Korea, he quickly **got** ________ **to** the sound of the language.
5 I've ________ **up on my** Arabic because I'm going to Riyadh next week.
6 Penny's lucky – she **has an** ________ **for** languages. She learns them much more easily than me.
7 After about a year, he found he could ________ **a conversation** in Italian without too much effort.
8 Unless I **put** a new piece of language **into** ________ immediately, I find I forget it.
9 People tend to give up on learning a second language too easily. You need to ________ **at it** if you want to succeed.
10 She spent six weeks in Poland and really ________ herself **in** the language and culture.
11 It's easy to ________ **up phrases** like "hello" and "excuse me" wherever you are in the world.
12 The sounds of Finnish are unique, so I found it difficult to ________ **to grips with** the pronunciation.
13 I need to practice my speaking now that I'm back. I'm sure I'm ________.

b Match the verbs 1–6 with the phrases a–f.

1 ☐ hold — a new ideas
2 ☐ grasp — b a level/degree of competence
3 ☐ get — c a conversation
4 ☐ put — d accustomed to
5 ☐ acquire — e into practice
6 ☐ attain — f a new/second language

c Now go back to p. 9.

Noun forms

d Complete the chart with the missing noun forms. Use a dictionary to help you if necessary.

Adjective	Noun	Verb
1 interactive		interact
2 distracted distracting		distract
3 dedicated		dedicate
4 limited		limit
5 motivated motivating		motivate
6 necessary		necessitate
7 capable		–
8 mental		–
9 reluctant		–
10 interfering		interfere
11 competent		–
12 literate		–
13 exposed		expose
14 –		acquire
15 insightful		–
16 prestigious		–
17 disciplined		discipline

e 01.08 **Pronunciation** Listen to some of the adjectives and nouns in the chart.

1 Which nouns have more syllables than their adjectives?
2 Notice the stressed syllables in the adjectives. Practice saying the words and underline the stressed syllables in the nouns. Listen again and check.
3 Notice that the stress sometimes changes in the noun. Choose the correct option to complete the rule.

In nouns with the suffixes *-tion* and *-ity*, the stressed syllable is always *the first syllable / the syllable before the suffix.*

Learning Tip Organizing your records of word families by suffix can make features such as sound and spelling relationships easier to remember.

f What other nouns do you know with the suffixes *-tion* and *-ity*? Make a list and practice saying the words.

g Now go back to p. 10.

2B Verbs of movement

a They **soared** into the air.

b She **hurtled** down the slope.

c They **zoomed** / **whizzed** along the road.

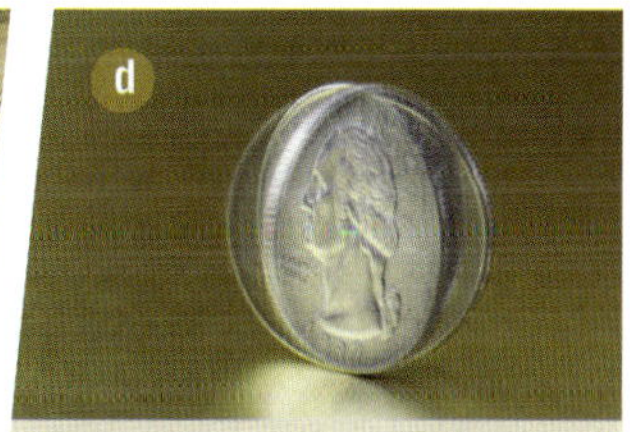
d It **rolled** across the floor.

e He **plunged** into the water.

f They **whirled** around the room.

g It **whooshed** through the station.

h

i

j

k

l

m

n

o

p

q

a 02.13 Match the sentences 1–10 with the pictures h–q. Listen and check.

1 ☐ He **crawled** up the stairs.
2 ☐ They **marched** through the square.
3 ☐ She **leaped** over the rocks.
4 ☐ It **drifted** out to sea.
5 ☐ He **crept** into the house.
6 ☐ He **limped** off the field.
7 ☐ He **staggered** across the desert.
8 ☐ We **slid** down the slope.
9 ☐ They **rushed** to catch the train.
10 ☐ They **strolled** through the park.

b Which verbs of movement in pictures a–q mean … ?

1 to move slowly
2 to move quickly
3 to move quietly
4 to move with difficulty

c Which verbs in **bold** in **a** are irregular past forms? What's the infinitive form of each?

d In pairs, take turns testing each other on prepositions of movement, using the sentences for pictures a–q. (Don't use picture h.)

He crawled ________ the stairs.

He crept ________ the house.

e Change the sentence *He*/*She*/*It* + (simple past verb of movement) *down the road* so that it matches the situations below. More than one verb may be possible.

1 He was a soldier. *He marched down the road.*
2 She was exhausted.
3 He didn't want anyone to hear him.
4 She was late for an appointment.
5 His right leg was injured.
6 She wasn't in a hurry.
7 He was on a sled.
8 It was a bird.
9 He was on a motorcycle.
10 I let go of my balloon.
11 It was an insect.

f Write a few sentences about an experience you've had that involved moving fast. Compare what you have written with other students.

I went on an incredibly fast ride at a theme park. The Nemesis hurtles along a track with lots of twists and turns. You whirl through the air at such high speed that you hit zero gravity. I lost both my earrings!

g Now go back to p. 25.

3B Landscape features

a 

b 

c 

d 

e 

f 

g 

a Read the extracts from the travel stories and match them with the photographs.

1 ☐ We made slow progress through the **mosquito-infested swamp**, knee-deep in mud. We avoided the **dark** [1]_________ **of stagnant water** and eventually reached the firmer ground beyond.

2 ☐ We visited **a remote village in the foothills**. In front of the cottage was a **rich green** [2]_________ where cows grazed. In the distance, beyond **wooded** [3]_________, the mountains rose up into the sky.

3 ☐ To the north lies **an untouched wilderness**. The **rocky** [4]_________ is unsuitable for farming. An **empty** [5]_________ stretches toward the distant mountains.

4 ☐ The **rugged coastline** is famous for its beauty. From where I stood, **sheer** [6]_________ dropped to the sea and, looking down, I saw **the mouth of a** [7]_________ in the **cliff** [8]_________.

5 ☐ Never before had I been to such an **arid desert**. On our third day, we came to some **huge sand** [9]_________. We knew there was no way our vehicle would be able to cross them.

6 ☐ We were deep in **the heart of the jungle** now. Quietly we moved through the **dense** [10]_________. Looking up, I saw the **forest** [11]_________ far above my head and heard the cries of monkeys and birds.

7 ☐ The island can only be described as **a tropical paradise**. The sight of **pristine** [12]_________ and **calm turquoise** [13]_________ made us forget our long journey in an instant.

Tip

Swamp, bog, and *marsh* all describe types of muddy wetlands.

- In a marsh, the main plant life is types of grasses.
- In a swamp, woody plants and trees can grow.
- In a bog, the soil is poor so there is less plant life.

b 03.05 Complete the collocations in **bold** in **a** with the nouns in the box. Listen and check.

dunes	plain	meadow	undergrowth
slopes	canopy	pools	cliffs	waters
cave	face	ground	beaches

c Ask and answer the questions.

1 Which of the words and phrases in **a** and **b** could describe places in your country?
2 Which other types of environment have you visited in other countries?
3 What's your favorite and least favorite type of environment to be in?

d Now go to p. 36.

4A Instinct and reason

a 04.01 Listen to sentences 1–10. Match the words and phrases in **bold** with their meanings.

1 ☐ I'm a very **rational** thinker.
2 ☐ **On impulse**, I married someone I'd only just met.
3 ☐ I know **subconsciously** when people are lying to me.
4 ☐ If I need to decide quickly, I always go with my **gut instinct**.
5 ☐ It's important to **weigh** the pros and cons before taking action.
6 ☐ I **had a hunch** that I should resign, and I was right.
7 ☐ I'm successful in business because I think **logically.**
8 ☐ I always **think twice** before trusting a stranger.
9 ☐ I'll need time to **think it over** before I decide.
10 ☐ I love making **spontaneous** decisions. They're more fun!

a an intuitive feeling ×2
b step by step, using reasons
c think carefully ×3
d without planning ×2
e without being aware
f based on facts, not emotions

b 04.02 **Pronunciation**

1 Listen to the pronunciation of the letters in **bold** in these words. Which sound has more than one syllable?

1 /ʃəs/	2 /iəs/	3 /dʒəs/
cau**tious**	spontan**eous**	gor**geous**

2 04.03 Copy the chart in **b1** into your notebook. Then add these words to the correct columns. Listen and check. Practice saying the words.

subcon**scious** presti**gious** hilar**ious** coura**geous** ambi**tious**
simultan**eous** pre**cious** cur**ious** outra**geous** conscien**tious**

c The words in **bold** below are about the mind and feelings. What is the difference between them? Use a dictionary to help you.

1 He's a very **reasonable** / **rational** person.
2 She's a very **sensitive** / **sensible** person.
3 He's very money-**conscious** / **conscientious**.
4 She's very **self-conscious** / **self-confident**.

d Which adjective in each pair in **c** do you think describes you better?

e Now go to p. 45.

4B Memory

1 I only ever **have a v_________ memory of** my journey to work. I do it on auto-pilot.

2 I **have a p_________ memory of** my cat getting run over when I was a child.

3 Once the city was rebuilt, the storm **became a d_________ memory** for most people.

4 Their trip to Venice **was a l_________ memory**, full of magic.

5 I **have a v_________ memory** of our team winning the World Cup when I was a kid.

6 He **has a p_________ memory** and can paint places he hasn't seen since childhood.

a 04.11 Complete the sentences with the correct adjectives. Listen and check.

b 04.12 Match 1–7 with a–g to make complete sentences. Check the meaning of any expressions in **bold** that you don't know. Listen and check.

1 ☐ I **vaguely remember** seeing that movie years ago,
2 ☐ If I think of my time in New York,
3 ☐ I told him you were coming today,
4 ☐ The smell of freshly baked bread always **triggers a memory** of
5 ☐ Before going into class, she reads the roster
6 ☐ If you **cast your mind back** to the last meeting,
7 ☐ I'll always **treasure the memory** of

a but it must have **slipped his mind.** Sorry he's not here.
b the warm welcome they gave us. It was a very special occasion.
c but I have no idea what it's about.
d staying with my grandmother during school breaks.
e the first thing that **comes to mind** is a yellow taxi.
f you'll remember we agreed to increase the fee by $10.
g to **refresh her memory** of her students' names.

c Now go back to p. 49.

5A Crime and justice

a 05.06 Listen to the sentences. What is the difference between the legal terms in **bold**? Talk about the meanings with a partner.

1 a Thousands of dollars in cash were found on the premises, and a 35-year-old woman was **arrested on suspicion of** money laundering.
  b When the missing money was noticed, they **made an allegation of** fraud against him.

2 a She is **being held in custody** while waiting for her trial.
  b He's **been convicted of** murder and sent to prison.

3 a The defense **showed evidence in court** that supported the accused's alibi.
  b She **testified in court** that she had seen the accused running from the scene of the crime.

4 a He was given a lighter prison sentence because he **pleaded guilty to** the crime.
  b Despite a strong defense case, he **was found guilty of** the crime.

Learning Tip

When you record new words and expressions in your vocabulary notebook, it is useful to make a note of others that have a similar but slightly different meaning. This can help avoid confusion when you want to use the new language.

b Look at the phrases in **bold** in **a**. In your country, who does each thing? Who do they do it to? Use the words in the box to help you.

judge	victim
jury	defense lawyer
police officer	prosecution
criminal	someone else
witness	

c 05.07 Listen to the sentences. Which of these forms of punishment and rehabilitation are possible in your country's legal system?

a He was **sentenced to life imprisonment**.
b He had to **do community service**.
c She **served a reduced sentence for good behavior**.
d The judge insisted that she **serve the full ten years**.
e The company was **fined** a six-figure sum.
f He was **banned from driving**.
g They suggested he be **brought face-to-face with his victim**.
h All prisoners receive either **one-on-one** or **group counseling**.
i Prisoners with mental health issues **receive psychiatric help**.
j It is necessary to hold some prisoners **in solitary confinement**.

d Order the forms of punishment and rehabilitation in **c** from 1 (= least harsh) to 10 (= most harsh), in your opinion. Compare your order with a partner.

e Talk about which crimes or types of criminals might receive each form of punishment or rehabilitation in **c**.

Prisoners who are a danger to other inmates might be held in solitary confinement.

f Now go back to p. 58.

6A Adjectives: Describing images

a 06.01 Complete the sentences below with the adjectives in the box. Listen and check. Sometimes more than one answer is possible.

playful	exotic
powerful	iconic
humorous	gritty
raw	evocative
meaningful	ironic
well-composed	nonsensical

1. The strength of emotion in this close-up of her face seemed to almost hit me. It's a truly ________ image.
2. He appears to be lifting a car with one hand. It's just not possible – it's completely ________.
3. The kittens are loving that ball of wool! It's an extremely ________ photo.
4. The photographer has captured ________ scenes of inner-city poverty. It isn't pretty.
5. It's a very ________ photo. There's a perfect balance between the foreground and the sky and the land.
6. These photos make a more ________ statement about man's impact on the environment than words could.
7. This is the most gently ________ photo in his portfolio. The expression on the man's face really makes me smile.
8. For me, the most wonderfully ________ photo in the exhibition is the frozen desert. It's another world for me.
9. It's a very ________ image. You can't look at it without feeling something.
10. This photo was taken just after he lost the game. The ________ emotion is painful to look at.
11. The picture of Neil Armstrong stepping on to the moon in 1969 is truly ________.
12. The rather ________ expression on the woman's face seems to be saying, Oh, well, life's like that.

b Notice the suffix in these adjectives:

- play**ful**
- power**ful**
- meaning**ful**

Underline more adjective suffixes in **a**. Which adjective doesn't have a suffix? Think of two more adjectives which have each suffix you underlined.

c 06.02 Match sentences 1–6 with a–f. Listen and check.

1 ☐ The angle of this photo shows off the iconic architecture of the new art gallery.

2 ☐ In this powerful photo, the house stands alone against its environment.

3 ☐ I like this photo of the room where everything is neatly arranged.

4 ☐ In this photo, he's wearing an exotic costume with feathers and gold ribbons.

5 ☐ All the pictures in the exhibition are virtually the same.

6 ☐ You need the perfect flower and the perfect light.

a It's not too **cluttered**.
b It looks **sensational**.
c It's quite a **bleak** image.
d It gets a little **repetitive**.
e If these elements are right, you can create an absolutely **flawless** image.
f It all looks very **elaborate**.

Tip

Many adverbs of degree and adjectives form very strong collocations. For example, we say *utterly miserable* and *incredibly elaborate*, but ~~*utterly elaborate*~~ isn't a natural collocation. It's a good idea to note adverb + adjective collocations in your vocabulary notebook.

d Underline the adverb of degree + adjective collocations in the sentences in **a**.

e Which of the adverbs of degree in the box can be used with which adjectives in **bold** in **c**?

incredibly	pretty	a little	wonderfully
extremely	utterly	rather	truly

f **Communication 6A** Now go to p. 134.

7A Compound adjectives: Parts of the body

> **Tip**
> Compound adjectives are formed in many ways:
> - noun + adjective: ***world-famous*, *self-confident***
> - adjective + noun + *-ed*: ***short-sleeved*, *cold-blooded***
> - adjective + participle: ***good-looking*, *long-running***
> - adverb + participle: ***hard-working*, *well-written***
> - noun + participle: ***heartbreaking*, *self-made***
>
> Unless they have become one word, e.g., *heartbreaking*, the forms listed here always require a hyphen (-) between the two parts.

> **Tip**
> Compound adjectives are usually well-established collocations.
> *The novel is* ***heartbreaking*** / ***mind-blowing***. NOT ~~*The novel is* ***heart-opening*** / ***mind-breaking***~~ etc.
>
> Many have idiomatic meanings. For example, if a person is ***tongue-tied***, it does not literally mean that their tongue is tied. It means they find it difficult to speak because they are shy, nervous, or embarrassed.

a 07.01 Look at examples 1–4 and then complete 5–9. Listen and check.

- **adjective + noun + *-ed***
  1. He considers other points of view – he has an open mind. ➜ He's **open-minded**.
  2. She will always help her friends – she has a warm heart. ➜ She's **warm-hearted**.
- **noun + present participle**
  3. Carrying boxes upstairs nearly broke my back. ➜ It was **backbreaking** work.
  4. The sight of elderly people in love always warms my heart. ➜ It's a **heartwarming** sight.
  5. She always uses her left hand. ➜ She's …

  6. Don't expect any sympathy – he has a very hard heart. ➜ He's …

  7. She made the decision with a clear head. ➜ She's …

  8. Thai food makes my mouth water. ➜ It's …

  9. The sight made my jaw drop. ➜ The sight was …

b 07.02 Match the words in the boxes to make compound adjectives that can replace the definitions in *italics*. Use some words more than once. Listen and check.

half near hair	sighted	headed
absent narrow	raising	hearted
light mind	boggling	minded

1. Everyone in the village disapproves of my lifestyle. They're all so *unwilling to accept different ideas.*
2. He agreed to help us move the furniture, but it was very *lacking in enthusiasm.*
3. He may forget to call you. He's rather *likely to forget things because he's thinking about something else.*
4. Can you tell me what that sign says? I'm afraid I'm *unable to see distant things clearly.*
5. After eating nothing for ten hours, I began to feel a little *as if I might lose my balance.*
6. I'm fed up with serious movies. I'd like to see something more *happy and not too serious.*
7. The brakes on the bus weren't working properly, so it was a *terrifying* journey.
8. Did you know there are 100 billion stars just in our own galaxy? It's *almost impossible to imagine.*

c 07.03 **Pronunciation**

1. Listen to the two pairs of compound adjectives. Underline the main stress. Is it on the first or the second word?

   mind-boggling   open-minded
   heartwarming   half-hearted

2. Underline the main stress in these patterns. Practice saying the compound adjectives in **a**.
   - adjective + body part + *-ed*
   - body part + present participle

d Find someone in the class who:

1. is left-handed
2. ate something mouthwatering yesterday
3. has done a backbreaking job at some time in their life
4. thinks they're open-minded
5. thinks they're absent-minded
6. has been on a hair-raising journey
7. knows a mind-boggling fact
8. has never felt tongue-tied.

e Now go back to p. 81.

8B Aging and health

a 08.07 Listen to the words and phrases in the box.

a glowing complexion	smooth skin	saggy skin	oily skin	dry skin	wrinkles / fine lines	freckles	a rash	blotches	spots/acne	firm skin	clear skin

Which words in the box are usually associated with … ?

- youthful skin
- mature skin
- all ages

b Complete the collocations in **bold** with as many words and phrases as possible from the box in **a**. Compare your ideas with a partner. Are they the same?

1 Sun exposure can **cause** …
2 If you have an allergic reaction, your skin might **break out in** …
3 **Anti-aging creams** are designed to **prevent** …
4 Young people are often **prone to** …
5 Most people hate it when they start **getting** …
6 A **facial** can be helpful if you **have** …
7 If you want to be a model, it helps to **have** …

c 08.08 Match 1–9 with a–i. Listen and check.

1 ☐ He was **showing his age**. His
2 ☐ Her **eyesight is deteriorating** and
3 ☐ **Yellowing teeth**? Try our new
4 ☐ **Moisturizing** daily combined with **weekly facials**
5 ☐ **Tooth loss** and **heart trouble** are
6 ☐ **Strengthening** and **toning** exercises
7 ☐ **Poor circulation** can be improved by
8 ☐ **Weight loss** can be aided by
9 ☐ There's no need to resort to painful **injections**

a **whitening** toothpaste. You'll be amazed.
b **regular cardiovascular exercise**.
c **eating a varied and balanced diet**.
d helps to **tighten** and **plump** the skin.
e **hair was thinning** and **graying** around the temples.
f like yoga and Pilates help to give you energy.
g or **plastic surgery**.
h not inevitable parts of aging.
i she **has arthritis** in her knees.

d Look at the words and phrases in **bold** in **c**. Complete the chart.

Anti-aging treatments/effects	
Superficial effects of aging	
Health problems caused by aging	
Healthy living	

e Answer the questions about the things in **d**.

1 What anti-aging techniques do you think are reasonable steps to take to stop the aging process?
2 Do you think that any of the superficial effects of aging can be prevented/cured?
3 Which health problems caused by aging have affected people you know? What happened?
4 Which healthy living technique is the most important? Can you add any more to the chart?

f Now go to p. 96.

9B Describing buildings

a Complete the sentences with the adjectives in the box. Sometimes more than one answer is possible.

imposing	nondescript	graceful
innovative	tasteless	over the top
out of place	stunning	dated

1 The planning commission favored an original design by a young architect because they wanted a striking and _________ town hall to bring a modern edge to their city.
2 As the town is fairly small, the large castle on the hill is really too _________ and seems _________.
3 I'm sorry, but there's nothing remarkable or new about the design of those houses – they're totally _________ and pretty _________.
4 I really like the gold leaf in the ceiling decorations, but for some people it's _________ and _________.
5 The _________, elegant lines of the building are very pleasing to the eye. It's _________.

b 09.10 Match words 1–10 with the pictures below. Listen and check.

1 ☐ cabin
2 ☐ skyscraper
3 ☐ power station
4 ☐ subdivision
5 ☐ warehouse
6 ☐ penthouse
7 ☐ studio
8 ☐ cottage
9 ☐ mansion
10 ☐ strip mall

c Put the words in **b** in these groups.

1 places that can be homes
2 places that are businesses
3 places that can be both

d Answer the questions.

1 Which residential buildings are common in your country? Which are less common?
2 If you had a lot of money, would you live in a mansion, a penthouse, or neither? Why?
3 If you had to live in a small space, would you prefer a cabin or a studio? Why?

e Now go back to p. 107.

10A Communication verbs

a 10.02 Complete the sentences with the verbs in the box. Listen and check.

address presented go into demonstrated made move on to illustrate

1 She ________ **her understanding** of complex social issues by explaining them in everyday language.
2 I've been invited to ________ **an audience** of business experts at a conference in London.
3 If you sense the audience is getting bored, you should ________ **a new subject** to keep their interest up.
4 Every time she got the wrong slide, she ________ **comments under her breath** that I couldn't hear.
5 She ________ **key information** in easy-to-read charts.
6 It really helps if you can ________ **the points** you want to make with specific examples.
7 Don't ________ **too much detail** during your presentation – people can only process so much new information.

b Match the phrases in **bold** in 1–8 with the definitions a–h.

1 ☐ She began by **paying tribute to** all the teachers who had inspired her throughout her school years.
2 ☐ During the speech, he **asserted** his right to express his opinion even if it wasn't a popular one.
3 ☐ He **backed up** the arguments he made by providing examples from recent research.
4 ☐ She **summarized** the key ideas in her presentation with a list of bullet points.
5 ☐ He saw his speech as an opportunity to **voice concerns about** the rise in crime in his neighborhood.
6 ☐ The leader of the opposition **attacked** government policies in a speech that focused on the rise in unemployment.
7 ☐ In her presentation, she **sold the idea** of more flexible working hours to her managers.
8 ☐ She **concluded** by encouraging more people to try one of their free community education courses.

a to criticize a person or people strongly
b to say the most important facts in a short and clear way
c to publicly praise somebody in front of an audience
d to end a speech or presentation
e to persuade a person or people that something is a good plan
f to publicly say what you think about worrying issues
g to prove that something is true
h to make a statement strongly

c Think of people you know or in the media who do / have done the things below. Tell a partner about what happened.

1 attack government policy
2 have paid tribute to another person
3 often go into too much detail
4 sometimes make comments under their breath
5 often voice concerns about something
6 sell their ideas well

d Answer the questions.

1 Have you ever addressed an audience of more than 100 people? If so, how did it feel? If not, how would you feel doing this?
2 If you were giving a presentation, what could you use to illustrate the finer points of a topic to other people?
3 Do you ever make throwaway remarks? If so, do other people take them seriously? If not, why don't you do this?
4 Who's an influential person from your past that you would feel comfortable paying tribute to? What would you say about them?
5 What do you think is a good way to back up your opinion on something?

e Now go back to p. 116.

10B Superstitions, customs, and beliefs

a 10.12 Complete the sentences with the words and phrases in the box. Listen and check.

make a wish   traditionally   customary   good fortune
good luck charm   ward off evil

1 She wore a ________ around her neck until the day she died at the ripe old age of 104.
2 I had the ________ to invest at exactly the right time and made millions.
3 The cautionary tales are ________ told by each generation of parents to teach their children morality.
4 It is ________ to decorate the house with branches from pine trees at this time of year.
5 They sprinkle the beans and then sweep every room to banish demons and ________ .
6 Children ________ and try to blow out the candles. It will come true if they manage to blow them all out.

b 10.13 The words in the box are all used for talking about beliefs. Check (✓) the ones you think you know. Try saying the words. Then listen and check.

gullible   convinced
plausible   convincing
persuasive   far-fetched
dubious

c Use the words in **b** to replace the definitions below in *italics*. Use a dictionary to help you. There may be more than one possible answer. Which words are very similar in meaning?

1 My friend says a fortune teller's advice led him to success, but I don't find this very *easy to believe*.
2 People who believe in good luck charms must be very *ready to believe anything people tell them*.
3 When she talks about magic, I'm sure what she says is true. She's very *able to make other people believe her*.
4 The idea that horseshoes bring you luck doesn't seem very *likely to be true* to me.
5 I think most things that fortune tellers say are *unlikely to be true*, to say the least.
6 My grandmother was absolutely *certain in her belief* that black cats were unlucky.
7 People's stories about seeing ghosts usually sound rather *difficult to believe* to me.

d Answer the questions.

1 Which of the beliefs in the pictures 1–3 do you find ... ?
   • convincing • plausible • dubious • far-fetched
2 As a child, how gullible were you? Can you think of an example?
3 Who do you know (personally or someone well known) who you'd describe as a persuasive person?
4 "People who are convinced they're right are usually wrong." How true do you think this is?

e Now go back to p. 119.

1D Expressing opinions

Disagreement	Agreement
That's nonsense. *That simply isn't true.* *There's no way …* *You're missing the point.* *That's easy to say, but …* *How can you possibly think that?* *That's a load of garbage.* *That doesn't make sense.*	*You're absolutely right …* *That makes a lot of sense.* *You've hit the nail on the head.* *I would go along with that.*
Uncertainty	**Partial agreement/disagreement**
I'm of two minds about this/that. *I have mixed feelings about this/that.*	*You've got a point, but …* *On the other hand, I do feel …* *It's true that … but …* *I agree up to a point …*

a Read Eva's post and then complete the replies (1–6). Check your answers in the chart.

b Which of the replies include words or phrases that soften the opinion? What words or phrases could you add to soften the other opinions?

c Which opinion do you agree with the most? Which opinion do you agree with the least? Why?

d Now go to p. 17.

EVA

The trouble with English is it's such a complicated, difficult language and it doesn't have any rules. I think they should create a simpler form of English that could be used internationally and would be easier to learn. It should definitely have simpler grammar, maybe just three tenses. And a more sensible spelling system!

Or they should choose an easier language to be the international language, like Spanish, say. Half the world speaks Spanish already. Or how about Swahili or Malaysian? They've both got nice, simple grammar.

1 How **can you** __________ that? You're completely **missing** __________. English is a beautiful, rich language, and that's exactly why people want to learn it.

2 Well, **that's easy** __________, but you can't just "create" a language. People speak the languages they choose to. And you say "half the world speaks Spanish." Well, **that simply** __________ – 400 million people isn't half the world!

3 I must say I think **you're** __________ about the difficult spelling. I had to learn English in school, so **I'd definitely** __________ **with that**! But **I have** __________ **about** simplifying the grammar – it would make it easier to learn, but I don't think you can express complex ideas using just three tenses.

4 I'm sorry, but **that's** __________. Of course English has rules – all languages do.

5 What you're saying **doesn't really** __________. Why would you need to "create" a global language? No one has to speak English, so if people speak it, obviously it means they want to and they find it useful.

6 Good comment – I think **you've hit the nail** __________. Spanish would make a much better world language. It's a beautiful language and easy to learn. I say go for it! (My mother tongue is Spanish, by the way! 😊)

2D Linking: contrast and concession

Offering alternatives	Comparing	Conceding
however *on the other hand* *alternatively*	*however* *on the other hand* *by comparison* *although* *unlike* *in contrast to* *when compared to*	*however* *nevertheless* *regardless (of)* *although* *even though* *for all that* *in spite of* *despite*
Opposing		
on the contrary		

a Complete the sentences below with the transition words in the box.

however when compared to on the contrary
regardless of by comparison even though

1 ____________ the effort that has been put into planning the program, attendance at activities has been disappointingly low.
2 I would recommend reserving a table at a local restaurant. ____________, if we are concerned about the budget, we could organize a potluck dinner where everyone brings something to eat.
3 The social evening at the theater was incredibly popular. ____________, the turnout for the student party was extremely low.
4 ____________ we used high-end caterers for the student dinner, the food was bland and overcooked.
5 Most students clearly indicated that the picnic in the park was not boring at all. ____________, they said it was the activity where they had had the most fun.
6 Our club includes at least one activity per week. ____________ clubs at other institutions, it is very full and extremely varied.

b Which other transition phrases from the table are possible in each blank?

c Rewrite these sentences using the transition in parentheses.

1 Even though the class was large, it was still possible to get individual attention. (despite)
2 The teacher we had was very strict. By comparison, my old teacher was very easygoing. (unlike)
3 I was very disappointed with the lunches. However, the evening meals were great. (although)
4 In spite of it raining every single day, I enjoyed everything that we did. (for all that)
5 In spite of several injuries, spirits were high among the groups. (nevertheless)

d Complete the examples with your own ideas.

1 Most students say that the club is an important part of their time at the university. On the other hand, …
2 Regardless of their heavy study commitments, students …
3 Feedback has generally been positive. Nevertheless, …

e Now go back to p. 29.

Sacsayhuamán

3D Writing briefly

a Read the description of a visit to the citadel of Sacsayhuamán near Cusco. Where might you find this style of writing? Why? Choose more than one answer.

1 an informal tourist review written for a website
2 an official review written in a travel guide
3 a travel blog written for yourself or your friends
4 a message to friends on social media
5 a newspaper article about a visit to Cusco

> Walked up to the citadel in the afternoon. Lots of narrow windy streets, great view from the top. Took hundreds of photos! Fabulous city. Definitely planning to come back here next year.

b In the first sentence, the word *We* or *I* has been left out:

~~We~~ walked up to the citadel in the afternoon.

What words have been left out in the other sentences?

c What words have been left out to make these reviews shorter?

1 Not much to do here in the evenings, and food in most places overpriced. Quite a disappointing place to visit.
2 Been to most resorts in Mexico but nowhere as impressive as Tulum.
3 Best time to visit: late fall, no tourists, great weather.
4 Went to Budapest last year. Much more interesting and more reasonable prices.

d How could you reduce these sentences for an online review?

1 It would be a great place for a honeymoon because it's so romantic.
2 There was so much to take photos of. It was a good thing I had my camera with me.
3 We arrived late and we couldn't find anywhere to eat. I wasn't very impressed!
4 You should go early to beat the heat. There's a beautiful beach at the foot of the cliff, which is great for cooling off.

e Write a short review (about three sentences) of a tourist attraction you visited recently. Use the same style as in the review of Sacsayhuamán on p. 170.

f Show your review to your partner and answer any questions.

g Now go back to p. 41.

Tulum, Mexico

4D Showing time relationships

= immediately	*The moment …* *The instant …* *No sooner had … than …*
= a short time later	*Before long, …* *… was closely followed by …* *Shortly after …*
= a long time later, or longer than expected	*It wasn't until … that …* *It was only … that …* *Not until … (did) …* *In time …* *Subsequently, …*

a Change these sentences, beginning with the words in parentheses.

1 I saw her paintings. I immediately knew she would be a famous artist. (The moment)
2 He graduated, and then he got a high-paying job on Wall Street. (Shortly after)
3 As soon as I started asking questions, she got up and left the room. (No sooner)
4 We were both laid off, and then we decided to form a business partnership. (It wasn't)
5 Years later I decided to take up horseback riding again. (It was only)

b Connect these ideas in any suitable way, using time expressions.

1 We met – we fell in love.
2 I got home – I realized that I'd had my wallet stolen.
3 I arrived in New York – I began to feel at home there.
4 We went into business together – I discovered that he had a secret life.
5 She started training for super-marathons – she developed a pain in her knee.

c Compare your sentences in **b** with other students. Are your sentences similar or different in meaning?

d Write two or three sentences about each of these events, using expressions to show the time relationship.

1 two events in your life that happened
2 an event that happened a short time after another earlier one
3 an event that happened a long time after another earlier one

No sooner had I turned 17 than my dad bought me an old van to fix up. I didn't know how to do anything mechanical, but before long, I had treated the rust and painted the bodywork.

e Show your sentences to your partner and answer any further questions about the events.

f Now go back to p. 53.

5D Linking: addition and reinforcement

Adding an idea in a new sentence		Adding two ideas in the same sentence
In addition ...	*Furthermore ...*	*In addition to ...*
What's more ...	*Above all ...*	*As well as ...*
Besides ...	*... also ...*	*Besides ...*
Moreover ...		*Beyond ...*

a Cover the chart. Complete the sentences with one word in each blank. Check your answers in the chart.

1 **As well** _________ doing online research on social media, companies usually contact previous employers.
2 Many people are careful about the information they post on social media. _________ **addition**, they often have a private profile under a different name that employers will not recognize.
3 _________ being unethical, using information from social media as a basis for discrimination against a job applicant is illegal in many countries.
4 The private life of employees should remain private. _________ **more**, employers have no right to try and control what employees do in their own time.
5 There should be laws to restrict how much information companies can look for. _________ **all**, they should be banned from fishing for negative information.
6 Companies argue that information that is freely available online can be seen by anyone. _________, they point out that applicants are free to do research on a company.

b Replace the words in italics with transition words and phrases from the chart. Make any other necessary changes.

It is common practice for companies to get useful information about their customers when they sign up for a free offer. Customers accept the free offer, *and* they have to agree to certain terms and conditions that they don't read carefully. Companies are then entitled to bombard these customers with spam. *And* they might pass on information to other companies who will send out more spam.
It's always important to read what you sign up for and bear in mind that nothing is completely free. *And most importantly*, make sure you are aware of consumer rights in your country so you can challenge companies who use information about you in an unethical way.

c Add an extra idea to two of these sentences, using an addition word/phrase or a reinforcement word/phrase.

1 I always think carefully about what I write in emails.
2 A lot of companies do not allow their employees to access social media during work hours.
3 I always ask my friends not to post photographs of me on their social media pages.

d Now go back to p. 65.

6D Formal letters; Giving a positive impression

Formal letters
Dear Sir/Madam:
I am writing in response to ...
I would like to express my (interest in / dissatisfaction with, etc.) ...
Please find attached ...
I look forward to hearing from you.
Sincerely,

Giving a positive impression
I am very much in touch with ...
I enthusiastically maintain my knowledge of ...
I played an active role in ...
I have been able to ...
I have taken a keen interest in ...
I feel that, with my ... , I would be very well qualified to ...

a Look at these extracts from letters. Cross out one word or phrase in each group in *italics* that is less suitable for a formal letter.

1 I *believe / am certain / guess* that my knowledge of local sporting events will enable me to *do / write / contribute* well-informed reviews.
2 I am *writing in response to / answering / replying to* your advertisement, which *was / appeared / was published* in the March issue of your magazine.
3 I look forward to hearing from you *in due time / in a bit / soon.*
4 I'm *an enthusiastic supporter / a real fan / a keen follower* of the local soccer team.
5 *Here are / I am attaching / Please find attached* some sample photos that I took recently.
6 I have *considerable / tons of / extensive* experience of restaurant work.
7 I *am able to be completely flexible / am free any time / can offer a good deal of flexibility* with regard to working hours.
8 I spent some time working on a school magazine and *acquired / developed / picked up* some *relevant / priceless / valuable* editorial skills.

b Add additional formal and positive expressions from **a** to the chart.

c Read the ad and Andy's application email. Rewrite it so that it is in a more formal style.

Dear Sir/Madam:
I am writing ...

STAFF NEEDED for a bookstore near the university. Flexible working hours, ideal as a part-time job for students.

To apply, please send an email to:
www.greenstreetbooks.net

job application — Andy_résumé

Hi there,

Saw your job ad in the student paper and I'd really like to work for you. I'm doing world literature in college, so I know quite a bit about books written by all kinds of people. I'm really into novels and travel books and that'll be useful, won't it? I've never worked in a bookstore before, but I've done café work and I spent a bit of time working in a sporting goods store, so I know all about selling stuff to people. I'm also a nice guy and I've got lots of friends – I can chat with anybody.

So I think I'm just the kind of guy you're looking for. Here's my résumé.

I could work whenever you like, mornings or evenings, it's all the same to me.

Hey, get in touch.

Andy

d Now go back to p. 77.

7D Linking: highlighting and giving examples

a Add a transition word or phrase from the chart where there is a ^ in 1–7. Often more than one answer is possible.

1 The team is getting along better now. ^ they have decided to have a team dinner once a month.
2 It is already possible to perceive benefits from the training for the company, ^ the increased productivity of the team.
3 The team's productivity has gone up by 10%, ^ the increased number of completed tasks in the past month.
4 Everyone's active listening skills have improved. Masha ^ has become a good listener since doing the program.
5 Sam and Pablo now work together more effectively. Sam makes a point of consulting Pablo about workflow issues, ^ prioritizing tasks on the schedule.
6 The team now deals with tasks in hand. ^ they focus more on getting things done and less on team politics.
7 The program has also resulted in an improvement in the way all team members deal with people outside the team, ^ their friendlier manner with support staff.

Transition words for highlighting and giving examples	
for instance	*specifically*
as demonstrated by	*as detailed in*
as shown by	*namely*
such as	*especially*
in particular	

b You are the social programming coordinator for a staff/student social club that is experiencing problems. Complete these sentences with your own ideas.

1 There has been little uptake of the program lately. For instance, …
2 Overall participation in the program in the past year has decreased, as detailed in …
3 Activities that involve … are especially …
4 Activities such as … are …

c Write sentences about the English language progress you and your classmates have made. Use transition words for highlighting and giving examples of particular achievements.

The ability of the class is improving, in particular our speaking skills.

d Now go back to p. 89.

8D Using persuasive language

Neutral language	Persuasive language
in the city center	*in the* ***heart*** *of the city*
a different experience	*a* ***unique*** *experience*
high standards	***exacting*** *standards*
well-trained	***highly*** *trained*
make a dish	***create*** *a dish*
We promise to …	*Our* ***commitment*** *to you is …*
our basic idea	*our* ***core values***

Writing Tip

Many of the texts you read online are for promotion, and their aim is to persuade you to buy something, do something, or go somewhere. Notice how they use persuasive language, which makes things seem better, more positive, or more important.

a Choose the two words or phrases in *italics* in each sentence that work best as persuasive language.

1 Try one of our *freshly / lovingly / well-* prepared salads.
2 All our staff work to the *most exacting / highest / required* standards.
3 We *serve / offer / sell* light meals and snacks throughout the day.
4 Café Colombia is a *nice / perfect / ideal* place to meet your friends after work.
5 You can have *complete / some / total* confidence in our specialist products.
6 Why not spend a weekend *away from it all / in the countryside / far from the bustle of the city*?

b The sentences below promote different products and places. Which are for … ?

- a music venue
- a duty-free shop
- an airport lounge
- a bank
- a language school
- a furniture store
- a hotel

1 *With good furniture* and each with its own individual character, our rooms offer a *really quiet* atmosphere in which to unwind after a hard day's work.
2 Our beds are *of good quality* and will *be usable for many years.*
3 We have *a lot of* perfumes, and our brands are *known everywhere.*
4 The Basement is *a good place* for parties and live music events.
5 Our *well-*equipped classrooms and *good* teachers will ensure that your course is *different from the usual.*
6 *You're welcome* in our executive suite, where you can *spend* your time between flights in *comfortable* surroundings.
7 *We aim* to provide *a safe place* for your financial investments.

c Replace the words in *italics* in **b** 1–7 with the phrases in the box to make the sentences sound more positive.

tastefully furnished   a unique learning experience
manufactured to the highest standards
an extensive range of   an ideal venue
highly qualified   truly relaxing   our mission is
globally recognized   a secure home   luxurious
stand the test of time   a warm welcome awaits you
fully   while away

d Choose a place in your town (a store, a shopping mall, a sports facility, a hotel, a school or college). Write two sentences to promote it. Try to describe it as positively as possible.

e Read your sentences aloud and listen to other students. What positive features are they promoting?

f Now go back to p. 101.

9D Linking: reason and result

Reason	Result
One key factor is … / One of the (main) reasons is … *… because of / due to …* *… as a (direct) result / consequence of …*	*lead to / result in / cause / mean that …* *As a (direct) result / consequence …* *Consequently …* *… thus / thereby / hence / therefore …*

a Complete the sentences with the reason and result language in the box.

due to resulted in thus cause
thereby one of the main reasons

1 ____________ people leave small towns is the lack of a lively cultural life.
2 Climate change has negatively affected rural environments and ____________ urban migration.
3 At first, one or two family members move to the city and do well. ____________ more family members join them, motivated by the hope to also do well.
4 There is sometimes disharmony in city neighborhoods ____________ the pressure urban migration puts on infrastructure and amenities.
5 Dramatic population decreases can ____________ the social fabric of rural communities to disappear altogether.
6 The exodus of inhabitants from small towns leads to less demand for goods and services, and ____________ the closure of many businesses.

Writing Tip

There are small differences in use between *thus* / *therefore* and *thereby*:
The government raised taxes, ***thereby/thus/~~therefore~~*** *raising a lot of money.* = direct result of action
The government raised taxes. ***Therefore,/Thus,/~~Thereby,~~*** *starting a business is a bad idea.* = logical conclusion

b Correct the reason and result language in these examples.

1 The recent arrival of large numbers of people from the countryside leads to the current shortage in housing.
2 Increased pressure on city infrastructure often causes that there is a rise in taxes.
3 There are fewer jobs in small towns because the closure of so many businesses.
4 As a result the arrival of immigrants, city schools have many more children enrolled.
5 Youth unemployment is very high in the town, thereby there's a lot of competition for jobs.

c Write four sentences about present or future changes in your neighborhood, using reason and result language.

In my neighborhood, a new sports center will be built due to the fundraising efforts of the local community. As a consequence, …

d Now go back to p. 113.

10D Movie reviews; Concise description

Ways to give information concisely	Examples
1 Add phrases between commas	*Roy McBride,* ***a young astronaut****, goes in search of his father.*
2 Add phrases before noun	***Young astronaut*** *Roy McBride goes in search of his father.*
3 Use past participle clauses	Ad Astra, ***directed by James Gray****, blends sci-fi with personal feeling.*
4 Use present participle clauses	*Roy McBride,* ***wanting to reach his father****, hijacks a spaceship.*

a Use one or more of the ways shown in the chart to make these sentences more concise.

1 The first *Blade Runner* movie, which is directed by Ridley Scott, is a sci-fi classic.
2 When he realizes that his father is probably still alive, he decides he must reach him at all costs.
3 Alfonso Cuarón, who is a Mexican director, is planning to make a new movie.
4 Because she is determined to solve the crime, she works on the case night and day.
5 Jo March, who is the second oldest sister, is played by Saoirse Ronan.
6 Panem, which is a totalitarian country that is set in the future, is divided into 12 districts.
7 Because they are trapped in the mountains and because they know their food is running out, they send four people off to get help.

b Write about a movie you saw recently.

Write some basic information about it (name, director, outline of the story) in only three sentences.
Include at least two of the ways shown in the chart to make the information more concise.

c Read your sentences aloud, but don't say the name of the movie. Can other students guess the movie?

d Now think of a movie you did not enjoy. Replace the words in *italics* with your own ideas and continue each sentence concisely.

James Gray's latest movie, *Ad Astra,* is the *exciting and absorbing* story of … .
A critical and box office hit, the movie has …
Brad Pitt is perfectly cast in the role of …
Tommy Lee Jones is also *superb* as …
The movie provides a subtle portrayal of …
The plot focuses on …
It's an *original, thought-provoking* movie, and *certainly worth seeing.*

e Now go back to p. 125.

Verb patterns

When followed by another verb (and object) (and indirect object), individual verbs follow different patterns:

verb + sb/sth + base form
*She **makes me wash** the dishes.*
*I **saw the bus arrive**.*

verb + infinitive
*She **agreed to give** a presentation next week.*
*He **tends not to be** comfortable with new people.*

verb + sb/sth + infinitive
*I **asked the guests to wait** outside.*
*They **want him to come** to the party.*

verb (+ sb/sth) + verb + *-ing*
*He **admitted cheating** on the test.*
*He **hates us visiting** unannounced.*

verb + preposition (+ sb/sth) + verb + *-ing*
*I'm **concentrating on studying** this weekend.*
*She **insisted on him leaving** at three.*

**Some verbs have different meanings in different patterns.*

admit	verb + verb + *-ing*
admit to	verb + preposition (+ sb/sth) + verb + *-ing*
advise	verb + sb/sth + infinitive verb + verb + *-ing*
agree	verb + infinitive
aim	verb + infinitive
allow	verb + sb/sth + infinitive verb + verb + *-ing*
anticipate	verb + verb + *-ing*
appear	verb + infinitive
appreciate	verb (+ sb/sth) + verb + *-ing*
approve of	verb + preposition (+ sb/sth) + verb + *-ing*
argue about	verb + preposition (+ sb/sth) + verb + *-ing*
arrange	verb + infinitive
ask	verb + (sb/sth) + infinitive
attempt	verb + infinitive
avoid	verb (+ sb/sth) + verb + *-ing*
beg	verb + (sb/sth) + infinitive
begin	verb + infinitive
believe in	verb + preposition + verb + *-ing*
can afford	verb + infinitive
can't help	verb + verb + *-ing*
can't stand	verb (+ sb/sth) + verb + *-ing*
care about	verb + preposition + sb/sth + verb + *-ing*
challenge	verb + sb/sth + infinitive
choose	verb + (sb/sth) + infinitive
claim	verb + infinitive
consider	verb + verb + *-ing*
continue	verb + infinitive verb + verb + *-ing*
*dare	verb + infinitive (be brave enough) verb + (sb/sth) + infinitive (challenge sb)
decide	verb + infinitive
demand	verb + infinitive
deny	verb + verb + *-ing*

demand	verb + infinitive
deserve	verb + infinitive
discuss	verb (+ sb/sth) + verb + *-ing*
dislike	verb (+ sb/sth) + verb + *-ing*
encourage	verb + sb/sth + infinitive
enjoy	verb (+ sb/sth) + verb + *-ing*
expect	verb (+ sb/sth) + infinitive
fail	verb + infinitive
feel (sense)	verb + sb/sth + base form
feel like	verb + preposition + verb + *-ing*
finish	verb + verb + *-ing*
*forget	verb + infinitive (an obligation) verb + verb + *-ing* (an event)
forget about	verb + preposition (+ sb/sth) + verb + *-ing*
forbid	verb + sb/sth + infinitive verb + verb + *-ing*
force	verb + sb/sth + infinitive
get (opportunity)	verb + infinitive
*go on	verb + infinitive (do a new activity) verb + verb + *-ing* (continue same activity)
happen	verb + infinitive
hate	verb (+ sb/sth) + infinitive verb (+ sb/sth) + verb + *-ing*
hear (noise)	verb + sb/sth + base form
help	verb (+ sb/sth) (+ *to*) + base form
hope	verb + infinitive
imagine	verb (+ sb/sth) + verb + *-ing*
insist on	verb + preposition (+ sb/sth) + verb + *-ing*
instruct	verb + sb/sth + infinitive
intend	verb (+ sb/sth) + infinitive
invite	verb + sb/sth + infinitive
involve	verb (+ sb/sth) + verb + *-ing*
keep	verb + verb + *-ing*
learn	verb + infinitive
let	verb + sb/sth + base form
like	verb (+ sb/sth) + infinitive verb (+ sb/sth) + verb + *-ing*
long	verb + infinitive
love	verb (+ sb/sth) + infinitive verb (+ sb/sth) + verb + *-ing*
make	verb + sb/sth + base form
manage	verb + infinitive
mention	verb (+ sb/sth) + verb + *-ing*
mind	verb (+ sb/sth) + verb + *-ing*
miss	verb (+ sb/sth) + verb + *-ing*
motivate	verb + sb/sth + infinitive
need	verb (+ sb/sth) + infinitive
notice	verb + sb/sth + base form
object to	verb + preposition (+ sb/sth) + verb + *-ing*
offer	verb + infinitive
order	verb + sb/sth + infinitive
pay	verb + sb/sth + infinitive
permit	verb + sb/sth + infinitive verb + verb + *-ing*

persuade	verb + sb/sth + infinitive
plan	verb + infinitive
plan on	verb + preposition + sb/sth + verb + *-ing*
postpone	verb + verb + *-ing*
practice	verb + verb + *-ing*
prefer	verb (+ sb/sth) + infinitive
prepare	verb (+ sb/sth) + infinitive
pretend	verb + infinitive
proceed	verb + infinitive
propose	verb + infinitive
recall	verb + verb + *-ing*
recommend	verb + verb + *-ing*
refuse	verb + infinitive
regret	verb + verb + *-ing*
*remember	verb + infinitive (an obligation) verb (+ sb/sth) + verb + *-ing* (an event)
remind	verb + sb/sth + infinitive
require	verb + sb/sth + infinitive
resent	verb (+ sb/sth) + verb + *-ing*
resist	verb (+ sb/sth) + verb + *-ing*
resume	verb + verb + *-ing*
risk	verb (+ sb/sth) + verb + *-ing*
say	verb + infinitive (instructions)
see	verb + sb/sth + base form
seem	verb + infinitive
start	verb + infinitive
*stop	verb (+ sb/sth) + infinitive (purpose of stopping) verb (+ sb/sth) + verb + *-ing* (activity)
succeed in	verb + preposition + verb + *-ing*
suggest	verb + sb + base form verb + verb + *-ing*
swear	verb + infinitive
talk about	verb + preposition (+ sb/sth) + verb + *-ing*
teach	verb + sb/sth + infinitive
tell	verb + sb/sth + infinitive (instruction)
tend	verb + infinitive
think about	verb + preposition (+ sb/sth) + verb + *-ing*
threaten	verb + infinitive
tolerate	verb (+ sb/sth) + verb + *-ing*
*try	verb + verb + *-ing* (a new activity) verb + infinitive (unsure of success)
understand	verb (+ sb/sth) + verb + *-ing*
urge	verb + sb/sth + infinitive
want	verb + sb/sth + infinitive
warn	verb + sb/sth + infinitive
watch	verb + sb/sth + base form
worry about	verb + preposition (+ sb/sth) + verb + *-ing*
would like / love / hate / prefer, etc.	verb (+ sb/sth) + infinitive

Phonemic symbols

Vowel sounds

/ə/	/æ/	/ʊ/	/ɒ/
teacher	man	put	got
/ɪ/	/i/	/e/	/ʌ/
chip	happy	men	but

/ɜ/	/ɑ/	/u/	/ɔ/
shirt	part	who	walk

Diphthongs (two vowel sounds)

/eə/	/ɪə/	/ɔɪ/	/ɑɪ/	/eɪ/	/ʊʊ/	/ɑʊ/
hair	near	boy	fine	late	coat	now

Consonants

/p/	/b/	/f/	/v/	/t/	/d/	/k/	/g/	/θ/	/ð/	/tʃ/	/dʒ/
pill	book	face	van	time	dog	cold	go	thirty	they	choose	jeans
/s/	/z/	/ʃ/	/ʒ/	/m/	/n/	/ŋ/	/h/	/l/	/r/	/w/	/j/
say	zero	shop	usually	me	now	sing	hot	late	red	went	yes

Irregular verbs

Infinitive	Past simple	Past participle
arise	arose	arisen
bear	bore	borne
beat	beat	beaten
bend	bent	bent
bet	bet	bet
bid	bid	bid
bind	bound	bound
blow	blew	blown
burn	burned/burnt	burned/burnt
burst	burst	burst
cling	clung	clung
deal	dealt	dealt
dwell	dwelt	dwelt
feed	fed	fed
flee	fled	fled
forbid	forbade	forbidden
foresee	foresaw	foreseen
hang	hung	hung
lay	laid	laid
lead	led	led
leap	leaped/leapt	leaped/leapt
lie	lay	lain
light	lit	lit
offset	offset	offset
overdo	overdid	overdone

Infinitive	Past simple	Past participle
overhear	overheard	overheard
overtake	overtook	overtaken
rebuild	rebuilt	rebuilt
rethink	rethought	rethought
rise	rose	risen
seek	sought	sought
set	set	set
shake	shook	shaken
shine	shined/shone	shined/shone
shoot	shot	shot
shrink	shrank	shrunk
shut	shut	shut
sink	sank	sunk
smell	smelled/smelt	smelled/smelt
sow	sowed	sown
spin	spun	spun
split	split	split
spread	spread	spread
swear	swore	sworn
sweep	swept	swept
swing	swung	swung
tear	tore	torn
undo	undid	undone
upset	upset	upset
wind	wound	wound

Acknowledgments

Author
The authors and publishers acknowledge the following sources of copyright material and are grateful for the permissions granted. While every effort has been made, it has not always been possible to identify the sources of all the material used, or to trace all copyright holders. If any omissions are brought to our notice, we will be happy to include the appropriate acknowledgements on reprinting and in the next update to the digital edition, as applicable.

Key:
U = Unit, C = Communication, V= Vocabulary, W= Writing.

Text
U1: Guardian News & Media Ltd for the adapted text from 'Thomasina Miers: learning Spanish on a Mexican food odyssey – video', *The Guardian*, 02/04/2015. Copyright © 2015 Guardian News & Media Ltd. Reproduced with permission; **U2:** Solo Syndication for the extract from 'We all crave it, but can you stand the silence? The longest anyone can bear Earth's quietest place is 45 minutes' by Ted Thornhill, *Mail Online*, 03/04/2012. Copyright © 2012 MailOnline. All rights reserved. Distributed by Solo Syndication; Guardian News & Media Ltd for the adapted text from 'Experience: I've been to the quietest place on Earth' by George Michelson Foy, *The Guardian*, 18/05/2012. Copyright © 2012 Guardian News & Media Ltd. Reproduced with permission; Wright's Media, Inc for the adapted text from 'Why Some of Us Are Thrill-Seekers' by Angela Haupt, *U.S. News & World Report L.P*, 06/12/2012. Copyright © 2012 U.S. News & World Report. Distributed by Wright's Media, Inc. Reproduced with permission; **U3:** Adapted text from 'Pod Caribbean Children's Home - Belize - Volunteer Reviews': Linda and Malcolm – 2013 and 'Pod Community Projects - Ghana - Volunteer Reviews': Debbie – Child care, baby weighing and building. Copyright © 2013/2014 Personal Overseas Development Ltd. Reproduced with permission; Excerpt and Listening (Audio Script) from 'The Problem with Volunteering' by Daniela Papi, *BBC Radio 4: Four Thought*, 01/05/2013. Copyright 2013 © BBC Worldwide Limited. Reproduced with permission; Excerpt and Listening (Audio Script) from 'Journey of a lifetime, Mum Says 'You're a Long Time Dead" by Will Millard, *BBC Radio 4*, 13/09/2013. Copyright 2013 © BBC Worldwide Limited. Reproduced with permission; Excerpt from 'Surviving malaria on the Mano River', by Will Millard, *BBC News Magazine*, 13/09/2013. Copyright 2013 © BBC Worldwide Limited. Reproduced with kind permission; **U4:** Excerpt and Listening (Audio Script) from 'Glucosamine for osteoarthritis; Alcohol addiction; Gut instinct' Dr Mark Porter, *BBC Radio 4: Inside Health*, 12/02/2014. Copyright 2014 © BBC Worldwide Limited. Reproduced with permission; **U5:** Guardian News & Media Ltd for the adapted text from 'Inside Halden, the most humane prison in the world' by Amelia Gentleman, *The Guardian*, 18/05/2012. Copyright © 2012 Guardian News & Media Ltd. Reproduced with permission; Guardian News & Media Ltd for the adapted text from 'Six surprisingly well-paid jobs' by Donna Ferguson, *The Guardian*, 07/08/2014. Copyright © 2014 Guardian News & Media Ltd. Reproduced with permission; **U7:** Excerpt and Listening (Audio Script) from 'A lie detector on your phone' by Ian Goldin, *Future 60 second idea, BBC World Service*, 16/06/2014. Copyright 2014 © BBC Worldwide Limited. Reproduced with permission; Excerpt and Listening (Audio Script) from 'A remote that can reduce street noises' by Anja Kanngiese, *Future 60 second idea, BBC World Service*, 26/09/2013. Copyright 2013 © BBC Worldwide Limited. Reproduced with permission; Excerpt and Listening (Audio Script) from 'Job candidates must wear masks' by Maurice Fraser, *Future 60 second idea, BBC World Service*, 25/02/2012. Copyright 2012 © BBC Worldwide Limited. Reproduced with permission; Solo Syndication for the extract from 'Rise of the Machines: Meet Bina48, the robot who can tell jokes, recite poetry and mimic humans with startling ease' by Emily Anne Epstein, *Mail Online*, 19/07/2012. Copyright © 2012 MailOnline. All rights reserved. Distributed by Solo Syndication; Excerpt from 'Rewire: Digital Cosmopolitans in the Age of Connection' by Ethan Zuckerman. Copyright © Ethan Zuckerman. Reproduced with permission of WW.Norton & Company,Inc.; Guardian News & Media Ltd for the adapted text from 'This column will change your life: loneliness and temperature' by Oliver Burkeman, *The Guardian*, 01/06/2013. Copyright © 2014 Guardian News & Media Ltd. Reproduced with permission; **U8:** Excerpt and Listening (Audio Script) from 'Can extreme calorie counting make you live longer?' by Peter Bowes, *BBC World Service*, 24/03/2013. Copyright 2013 © BBC Worldwide Limited. Reproduced with permission; Excerpt from 'Segmented sleep: Ten strange things people do at night' and The myth of the eight-hour sleep', by Stephanie Hegarty, *BBC News Magazine*, 22/02/2012. Copyright 2012 © BBC Worldwide Limited. Reproduced with kind permission; Guardian News & Media Ltd for the adapted text from 'Aubrey de Grey: We don't have to get sick as we get older' by Caspar Llewellyn Smith, *The Guardian*, 01/08/2010. Copyright © 2010 Guardian News & Media Ltd. Reproduced with permission; **U9:** Text about Jeanne Gang. Reproduced with kind permission of Studio Gang; **U10:** Text about Scott Berkun. Reproduced with kind permission of Scott Berkun.

Photographs
The following photographs are sourced from Getty Images.
U1: Barcroft/Barcroft Media; Sam Edwards/OJO Images; Arseniy Rogov/iStock Editorial/Getty Images Plus; Mediaphotos/E+; Richard Drury/Stone; Universal History Archive/Universal Images Group; MCT/Tribune News Service; Sjale/iStock/Getty Images Plus; Jetta Productions Inc/DigitalVision; JohnnyGreig/E+; Image Source; Grant Faint/The Image Bank; Istetiana/Moment; Violet-blue/iStock/Getty Images Plus; Mike Powell/Allsport Concepts/Getty Images Plus; Tim Kitchen/The Image Bank/Getty Images Plus; Alex Mares-Manton; Westend61; Jaturon Ruaysoongnern/EyeEm; **U2:** CharlieChesvick/E+; Alacatr/iStock/Getty Images Plus; Fabrice Lerouge/Onoky; Scott Olson/Getty Images News; Stock_colors/E+; Macsnap/iStock/Getty Images Plus; Dan Herrick/Lonely Planet Images/Getty Images; Philartphace/iStock; Oliver Furrer/Stone; Yuin Lu Hoo/E+; Alexander_Safonov/iStock/Getty Images Plus; Ariel Skelley/DigitalVision; Marcos Calvo/iStock/Getty Images Plus; Mayo5/E+; Steve Bly/The Image Bank/Getty Images Plus; Vuk Ostojic/Moment; Icon Sports Wire; Brazzo/E+; Naumoid/iStock/Getty Images Plus; Aldomurillo/E+; DragonImages/iStock/Getty Images Plus; Westend61; Recep-bg/E+; **U3:** Phil Clarke Hill/Corbis New; Kryssia Campos/Moment; Nick Dolding/Stone; Demerzel21/iStock Editorial/Getty Images Plus; Janet Kimber/The Image Bank/Getty Images Plus; Kike Calvo/Universal Images Group; Paula Bronstein/Getty Images News; Fairfax Media; MikhailSemenov/iStock/Getty Images Plus; Konoplytska/iStock/Getty Images Plus; Banjongseal324/iStock/Getty Images Plus; Daniilphotos/iStock/Getty Images Plus; Halecr/iStock/Getty Images Plus; Franz Wogerer; DaveLongMedia/iStock/Getty Images Plus; Fizkes/iStock/Getty Images Plus; Joerg Steffens/OJO Images; Anna Gorin/Moment; Keren Su/Stockbyte; Javarman3/iStock/Getty Images Plus; **U4:** Tomohiro Ohsumi/Getty Images News; SelectStock/Vetta; Kate_sept2004/E+; Westend61; Laurence Berger/iStock/Getty Images Plus; Fstop123/E+; Yuri_Arcurs/E+; Greg Blomberg/EyeEm; Cavan Images/Cavan; Daniel Allan/Cultura; Peathegee Inc; **U5:** Giuseppe Cacace/AFP; Junge, Heiko/AFP/Getty Images; Abzee/E+; Christopher Murray/EyeEm; Karyn Nishimura-Poupee/AFP; GS Visuals/Cultura; LaylaBird/E+; GlobalStock/E+; XiXinXing; Burnsboxco/iStock/Getty Images Plus; Jacobs Stock Photography Ltd/DigitalVision; Galina Zhigalova/iStock/Getty Images Plus; MangoStar_Studio/iStock/Getty Images Plus; SanneBerg/iStock/Getty Images Plus; Tim Robberts/DigitalVision; SolStock/E+; GCShutter/E+; **U6:** Getty Images/Handout/Getty Images Entertainment; Mireya Acierto/Getty Images Entertainment; Igor Ustynskyy/Moment; Jesus Trillo Lago/iStock/Getty Images Plus; Westend61; Plume Creative/DigitalVision; Simonkr/E+; Runstudio/Moment; Fizkes/iStock/Getty Images Plus; Manuel Sulzer/Cultura; Grandriver/E+; SolStock/E+; **U7:** BSIP/Universal Images Group; VCG/Visual China Group; Fort Worth Star-Telegram/Tribune News Service; Jacobs Stock Photography Ltd/DigitalVision; Jose Luis Pelaez Inc/DigitalVision; Westend61; Roydee/E+; Eclipse_images/E+; MarianVejcik/iStock/Getty Images Plus; Creative-Family/iStock/Getty Images Plus; Maskot/DigitalVision; Mohamad Itani/Photodisc; Hinterhaus Productions/DigitalVision; Andresr/E+; Muntz/The Image Bank/Getty Images Plus; Sturti/E+; ColorBlind Images/The Image Bank/Getty Images Plus; Philipp Nemenz/DigitalVision; Jupiterimages/Photos.com/Getty Images Plus; Klaus Tiedge; **U8:** Laflor/E+; Tara Moore/Stone; Skaman306/Moment; Monkeybusinessimages/iStock/Getty Images Plus; JohnnyGreig/iStock/Getty Images Plus; Westend61; Ajr_images/iStock/Getty Images Plus; BSIP/UIG; Motortion/iStock/Getty Images Plus; Cuiphoto/iStock/Getty Images Plus; GlobalP/iStock/Getty Images Plus; DanielPrudek/iStock/Getty Images Plus; GMint/iStock/Getty Images Plus; Evgeniy1/iStock/Getty Images Plus; Hindustan Times; Malikov Aleksandr/iStock/Getty Images Plus; SergeyChayko/iStock/Getty Images Plus; Fascinadora/iStock/Getty Images Plus; Supamas lhakjit/iStock/Getty Images Plus; JohnArcher/iStock/Getty Images Plus; Alvarez/E+; By_nicholas/E+; Simonlong/